Law School Survival Guide

VOLUME I of II

Outlines and Case Summaries for:

Torts • Civil Procedure

Property • Contracts and Sales

t

LAW SCHOOL SURVIVAL GUIDE
Outlines and Case Summaries
Volume I of II
2016 Edition

Published by Teller Books
Manufactured in the U.S.A.

ISBN (13) (paperback): 978-1-68109-074-0
ISBN (10) (paperback): 1-68109-074-0
ISBN (13) (ePub): 978-1-68109-075-7
ISBN (10) (ePub): 1-68109-075-9

t TellerBooks

www.TellerBooks.com

DISCLAIMER: Although this book is designed to provide readers with rigorously researched information, it is not intended to constitute legal advice. Rather, it aims to serve as a general overview of the law that will help readers to understand basic legal principles and find further information, if necessary. It does not lay out all of the legal nuances and details that may make the difference in any potential case.

Some judicial decisions discussed in this book, due to their ambiguity, are subject to different interpretations. Other authors may come to conclusions different from those presented herein. No representation is therefore made that these materials reflect a definitive statement of the state of the law or of the views that will be applied by any court in any particular case or jurisdiction.

The law changes with remarkable swiftness as new statutes are passed and innovative judicial decisions are handed down. The information in this volume could therefore become obsolete with remarkable speed. For up-to-date legal advice, readers are encouraged to seek the counsel of a qualified attorney or other professional.

SUMMARY OF CONTENTS

Look for all of these titles in the

TellerBooks

Law School Survival Guides Series

(Outlines and Case Summaries)*:

TORTS

PROPERTY

CIVIL PROCEDURE

INTERNATIONAL LAW

CONTRACTS AND SALES

CONST. CRIMINAL PROCEDURE

BUSINESS ORGANIZATIONS

CONSTITUTIONAL LAW

CRIMINAL LAW

FAMILY LAW

EVIDENCE

*Available in paperback,
ePub, Kindle,
Nook and pdf formats.

TABLE OF CONTENTS

ABBREVIATIONS

3PP................... Third-party plaintiff
3PD.................. Third-party defendant
A .... The grantee of a present estate or future interest
AP .... Adverse possession
A/R.................. Assumption of the risk
B...................... Buyer
BFP .... *Bona fide* purchaser or *bona fide* purchase
C...................... Constitution
CIF .... Cause-in-fact
Cl. .... Clause
CLEO............... State Chief Law Enforcement Officer
Court (cap.)....... The United States Supreme Court
CR.................... Contingent remainder
CSD .... Common Scheme of Development
CSI................... Compelling state interest
Ct. .... Court
ED.................... Emotional distress
EI .... Executory interest
ES.................... Equitable Servitude
FI...................... false imprisonment
FLSA .... Fair Labor Standards Act
FMLA .... Family and Medical Leave Act
FQJ................... Federal question jurisdiction
FRAP .... Federal Rules of Appellate Procedure
FRCP .... Federal Rules of Civil Procedure
FRCrP .... Federal Rules of Criminal Procedure
FRE.................. Federal Rules of Evidence
FS.................... Fee simple absolute (fee simple)
FSCS................ Fee simple on condition subsequent
FSD.................. Fee simple determinable
FS EL............... Fee simple on executory limitation
FT.................... Fee tail
IIED .... Intentional infliction of emotional distress
IT .... Intentional tort
JMOL............... Judgment as a matter of law
JNOV................ Judgment *non obstante veredicto*
J/SL.................. Joint and several liability, or jointly and severally liable
JT .... Joint tenant/tenancy
K .... Knowledge (criminal law) or Contract (all other law)
KSC .... Knowledge to a substantial certainty
L...................... Loss in value
L1.................... First landlord
Lat.................... Latin
LE .... Life estate
LED .... Life estate determinable
LLC .... Limited liability company
LLP .... Limited liability partnership
LRM .... Least restrictive means
MPC................. Model Penal Code
MSAJ............... Motion to set aside the judgment
N .... Negligence
N.B. .... *Nota bene*
NIED .... Negligent infliction of emotional distress
O .... Original owner, or grantor (in present estates and future interests)
OLQ................. Owner of the *locus in quo*
OO .... Original owner
P...................... Purpose or purchaser
PE .... Privity of Estate
PJ .... Personal jurisdiction
PJI................... Pattern Criminal Jury Instruction
PK .... Privity of Contract
R...................... Recklessness
RAP .... Rule against perpetuities
RC.................... Real Covenant
Restatement ...... Restatement (of Contracts, Torts, Judgments, etc.)
RFRA............... Religious Freedom Restoration Act of 1993
RIL................... *Res ipsa loquitur*
RPP.................. Reasonable prudent person
Rule .... Federal Rule of Evidence or Federal Rule of Civil Procedure
§ .... Section

ABBREVIATIONS

S	Sub-lessee or seller
SF	Statute of Frauds
SJ	Summary judgment
SL	Strict liability, or statute of limitations
SMJ	Subject matter jurisdiction
SP	Specific performance
T1	First tenant
TE	Tenant/tenancy by the entireties
TO	True owner
UCC	Uniform Commercial Code
USC	United States Code
VR	Vested remainder
VR SD	Vested remainder subject to divestment

CHAPTER 1.
CONTRACTS AND SALES

I. INTRODUCTION

A. DEFINING CONTRACTS

1. The Restatement (Second) of Contracts § 2 establishes the following definitions:

   a. *Promise*: a manifestation of intention to act or refrain from acting so made as to justify a *promisee* in understanding that a commitment has been made.

   b. *Promisor*: the party making the promise.

   c. *Promisee*: the party receiving the promise.

   d. *Beneficiary*: the party that will benefit from a performance, when this person is not the promisee.

2. "A contract is a promise or set of promises, for breach of which the law gives remedy, the fulfillment of which is a legal duty" (§ 1 Restatement).

3. "An agreement is a manifestation of mutual assent by two or more persons. A bargain is an agreement to exchange promises or exchange a promise for a performance or to exchange performances" (§ 3 Restatement).

4. A contract can be made orally or in writing, or inferred from conduct (§ 4 Restatement).

B. SOURCES OF THE LAW ON CONTRACTS

1. The case law, which can vary from state to state.

2. In the sales of goods, the Uniform Commercial Code (UCC).

   a. This is a uniform law that that all of the states have adopted.

   b. However, Louisiana has not adopted the UCC in all of the ways suggested its drafters.

   c. The UCC applies to contracts for the sale of goods (art. 2) and for leases (art. 2A).

   d. The UCC also deals with negotiable instruments (art. 3), bank deposits (art. 4), letters of credit (art. 5), investment securities (art. 8).

   e. The present text will limit itself to discussing sales of goods and will make some mention of the UCC provisions with respecto to leases.

3. Furthermore, secondary sources such as the Restatement (Second) of Contracts, legal treatises, and scholarly articles may apply.

C. CLASSES OF CONTRACTS

1. Bilateral contracts are accepted by return promise.

   a. Example: a contract in which A promises to sell B land at a particular price if B promises to purchase the land at that price.

2. Unilateral contracts are accepted by performance.

    a. Example: A promises to pay $10 to whoever finds and brings him his lost dog.

    b. The person who finds and brings the dog, without notifying A of his acceptance or promising to bring A the lost dog, is entitled to the $5 at the time he brings the lost dog.

II. MUTUAL ASSENT

A. THE OBJECTIVE THEORY OF ASSENT

1. An Objective Meeting of the Minds: the Reasonable Person Standard

    a. For there to be a valid contract, there must be a "meeting of the minds."

    b. *Actual mutual assent* is not required; it is the *expression* of assent through behavior that matters.

    c. What is important in the objective theory of assent is not the inner motives of the parties, but rather, their outward expressions.

    d. Determining the "secrets of the mind" is thus not necessary in determining mutual assent.

        i. *See Embry v. Hargadine, McKittrick Dry Goods* Co., where the defendant acted as though the plaintiff had his job contract back, but then fired him after two months. The court ruled in favor of the plaintiff, since the defendant expressed his assent through behavior and whether he intended to renew the contract was irrelevant.

    e. One must determine whether a *reasonable person* in the offeree's position would come to conclude that an offer or assent to an offer is being made.

    f. Even if the offeror is joking or intoxicated, if his outer conduct would lead a reasonable person to conclude that there was an agreement, then the promise is enforceable.

        i. *See Lucy v. Zehmer*, where a court held that if the defendant were sober enough to spend forty minutes discussing the terms of an agreement, then regardless of whether he was intoxicated, that promise was enforceable because of the manifestation of assent.

2. A Written Contract

    a. The commitment does not need to be memorialized as a written contract.

    b. A contract is enforceable as soon as there is a meeting of the minds.

        i. *See Sanders v. Pottlitzer Fruit Co.*, where after much negotiation, the plaintiff sends a letter offering apples, the defendant says it will take apples only if conditions are met, and the plaintiff accepts. The defendant then asks for the written contract to be sent, which it tries

CHAPTER 1
CONTRACTS AND SALES

to change. The plaintiff refuses to change it and sues to enforce the original contract. The court held that an agreement in the prior correspondences; a formally written contract is not required. Judgment for the plaintiff.

B.   THE OFFER

1.   Definition

    a.   An offer is a manifestation of willingness to enter into a bargain, so made as to justify another person in understanding that his *assent* to that bargain is invited and will conclude it (§ 24 Restatement).

2.   The Four Elements of an Offer

    a.   A Commitment

        i.   There must be a promise to enter into a contract, not an invitation to negotiate.

        ii.   Language such as "I offer" or "I promise" tends to indicate commitment; language such as "I consider" or "I quote" tends to indicate an invitation for offers.

        iii.   If offeror did not intend to make the offer, the objective test will be used: "would a reasonable person in the offeree's position know or should he have known that there was an offer?"

        iv.   To answer this question, the following will be considered:

            1)   Industry practices and prior practices between the parties.

            2)   Circumstances: was the offer made in jest? If so, would a reasonable person have construed it to be an offer?

                a)   *See Zehmer*, where the defendant said he was joking about selling his land, but the court held there was a commitment because a reasonable person would not have understood that he was joking.

    b.   Communicated

        i.   The offeree must have knowledge of the offer before being able to accept it.

        ii.   Example: A offers to buy B's car for $5,000. B, before he finds out about the offer, says that he will give A his car for the same price. Since A's offer was not communicated to B, B's communication is merely another offer; it does not constitution acceptance.

    c.   To an Identified Offeree

        i.   An offer is always personal; it cannot be transferred to a third party.

        ii.   The broader the medium for communicating the offer, the more likely the courts will construe the communication to be an advertisement.

        iii.   Advertisements are not offers, but rather, invitations to negotiate or make offers.

1) *See Nebraska Seed Co. v. Harsh*, where a farmer invited a company to buy about 1,800 bushels of seeds for $2.25 each, and the company accepted. When the farmer did not deliver, the company sued for breach of contract. The court held that there was never an offer, since the communication was not made to an identified offeree, but rather, to several. Furthermore, the delivery time and subject matter ("about" 1800 bushels) was indefinite.

2) *See also Leonard v. Pepsico*, where an advertisement was held not to be an offer, and furthermore, tested by the reasonable person standard, the content of the advertisement was an obvious joke, not a real offer.

iv. However, the Restatement (Second) of Contracts allows offers to be made to more than one person (§ 29 Restatement). The communication would be a valid offer if it can only be construed as being open to a single offeree.

1) For example, if a subject offers a reward to whoever finds and returns his lost dog, a court would treat the communication as an offer, since it is implicitly being communicated to an identified offeree: the first and only person to return the dog.

d. With Definite Terms

i. For an offer to be enforced, it must contain definite terms.

ii. Each category of contracts calls for different terms to be specified.

1) For contracts of *realty*, the **price** and the **land to be sold** (the amount and location) must be specified.[1]

a) The land must be identified as to both the amount and the location to be sold.

2) For employment contracts, the **duration** must be determined.

a) The duration may be manifested as a period of time (*e.g.*, a one year employment contract) or as a task (*e.g.*, a contract to repair a computer).

b) If the duration is not specified, the offeree is considered hired at will and can quit or be fired at anytime without being able to enforce any time provision.

3) For contracts for the sale of goods under the UCC, only the **quantity** must described (UCC Official Comment 1, § 2-201).

a) The indicated quantity need not be accurate, but the contract cannot be enforced beyond this quantity.

---

[1] With respect to the description of the land, the test turns on whether a court can identify the land to be sold in order to enforce the contract.

b) Other terms, such as the price, place of delivery, or time of delivery, can be determined by the UCC gapfillers.[2]

c) There are two exceptions to this rule:

    i) Requirements contracts (*e.g.*, "I will buy as many units as I need"); and

    ii) Output contracts (*e.g.*, "I will buy as many units as you produce").

d) If terms, such as place of delivery and time of delivery, are left unspecified, the court can fill these in with what is reasonable.

e) If the price is unspecified, the court can fill it in when: (i) there is no mention of price in the negotiation; (ii) the price was left to the parties to agree upon but they did not; or (iii) the price was left to be determined by the market.

    i) For example, if A offers to sell B ten widgets "for the price we agree to," the price can be determined by the court, since the price was left to the parties to agree upon.

    ii) However, if A offers to sell B ten widgets "for a reasonable price," a court cannot fill in the price because the offer does not fit into one of the three circumstances defined above.

    iii) Since price is not determined, it is not a valid offer and the agreement is unenforceable; the court is not going to try to determine what a reasonable price is.

3. Terminating an Offer

a. The offeree's power of acceptance is terminated in the following circumstances (§ 36 Restatement):

    i. The offeree **rejects** the offer or makes a **counteroffer**;

    ii. There is a **lapse of time** (must be reasonable);

    iii. The offeror directly or indirectly **revokes** the offer:

        1) The offer is considered to be indirectly revoked if the offeree receives reliable information that would lead a reasonable person to conclude that it has been revoked (*e.g.*, when the offeree learns that the offeror is searching for other purchasers).

        2) *See Dickinson v. Dodds*, where Dodds, the defendant, gave the plaintiff an option not bearing consideration that would remain open for two days to buy his house for 700 pounds.

---

[2] In the case of an open price term, see § 2-305 UCC; for the absence of a specified place of delivery, see § 2-308 UCC; for the absence of specific time provisions, see §2-309 UCC.

The plaintiff heard of Dodd's intent to sell the land to another purchaser, even though he never communicated a formal, direct revocation. The plaintiff then accepted the offer and sued for specific performance when the land was not delivered. Held: although Dodd's revocation was not directly communicated to the plaintiff, the offer was terminated the moment that the plaintiff heard about it indirectly.

    a) *N.B.*: if there had been any consideration on the option, real or recited, the offer would have been irrevocable until the agreed-to termination.

    iv. The offeror or offeree ***dies*** or is ***incapacitated***.

        1) If the offeror dies before the offeree accepts the offer, the offeree's power of acceptance is terminated and no contract is formed.

        2) However, if the offerree accepts just prior to the offeror's death, an enforceable contract is formed. Once there is a meeting of the minds, the death of either party does not invalidate the contract.

b. Exception: Options Contracts

    i. If an options contract is supported by consideration (or, in many courts, by recital thereof), the offeree's power of acceptance is not terminated through his rejection of the offer, counteroffer, death or incapacity, or through the direct or indirect revocation by offeror.

    ii. However, if there is no consideration, an options contract can be terminated in the same way that a regular offer can be terminated (rejection, lapse of time, revocation or death or incapacity).

c. Revocation of Unilateral Contracts

    i. In the case of unilateral contracts, where the offer is accepted by performance, the offeror may revoke the offer at any time before the offeree completes performance.

    ii. However, where there is a ***tender*** (unconditioned willingness to perform immediately coupled with a manifest ability to perform) or a ***beginning of performance*** (more than just preparation to begin performance), a binding option contract is formed that the offeror is unable to revoke.

    iii. The offer expires on its own if the offeree leaves the job uncompleted and a reasonable time lapses.

    iv. Examples

        1) Suppose A offers to pay B $50 to shovel his driving. If B shows up at A's home with a shovel and indicates that he is ready to begin performance, has a contract been formed?

            a) Since B tendered performance, a valid option contract is formed.

2) If B arrives at A's home and begins performing without informing A, has a contract been formed?

    a) A valid options contract is formed from the moment that B begins performance until he completes it.

3) If, without completing the job, B takes off, leaving the job incomplete, can A sue for breach of contract?

    a) No; since B can only accept A's offer by complete performance, no acceptance was ever made, and therefore, no contract exists.

4) What if B arrives at A's home, and, just before tendering performance, A shouts out that he revokes the offer. Is there nevertheless a contract?

    a) No; B's power of acceptance expires if A revokes before B tenders or begins performance.

    b) *See Petterson v. Pattberg*, where the defendant offered the plaintiff the opportunity to obtain full title to the plaintiff's home by selling the plaintiff the mortgage to the home in exchange for $4,850 to be paid to the defendant before a certain date. The plaintiff sold the title to third party, expecting to use the funds obtained to pay the defendant $4,850 to purchase the mortgage. The plaintiff went to the defendant's home, but before he could accept the offer and tender payment, the defendant revoked the offer. The court held that no contract was formed, since the defendant had revoked his offer just before tender had been made.

v. Thus, the defendant's obligations depend on whether the plaintiff has prepared for, tendered, begun, or completed performance.

Time	Preparation of Performance	Tender or Beginning of Performance	Completion of Performance
The Contract Formed	There is no contract.	There is a valid option contract from this moment to the moment in which performance is completed. The offer is irrevocable.	There is a valid contract; the offeree must fulfill his contractual obligation.
The Offeror's Duties	Specific performance, if there is an options contract. If there is no options contract, the offeror may be liable for damages through promissory estoppel if his revocation causes detrimental reliance on the offeree.	The offeror may not revoke the offer at any time. The offeree may, however, decide not to complete performance, at which point the option contract expires after reasonable time.	The offeror is obligated to pay the offeree.

C.   ACCEPTANCE

1.   Introduction

   a.   There are three kinds of contracts, each of which requires a different kind of acceptance:

      i.   Unilateral contracts, which are constituted through performance by the offeree;

      ii.   Bilateral contracts, which are created through a return promise;

      iii.   Contracts for the sale of goods, which are governed by the UCC, whether they are unilateral or bilateral.

2.   The Four Elements of Acceptance

   a.   Commitment

      i.   As with offers, acceptance must involve a commitment.

      ii.   The primary issues raised involve the objectivity test.

   b.   Communicated

      i.   For determining if an acceptance is communicated, an objective standard is applied; the subjective state of mind of the parties is irrelevant.

      ii.   The Mailbox Rule

         1)   An acceptance is effective upon *proper dispatch* (when it is *sent*, not received), unless:

            a)   The offer stipulates that acceptance is effective when received; or

            b)   There is a valid option contract (having real or recited consideration), in which case there is acceptance only through receipt (§ 63(b) Restatement).

         2)   Suppose A offers to sell B his car on January 1. On January 2, B sends a properly addressed letter accepting the offer, but revokes on January 3. On January 4, A receives the letter. Is there a contract?

            a)   A valid contract is formed the moment B sent the letter on January 2. At that moment, revocation was no longer possible.

         3)   Since it is the dispatch of the acceptance, not its receipt that counts, an offer is properly accepted even if the acceptance is lost in the mail and is never received by the offeror.

      iii.   Acceptance by Silence (§ 69 Restatement)

         1)   When an offer is made, the offeree's silence cannot be construed as acceptance, *unless*:

            a)   The offeree puts himself within the duty of needing to speak up in order to reject an offer (*e.g.*, if he states, "unless I say something by Friday at noon, I accept this offer," *not* when the offeror puts the offeree in this position, by stating, for example, "unless you say something by Friday, you will have accepted").

2) When industry standards or prior dealings establish acceptance by silence.

    a) *See Hobbs v. Massasoit Whip Co.*, where the plaintif, Hobbs, sues Massasoit for failing to have paid for eel skins that the plaintiff had shipped. The defendant argues that it had never accepted the offer, an argument rejected by the court, which holds that, given trade practices and prior dealings, it was reasonable to conclude that the defendant had in fact accepted the plaintiff's offer.

3) When the offeree silently accepts the offered benefits.

    a) The offeree's benefiting from the proposed services are enough to constitute acceptance and create a contract.

    b) For example, if a book club mails the offeree a book of the month, which the offeree reads, he will be considered to have accepted it. If he does nothing with it or throws it away, acceptance by silence will not be presumed.

c. Communicated in the Right Way

    i. The offeror is the "master of the offer" sets the terms under which acceptance can be properly made.

    ii. If he asks for for acceptance by mail, acceptance cannot be transmitted fax, for example. If he states acceptance is rendered by performance, a return *promise* will not suffice.

    iii. If the way in which communication should be made is not stipulated by the offeror, the courts will presume it to be any method that is not slower or less legally reliable than the way that the offer was made.

d. Unequivocal Acceptance that Does Not Vary the Terms

    i. Minority Approach

        1) This is the older common law approach known as the "Mirror Image Rule."

        2) To be valid, the acceptance must be *identical* to the offer.

        3) Any response varying the terms of the offer would be a counteroffer, not acceptance.

    ii. Modern Restatement Approach

        1) Some slight changes of the offer are tolerated if they do not set up a condition to the acceptance. Otherwise, they will be construed as counteroffers.

2) *See Ardente v. Horan*, where the plaintiff made a bid to buy the defendant's house for $250,000. The defendant accepted and sent the plaintiff a purchase and sales agreement, which the plaintiff signed and sent back with a letter asking for the furniture in addition to the house. The court held that the offer was the purchase and sales agreement. The plaintiff's signing it did not constitute acceptance, since the letter sent along with it constituted a condition and therefore, a counteroffer.

iii. UCC Approach

1) Change or modification does not constitute rejection and counteroffer, but rather, it is an acceptance (unless it is made expressly contingent on the offeror's acceptance of the new terms) (UCC § 2-207(1)).

2) Assuming that a contract is formed and the acceptance is not expressly conditional on offeror's acceptance of new or different terms, the following happens to the new terms in the acceptance:

a) When *both parties are merchants*, the new terms become part of the accepted offer *unless*:

i) The original offer limited itself to its terms;

ii) The new terms materially alter the original offer; or

iii) The offeror already has rejected or rejects the new trems within reasonable time (UCC § 2-207(2)).

b) When one or both parties are *non-merchants*, the terms common to the offer and acceptance become part of the contract and the new terms become "proposals for addition to the contract." (UCC § 2-207(2)).

iv. Last Shot Rule

1) The last shot rule is used to determine which terms to apply when there is a contract in which the terms of the offer were different from those of the acceptance.

2) Under the last shot rule, the terms of the "last shot" or last counteroffer apply whenever it is determined that there is a contract.

3. Acceptance by Performance in Unilateral Contracts

a. A unilateral contract is contemplated when language in the contract or custom, trade practices, or tradition require acceptance via performance.

b. Interpreting Ambiguities in a Contract

  i. When it is ambiguous whether the offeror intended acceptance by performance or by return promise, the courts will read the offer as creating a bilateral contract, inviting acceptance via return promise or performance (Restatement § 32, UCC § 2-206)

  ii. If the offeror states, for example, that B may purchase his car *only* if he comes to the offeror's home on a particular day and pays him, a unilateral contract is contemplated and acceptance can only be made if if the offeree shows up in person and pays. A return promise will have no effect.

  iii. However, if the word "only" is removed, it will no longer be unequivocally clear that acceptance can be made only by performance. A court will therefore interpret the contract to be bilateral and inviting acceptance via promise or performance.

 c. It may be easy to confuse acceptance in a bilateral contract with performance in a unilateral contract. In a unilateral contract, after the offeree accepts, he has no other obligations to discharge. In a bilateral contract, however, he has not yet performend, even though he has accepted.

  i. For example, if one party offers to sell his car for $5,000 and stipulates that the only way the offeree can accept is by doing a cartwheel, the offeree has not performed until he has paid the $5,000. The cartwheel is merely a way of manifesting acceptance.

  ii. In contrast, if the first party offers to give to the second his car, with the only way of acceptance being doing a cartwheel, there would be a unilateral contract where the offer is accepted by performance, since doing the cartwheel is the only duty mentioned.

 d. In unilateral contracts, there is no duty to give notice of acceptance.

  i. *See Carlill v. Carbolic Smoke Ball Co.*, where Carbolic offered a reward to any users of its product who might become ill. The court held that the offer was to be accepted by performance and did not require notice of acceptance. A contract was therefore formed upon Carlill's using the product, becoming sick, and thereafter notifying Carbolic and demanding 100 pounds. Carbolic was obligated to pay her.

  ii. Thus, although in bilateral contracts, notification of acceptance is required to create the contract, in unilateral contracts, no such notice is required, *unless:*

   1) The offeror requests notice of performance. Restatement § 54(1); or

   2) The offeree knows that the offeror will not have knowledge of his performance in reasonable time. In this case, if the offeror does not find out, his obligations are dismissed, *unless*:

    a) The offeree, under due diligence, tried to inform him;

          b)   The offeror finds out about the offeree's performance on his own in due time; or

          c)   The offer indicates that notification of acceptance is not required. Restatement § 54(2).

    iii.   For example, if A offers B $20 to shovel his driveway over the weekend, and then indicates that he will be out of town for a week, notification of B's performance will be required, since A will not find out about B's performance in reasonable time.

e.   Acceptance by performance to an offer done in jest does not create a contract if a reasonable person, in the place of the offeree, would have known that an offer was made in jest.

    i.   *See Leonard v. Pepsico*, where the court held that a valid offer was never made and therefore, no contract was formed by acceptance via performance.

D.   E-COMMERCE AND MUTUAL ASSENT

1.   Rules Applied

a.   The same rules that apply to traditional cases also apply to e-commerce cases.

b.   However, courts are challenged as to how to *apply* traditional rules to cases involving the internet and other new phenomena.

c.   In some cases, opening up a package constituted acceptance to terms and conditions of an agreement when a notification was included on the package.

2.   End User License Agreements (EULA's)

a.   In e-commerce, acceptance can be made by agreeing to the terms of a pop-up window from a web-site publisher warning end-users that entering a web-site or purchasing a program constitutes acceptance of a contract.

    i.   *See Caspi v. Microsoft*, where the plaintiff brings a class action lawsuit against Microsoft for breach of contract and fraud. The defendant moves to dismiss the action, on the basis that the plaintiffs signed a EULA and thereby agreed that the courts of Washington would have personal jurisdiction and venue. The court held that the forum selection clause that the plaintiffs agreed to when downloading the software was valid, since it was not fraudulent or based on undue bargaining power or forced litigation in a forum inconvenient to the parties. Motion to dismiss granted.

    ii.   *Compare Ticketmaster v. Tickets.com*, where the plaintiff sued the defendant for having violated the EULA on the plaintiff's homepage by copying information onto the defendant's web site. The court held that the EULA was not enforceable as it was, since: (i) agreeing to the EULA was never required by users of the web site (as it was in *Caspi*); and (ii) the EULA was located in a part of the page that could be overlooked by users. Motion to dismiss granted, with a chance to amend the complaint in case there was evidence that the defendants saw the EULA.

b. Thus, for a EULA to be binding, the parties that accept it must have seen and agreed to it before proceeding.

c. Mere notification of the existence of a EULA on a different web page, or "browse wrap," does not constitute the necessary notification to end-users.

d. Rather, there must be a "shrink wrap" or "click" wrap that forms a unilateral contract when opened or clicked by the end-user. Otherwise, no contract is formed.

   i. *See Specht v. Netscape Communications* and *Specht v. Netscape Communications* on appeal, where the defendant objected to the plaintiffs' suit by pointing out to the EULA, which required that disputes be resolved by arbitration. The court held that the EULA, tucked away on a distant page that required clicking several times to be viewed, gave insufficient notice to end-users, and therefore did not create a valid contract.

   ii. Shrink wrap or "click wrap" forms a unilateral contract when opened (or clicked); "browse wrap" is insufficient.

III. ENFORCEABILITY

A. CONSIDERATION

1. The Bargain Theory of Consideration

   a. Distinguishing Bargains from Gratuitous Promises

      i. The Bargain

         1) With the exceptions of §§ 82 – 94 of the Restatement, for a promise to be enforceable, it must be supported by consideration (§ 17 Restatement).

         2) For there to be consideration, there must be a *bargained for exchange*. The promise must induce the detriment *and* the detriment must induce the promise.

         3) In other words, the promisor makes the promise in exchange for the promisee's giving up of value and the promisee gives up something of value to induce the promise (§ 71 Restatement).

            a) In minority jurisdictions, in order to have consideration, in addition to promisee's detriment, the promisor's benefit is required.

      ii. Gifts

         1) In a gift, on the other hand, a promise is made, but the promisee does not undergo any detriment. Furthermore, the promisor was not inducing an exchange.

2)   Thus, gifts are not binding because of the absence of consideration.

        a)   *See Johnson v. Otterbein University*, where the court refused to enforce Johnson's promise of a $100 gift to the university, since gifts lack consideration.

3)   Even if a gift is conditioned, it is still a gift and is therefore not enforceable.

        a)   A condition is not to be confused with consideration. If the gift is made on a condition, it is not enforceable. If it is made in exchange for consideration, then it is not truly a gift, but rather, a bargain, and is enforceable.

        b)   To be enforceable, it is not enough that the promise be performable on a certain contingency (§ 24). There must be consideration.

        c)   For example, if A promises to pay $100 to B to go to college, there is consideration if A is inducing B to go to college and B does.

        d)   However, if B understands that A is offering him a gratuity conditioned on his going to college, then there is no consideration.

iii.   If a promise is exchanged for performance, the promise is enforceable even if the performance benefits the promisee.

    1)   In *Hamer v. Sidway*, the defendant promised to pay the plaintiff $5,000 if the plaintiff refrained from drugs, alcohol and gambling. The plaintiff fulfilled his side of the bargain, but the defendant never paid. In response to a legal suit that followed, the defendant argued that because the plaintiff's performance benefited him, it did not constitute consideration. The court, reasoning that a forbearance of legal rights always constitutes bargained for consideration, ruled in favor of the plaintiff.

2.   Discerning the Agreement: Illusory Promises

a.   Introduction

i.   An illusory promise is one that appears on its face to be so insubstantial as to impose no obligation on the promisor.

ii.   When an illusory promise is made, the promisor is not really bound to do anything; there is no bargain or exchange.

iii.   As a general rule, a conditional promise is unenforceable when the condition is entirely within the promisor's control. In such a case, the promisor's promise is illusory and lacks consideration.

b.   Conditions of Satisfaction

i. Many courts therefore consider *conditions of satisfaction* based on taste (*e.g.*, "I will pay you to pay my portrait *if I like the result*") to be illusory, since there is no objective standard.

ii. Others, however, consider them to be valid by employing a good faith standard (if it can be shown that the promisor did not pay because he was genuinely not satisfied, there will be no breach; otherwise, there will be a breach).

c. Examples of Illusory Promises Lacking Consideration

i. "I promise to buy your laptop for $2000 *if I feel like it* when the time comes."

ii. A and B agree that B will buy as many widgets *as she wants* from A over the month at $1 each.

1) B's promise is illusory and unenforceable, since she has not committed to doing anything.

iii. "I will give you the exclusive right to use and license my name if you give me 50% of all your profits."

1) *See Wood v. Lucy, Lady Duff-Gorden*, where the defendant (Lucy) gave the plaintiff (Wood) an exclusive license to her name. When the Wood sued for breach of contract, Lucy argued that there was no contract because Wood assumed no obligations and was not required to earn any profits; the promise was illusory. The court held that although it was not explicitly stated, Wood implicitly promised to use his best efforts to sell Lucy's name to clothing licensees, he had indeed assumed obligations. The contract was thus binding.

iv. "I will buy your strip mall for $1,000,000 if I can find satisfactory lessees in the market."

1) This is not an illusory promise because fulfilling it is not entirely within the promisor's control, but rather, depends on external conditions that can be objectively tested by the market.

3. Past Acts or Events

a. A promise made for past acts or events is not enforceable.

b. If something was given or performed before a promise was made, courts generally hold that it was not bargained for; past consideration is no consideration.

i. *See Moore v. Elmer*, where Moore predicted that Elmer would die, and Elmer *later* promised to pay Moore his mortgage if he died as predicted. Valid consideration was not made since the prediction (the alleged consideration) was made before the promise.

ii. If Elmer had promised to pay Moore for the correct prediction *before it was made*, the prediction would serve as consideration and a court would enforce Elmer's promise to pay.

c. However, the modern approach is to treat past consideration already received (past performance) as "moral consideration" and to thus enforce promises made in exchange for this consideration.

4. Moral Consideration (§ 86 Restatement)

a. There are some exceptions to the rule that a promise without consideration is unenforceable.

b. One of these exceptions involves ***moral consideration***, which applies to promises made for a past service that *substantially benefited* the promisor and *detrimented* the promisee.

c. In these cases, although the past services are not strictly considered to be consideration, the courts will enforce the promise.

    i. *See Webb v. McGowin* (Supr. Ct.), where Webb, in protecting his boss from a falling object, became crippled. Although McGowin promised to pay Webb for the rest of his life, his executor failed to make the disbursements to Web from McGowin's estate. The court conceded that McGowin's promise did not induce Webb's fall, and that there was therefore no consideration. However, the court enforced the promise by substituting consideration with "moral consideration."

        1) This court represents the majority view, which not all courts accept.

    ii. *Compare Mills v. Wyman*, where the defendant offered to pay the plaintiff for the expenses of having taken care of the defendant's son during the defendant's son's illness, but never paid. The court held that the plaintiff did not act in consideration of the defendant's later promise to pay. Moral would apply if the son were an infant or of a well-disposed son, but he was instead a major who did not consider himself to be part of the father's family. The defendant is not morally obligated to his estranged son and is thus not obligated to his (implied) moral contracts.

        1) Note the difference in this case from *Webb*. Whereas in *Webb*, there is a material benefit to the promisor (McGowin), whose life was saved, in *Mills*, the promisor (the father) received no such direct benefit.

d. The Restatement (Second) of Contracts treats moral consideration in § 86, which states that a promise made for a previously received benefit is binding to the extent necessary to prevent injustice.

5. Contractual Modification

a. Traditional Rule: Consideration is Needed

    i. Under the traditional common law, all contractual modifications require consideration to be binding.

      ii.   If one party promises the other extra compensation for the same performance, the promise is unenforceable, since there is no consideration for the new promise.

      iii.   This rule is based on the ***preexisting duty rule***, which holds that a promise to compensate for performance that was already within a preexisting duty is not enforceable.

            1)   *See Stilk v. Myrick* (Ct. of Common Pleas 1809), where a captain agrees to distribute wages of two deserters to the remaining crew members in order to compensate them for their work. When the promised extra wages are never paid, a crew member sues. The court held that a subsequent promise offering more compensation for the same performance is not enforceable. Since the crew members had a preexisting duty to work until the ship arrived safely, even if, as the contract foresaw, some of the crewmembers deserted, the promise of extra compensation is unenforceable.

      iv.   This is currently the majority rule for contracts, outside of those governed by the UCC (see *infra.*).

   b.   Modern Approach: Foreseeability Test

      i.   In some jurisdictions, actual consideration is not needed for contractual modifications undertaken when unforeseeable circumstances cause the costs of performance of one of the parties to rise substantially.

      ii.   Under these circumstances, the extra costs serve as consideration for the contractual modification.

            1)   *See Brian Construction and Development Co. v. Brighenti*, where a contractor hired a subcontractor and furnished him with plans and information on what the job requires. The subcontractor agreed to complete "all requisite work," but later discovered that there is much more work than either party foresaw. The parties agreed for all the work to be done for 10% more. When subcontractor failed to perform, the contractor successfully enforced the new contract, which was held to be supported by consideration.

            2)   *Compare Stilk*, where *it was foreseen* in the contract that sailors might desert the ship. In *Brighenti*, on the other hand, because the quantity of work required was not foreseen by either party, the new contract was binding and does not merely grant more compensation for the same performance.

      iii.   This rule reflects the approach of those few states that have abrogated the preexisting duty rule.

   c.   Cases in Which Consideration is not Needed

i. As an exception to the general rule, a modification of a contract with a preexisting duty is enforceable even if it has no consideration, under the following circumstances (§ 89 Restatement):

1) It is equitable in light of circumstances not anticipated by the parties.

   a) This rule reflects the modern approach of those states that do not follow the preexisting duty rule.

   b) Example: the modification of a contract will be enforceable, even if unforeseen costs significantly increase the costs of performance by one of the parties.

2) It is provided for by statute.

   a) This would be the case, for example, of the UCC: an agreement modifying a contract for the sale of goods needs no consideration to be binding (UCC § 2-209(1)).

   b) The foreseeability test is not applicable; the parties only need to show they were modifying the contract in good faith.

   c) A party would be considered to have acted in good faith, even if he foresees the possibility of prices going up, but is not certain, and prices actually do later go up.

3) It is required by justice in light of a material change of position in reliance on it.

B. ADEQUACY OF CONSIDERATION

1. Under § 79 of the Restatement (Second) of Contracts, if there is consideration, there need not be:

   a. A benefit to the promisor or a detriment to the promisee (the Restatement's language is slightly different from the case law here; focus on the language of the Restatement);

   b. Equivalence of values exchanged;

   c. Mutuality of obligation (it does not matter whose duty is greater).

2. Inadequacy of consideration is thus no defense to the creation of an otherwise valid contract; all that is required for valid consideration is a "peppercorn's worth of value," as long as it is a good faith bargained-for exchange.

3. Thus, if a party purchases a good that has considerably less value than that party anticipated, an enforceable contract is nevertheless created. It is not for the courts to determine whether the prices in a contract was fair.

   a. *See Hardesty v. Smith*, where the defendant purchases from the plaintiff the ability to use an improvement to a lamp. When the plaintiff sues to force the defendant to pay, the defendant claims that he did not get what he was paying for. The court held that there is an enforceable contract, regardless of the value and insufficiency of the consideration.

b.   *N.B.:* had the defendant returned the product, he may have been able to get his money back; but here, he sought to invalidate the contract while holding on to the goods.

C.   FORMALITIES MANIFESTING AN INTENTION TO BE LEGALLY BOUND

1.   Introduction

a.   Formalities have several functions. In the first place, they serve as evidence that a transaction took place.

b.   Additionally, they serve a cautionary function: the promisor is warned that he is engaging in an enforceable act of volition. He is made aware that the device being used will attain a certain result.

c.   Historically, formalities have either taken the place of or "imported" consideration. The modern trend has been to abandon such practices and to look to the substance of the bargain to determine whethere there was in fact an exchange.

2.   The Seal (Restatement § 95)

a.   Under the common law, an agreement made under seal was considered to be binding even if it was not supported by consideration because the seal makes it clear that the parties were meant to be bound.

b.   The seal was said to "import" consideration.

c.   In the modern law, however, seals are rarely considered to import or serve as a substitute for consideration.

i.   For promises involving the sales of good, the UCC does not recognize seals.

ii.   At least thirty four states have abolished seals or treat sealed written promises as unsealed; most others modify the effect of seals.

iii.   Even in those states that do or did recognize the seal, it imports only a *rebuttable presumption of consideration.*

1)   *See In re Conrad's Estate (Pa. 1938),* where the court showed suspicion of a plaintiff who sought payments for judgment notes after the defendant died. Although the judgment note included a seal that, at the time, imported consideration at that time, the court does not recognize the note as binding, because it was presented so late after it was written.

2)   *Compare Aller v. Aller (N.J. Sup. Ct. 1878),* where the court did enforce a sealed note.

3. Nominal Consideration

   a. Although the courts will not look into the adequacy of consideration, a disparity in value sometimes indicates that the consideration was not in fact bargained for but was a mere pretense. Such consideration is said to be "nominal consideration" (in name only) and does not satisfy the requirements of a bargain (Comment *d*, § 79 Restatement).

   b. Something of indeterminate value can be validly exchanged as consideration for a sum of money. However, something of nominal determinate value, such as a penny, cannot be considered to be consideration in exchange for something else of a much greater value.

   c. Such an exchange is no bargain, but rather, an unenforceable contract.

      i. *See Schnell v. Nell*, where the husband promises to give money to three parties stipulated by his wife. He exchanges his promise to pay later for one cent, his wife's love and affection, and her wish to have the money paid. The court rules that this nominal consideration is no consideration at all. This promise is really no more than a gift, for there is no bargain, and it is therefore unenforceable.

4. Recitals

   a. When consideration is not exchanged, but is recited in the contract, there is a rebuttable presumption of consideration (just as with seals).

   b. This is like nominal consideration, except that, rather than being exchanged, it is simply written down.

   c. Recital of consideration may be contradicted by parol evidence (oral or written evidence of the bargain that occurred before the final terms of the contract were laid down and were not made part of the final contract).

      i. *See Allen v. Allen*, where the court ruled that the consideration of $1 in a promise by a mother to her son and daughter regarding the proceeds of the sale of the house was just a pretense. The parties never intended for the consideration to be paid and the lower court did in fact find that it was not paid. The agreement was therefore not enforceable.

   d. However, the fact that consideration is not delivered does not automatically void a contract. Many courts will enforce an options contract even when the recited consideration is never delivered.

      i. *See, e.g., Smith v. Wheeler*, where the defendant, in exchange for $1, gave the plaintiff one year to decide whether he wanted to purchase property for $30,000. The defendant rescinded the option on the basis that $1 was recital of nominal consideration that was never paid. The court nevertheless enforced the options contract, holding that the recital of consideration was sufficient for options contracts.

ii. This view is reinforced by § 87 of the Restatement (Second) of Constracts, which states that an *options contract* is enforceable if it merely recites consideration, as long as it is:

    1) in writing;

    2) signed by the offeror;

    3) for a reasonable duration; and

    4) fair.

iii. The recital of consideration needs to *look* like a bargain; this formality is essential.

e. The UCC goes even further, by establishing the enforceability of firm offers (options contracts), even when they are exchanged for neither real nor recited consideration (UCC § 2-205). Options contracts are legally binding and cannot be revoked for the time stated or a reasonable time not exceeding three months if no time is stated, if:

i. They are made by a merchant;

ii. To buy or sell goods;

iii. In a *signed writing* (this serves as a formality that can be said to have "replaced" the need for real or recited consideration); and

iv. Gives assurance that it will be held open.

D. PROMISSORY ESTOPPEL (RESTATEMENT § 90)

1. Definition and Elements

a. Promissory estoppel, or "detrimental reliance," is yet another means by which a party may argue for the enforceability of a contract that lacks consideration. It can be thought of as a form of protection in situations of detrimental reliance.

b. A promise may be enforced to prevent injustice, even if it lacks consideration, if the promisor should have expected the promisee to have relied on the promise and if the promisee did in fact rely on it to his detriment.

c. There are thus four elements:

i. There is a promise;

ii. The promisor reasonably expects that the promise will induce the promisee's action or forbearance (this can be shown deductively— "it is natural that ..."—or inductively, "the facts show that ...");

iii. The promise does in fact induce such action or forbearance;

iv. The detriment resulting from the promise requires enforcement of the promise for justice.

d.   It is the same as equitable estoppel, except that equitable estoppel requires not a promise, but a representation of facts that lead to detriment.

e.   Not all jurisdictions recognize promissory estoppel, and many will struggle to find consideration before going to this doctrine.

2.   Promissory Estoppel as a Substitute for Consideration

a.   If a promise is made that induces the promisee to act in a way that detriments him, then even if the promise was not bargained for, it can be enforced under the doctrine of promissory estoppel.

i.   *See Ricketts v. Scothorn*, where the plaintiff successfully sues her grandfather's estate, requiring it to pay her the promissory note which induced her to leave her job to her detriment.

b.   A promise to make a gift may be enforceable, if the promise induces the promisee to act to his detriment.

i.   *See Allegheny College v. National Chautauqua County Bank of Jamestown*, where the court "created" consideration for Johnston's promise to pay $5,000 after she dies. Although Johnston considered the school's work in promoting Christian education as consideration for her promise, there was no bargain because her promise did not induce the Christian education. The court nonetheless found consideration in the detriment the school faced in relying on hre promise and in setting up Johnston's memorial fund.

c.   A pension that normally would be considered to be a gift can similarly become enforceable under the doctrine of promisory estoppel.

i.   *See Feinberg v. Pfeiffer Co.*, where Feinberg, in reliance of a promise to pay a pension of $200 per month for the rest of her life, left her job when she was ill with cancer. When that pension was later cut, she sued, claiming that she and her husband had relied on this income.

E.   **THE WRITING REQUIREMENT AND THE STATUTE OF FRAUDS**

1.   The Statute of Frauds (SF) was an English statute whose purpose was to avoid fraud and perjury.

2.   Today, the SF imposes the following requirements on certain contracts in order for them to be enforceable:

a.   To be evidenced in a ***writing***;

b.   That is ***signed*** by the party to be charged; and

c.   That sufficiently describes the ***essential terms of the contract***.

3.   The SF is an *affirmative defense*. Thus, if the defendant fails to plead that the oral contract on which the plaintiff is suing falls within the SF writing requirement, he waives the defense and the contract may be enforced.

4. The following contracts fall within the SF and therefore can only be enforced if evidenced by a writing:

    a. Contracts Made upon Consideration of Marriage

        i. These fall within the statute and must be written and signed.

        ii. In order to induce B to accept his offer to get married, A orally offers to purchase her a car. B accepts, but A never delivers. Can B enforce the contract?

            1) Since it was not made in writing. It cannot be enforced.

        iii. However, an agreement consisting only of "mutual promises of two persons to marry each other" *that does not include ancillary promises to transfer property* does not fall within the statute and is enforceable even when not written and signed (§ 124 Restatement (Second) of Contracts).

    b. The One-Year Provision

        i. *Service contracts that cannot be performed within one year* from the making of the contract are only enforceable if in a signed writing.

        ii. *See Boone v. Coe* , where Coe, the defendant farm owner promised the plaintiff that he could lease Coe's land for one year as soon as the plaintiff arrived to the defendant's land. The court held that the contract was within the SF, since its completion could *only* happen *after* one year from the date that the contract was formed. Since the contract was not in writing, the plaintiff was not entitled to damages.

    c. Contracts for the Sale of Land Interests

        i. Contracts conveying the following land interests fall within the SF and must be in a signed writings:

            1) Land *sale contracts*;

            2) Real estate *mortgages*;

            3) *Leases* of land[3];

            4) *Easements* (the right to make use of another's property); and

            5) Life *estates*.

        ii. Although *construction contracts* relate to land, they are not interests in land and therefore do not fall within the SF.

    d. Sales of Goods

        i. Contracts for *sales of goods for more than $500* ($5,000 under amended art. 2 UCC) fall within the SF.

        ii. *Exception*: if B keeps the good for more than ten days, the writing requirement is waived.

---

[3] However, in the majority of jurisdictions, when a lease lasts for less than one year, it is not within the SF.

e. Suretyship/Guarantyship

    i. This refers to contracts where a second party is answering for the duty of another (*e.g.*, a surety answering for the duties of a debtor).

    ii. The contract must have three elements to fall within the SF:

        1) There must be three parties (the creditor, the debtor and the surety);

        2) There must be two promises (the debt obligation promise and the collateral promise); and

        3) The collateral promise must be secondary to the first; it must not take effect until there is breach of the first promise. That is, the surety will only pay the debt if the debtor fails to do so.

5. The following ***exceptions*** allow for oral contracts to be enforced despite the violation of the SF:

a. Realty and Service Contracts

    i. *Complete Performance*: when there has been complete performance by either side.

        1) For example, B offers to pay C to write a memo that can only be completed in eighteen months, but never signs a contract. C writes it and seeks payment. Normally, C would be unable to enforce the contract. However, the SF writing requirement does not apply, since performance was complete.

    ii. *Part Performance*: when there has been part performance by either side that *unequivocally* evidences a contract.

        1) For example, A takes possession and improves or begins payment of land sold to him by B, but B repudiates the contract. Even in the absence of a written contract, the sale can be enforced because of A's part performance.

    iii. *Preparation for Performance*: when there has been preparation for performance that evidences the existence of a contract, the promisee may invoke promissory estoppel (§ 129 for land; § 139 generally).

        1) When the promisor expects the promise to induce actions of the promisee, the promise does induce these actions, and the promisee is detrimented, the promise can be enforced even if it does not comply with the SF requirements.

        2) Hypo: the lessee arrives to Texas and the lessor revokes the offer. The lessee sues. Is contract enforceable without a contract signed by Coe?

            a) Normally, no, since the contract could only have been performed more than one year after the agreement and since it does not fall within the two exceptions: *complete performance* or *part performance* (coming to

Texas is not the beginning performance; moving in and beginning to erect the barn is).

b) However, the lessee may invoke *promissory estoppel* for damages against the promisor for revoking his offer, to the extent that the lessee's preparations induced damages.

b. Sales of Goods

i. This section applies to the sale of goods for over $500 ($5,000 in amended art. 2) (UCC § 2-201).

ii. Between Merchants (UCC § 2-201(2))

1) The SF writing requirement does not apply to contracts when the purchaser receives an invoice and does not protest for over ten days. The seller may enforce the contract, even without a writing signed by the purchaser.

2) For example, purchaser P purchases ten computers from seller S. S sends an invoice for one hundred computers. P neither signs the invoice, protests, nor pays. S tries to enforce the contract and B defends on the basis that there was no written contract.

a) A court will hold that because B never protested, the SF does not apply.

b) The contract will be enforced.

iii. Between Non-Merchants (UCC § 2-201(3))

1) Specially Manufactured Goods (UCC § 2-201(3)(a))

a) The SF writing requirement does not apply when the offeree orders *specially manufactured goods*.

b) For example, if the plaintiff orders ten customized coffee mugs, but never pays, the seller S can enforce the contract, even if P never signed a written document. The SF does not apply because the goods were custom made.

2) Estoppel (UCC § 2-201(3)(b))

a) Estoppel applies when the party against whom the contract is being enforced admits to there having been a contract. He becomes "estopped" from asserting the SF defense.

b) One cannot admit that he made a promise while simultaneously invoking the SF defense on the basis that the promise was not in writing. The admission prohibits the SF defense.

3) Part Performance (UCC § 2-201(3)(c))

a) The SF defense similarly does not apply when payment is sent to and accepted by the seller, or goods are sent to and received by the purchaser.

b)   For example, if S sends P two computers, which P accepts without protesting. The contract is enforceable, even absent a signed contract, through the plaintiff's part performance by accepting, thereby waiving his SF defense.

c)   This exception is similar to that offered to merchants, except that the exception for merchants would apply *even if only the invoice were received.*

6.   Satisfying the Writing Requirement

a.   When an offer to sell property is made in writing, the mailed title and deed cannot become a binding contract upon oral acceptance of the offer. Written acceptance is necessary.

     i.   *See Schwedes v. Romain*, where the court did not accept as binding the plaintiff's oral acceptance of the defendant's written offer to sell property.

b.   Satisfying the writing requirement does not mean satisfying a strict, rigid standard; the contract can be evidenced in *any* writing, even by a note written to oneself in a journal.

c.   The writing must identify the subject matter of the contract and must be signed by the party against whom it is being enforced.

     i.   If the subject matter is not identified in the writing of a journal entry, then another journal entry from the same journal, whose subject matter can reasonably traced to the one where there was acceptance, can be used to create the necessary writing.

d.   Many questions have arisen with respect to whether emails and other electronic texts can be construed as satisfying the writing requirement.

     i.   *See In re RealNetworks*, where a digital EULA was considered to be a written contract for the purposes of the SF. Contrary to the plaintiffs' arguments, it can easily be saved to one's hard drive and printed.

7.   Satisfying the Signature Requirement

a.   The party being charged must have signed the writing in order for it to be enforced.

b.   For example, if A sues to enforce B's payment of $10,000 for a car sold to him, and all A can produce is an invoice with his own signature, the courts will not enforce.

c.   However, there are no strict, rigid rules for satisfying the signature requirement.

     i.   *See Parma Tile Mosaic and Marble Co. v. Estate of Fred Short*, where MRLS Construction Corp. sent a written notice that indicated "MRLS" but was not signed. MRLS argued that this did not satisfy the SF signature requirement. The court disagreed, holding that any symbol written or stamped on the document may constitute a signature, as long as the intent to be bound is manifested.

    ii.   With this broad definition of "signature," one can argue as to whether an email, or a voicemail can also constitute a signature.

8.   Interpreting a Writing: the Parol Evidence Rule

    a.   Common Law Approach

        i.   Under the parol evidence rule, supplementary oral or written evidence of any agreement prior to or contemporaneous with the laying down of the final terms of the contract cannot be used to contradict or vary the final agreement.

        ii.   However, such supplementary oral or written evidence can be used to clarify incomplete or vague contractual terms, even if the parol evidence is oral and the contract is written.

        iii.   If the terms of a contract are neither vague nor incomplete, parol evidence is inadmissible.

            1)   *See Thompson v. Libbey*, where the plaintiff sued when the logs that he ordered turned out to be of poor quality. During the trial, the defendant submitted parol evidence regarding the warranty that was not in the written agreement, which the lower court admitted. On appeal, the court reversed, excluding the parol evidence, since the terms of the written agreement were neither *incomplete* nor *vague*. The parol evidence was not necessary to clarify or determine the terms of the agreement.

        iv.   Under the parol evidence rule, collateral agreements that deal with issues not addressed in the final agreement are admissible, since they do not contradict or vary the terms of the final agreement.

    b.   UCC Approach for the Sale of Goods

        i.   The UCC does not allow written or oral evidence prior to the written *final expression of the agreement* to contradict that agreement or to contradict the terms "to which the confirmatory memoranda of the parties agree" (UCC § 2-202).

        ii.   Evidence of *consistent additional terms*, however, may be used to explain or supplement the final expression of the agreement, *unless the court finds the written agreement to be the complete, final, and exclusive statement of the terms* (usually through a merger clause).

        iii.   However, even if there is a merger clause, the final agreement may be *explained or supplemented* by course of performance, course of dealing, and usage of trade.

    c.   Compared

        i.   Both the common law and the UCC are based the idea that outside terms may not be used to contradict a fully integrated agreement.

ii. However, the UCC allows evidence of course of performance, course of dealing, and usage of trade *even if there is a fully integrated agreement.*

IV. CONDITIONS AND THE ABSOLUTE DUTY TO PERFORM

A. INTRODUCTION TO CONDITIONS

1. Definition

   a. A condition is an uncertain future event on which an obligation depends.

   b. When performance is based on an unsatisfied condition, nonperformance is not a breach of contract.

   c. Suppose, for example, that an insurance company promises to indemnify a client if (i) his home burns down; and (ii) he files a claim without thirty day. The insurance company's failure to pay would not constitute breach of contract if either of the conditions were not met.

2. Classification of Conditions

   a. Classification by Time of Occurrence

      i. Condition Precedent

         1) A condition precedent is an event whose occurrence or non occurrence triggers the obligation to perform.

         2) For example, if the promise is to shovel a driveway if it snows, the fact of snowing is a condition precedent that triggers the duty to shovel.

      ii. Condition Subsequent

         1) A condition subsequent excuses the duty to perform after the performance has begun.

         2) For example, if the promisor agrees to "work for you for one year, unless I am accepted to graduate school," the occurrence of admission to graduate school discharges the duty to continue working for a full year.

      iii. Condition Concurrent

         1) A condition concurrent is an occurrence that must occur at the same time as other occurrences.

         2) The parties may, for example, agree to exchange payment and a deed at a closing. The conditions in this case would be "I will give you the payment if you give me the deed" and vice versa.

   b. Express, Implied-in-Fact, and Constructive (Implied-in-Law) Conditions

      i. Express Conditions

        1)   Express conditions are mentiond in the contract.

        2)   No special language is necessary, but courts will more likely enforce express conditions if phrases such as "provided that" or "if" are included.

        3)   When a condition relates to time, the best way would be to include the phrase, "time is of the essence."

        4)   There are two kinds of express conditions:

            a)   *Simple express conditions*, where the event is outside the control of either party (*e.g.*, whether it will rain); and

            b)   *Promissory express conditions*, where one of the parties has some control over the occurrence of the event (*e.g.*, "I will buy the computer subject to my getting the finances").

   ii.   Implied-in-Fact Conditions

        1)   Implied-in-fact conditions are deduced by the facts in a case that make it reasonable that they were intended.

        2)   For example, it is implied that a fire insurance company will pay only for damage caused by a fire and not by a flood, even if this condition is not expressly made in the contract.

   iii.   Constructive (Implied-in-Law) Conditions

        1)   A constructive condition is is a legal fiction invented by the courts.

        2)   It is not derived from a contract, as in the case of an express condition, or from the intent of the parties or facts of a case, as in the case of an implid-in-fact condition.

3.   Other Conditions

   a.   Conditions of Satisfaction

      i.   Two standards can be used in measuring satisfaction.

      ii.   When the satisfaction involves utility or marketability (construction, manufacturing, etc.), an *objective standard* based on a reasonable person is employed.

      iii.   When the satisfaction relates to purely subjective tastes, a *subjective standard* based on *good faith* seen in the discussion on illusory promises is employed.

   b.   Certificates of approval

      i.   A party's paying another may be contingent on a certificate by a third party expert attesting that the work is in accordance with specifications.

      ii.   This would be the case of a condition that a contractor's improvements on a home are subject to the inspection and approval of an architect who indicates that the work is of adequate quality.

     c.   Conditions of time

         i.   The best way to make a time condition express would be to state "time is of the essence" (or similar terms such as "provided that" or "if") or to create an options contract.

         ii.   Without these "magic phrases," time is neither a condition nor a promise and therefore, if performance is late, the contract is not considered to have been breached, as long as performance is rendered in reasonable time.

4.   The Effect of a Condition

     a.   When a condition is not met, the party protected by the condition is not obligated to perform.

     b.   However, conditions will be ignored by the courts when they are prohibited by public policy.

         i.   *See Inman v. Clyde Hall Drilling Co.*, where the plaintiff Inman signed a contract agreeing that he would give the defendant thirty days notice if he made any claims against him. When he is fired, Inman sues for wrongful discharge. The defendant argues that Inman cannot sue because he did not meet the notice provision. Held: because the defendant's requirement is not contrary to public policy, and since courts should not alter the contracts of parties who are sufficiently capable of drafting them, the provision is a valid condition.

B.   **SATISFYING A CONDITION**

1.   Introduction

     a.   This section applies when one party's performance is *expressly* or *constructively* a condition precedent to the other party's counter-performance.

     b.   The standard of performance required depends on whether the condition is *express* or *constructive* (implied-in-law).

2.   Express Conditions

     a.   Perfect Performance

         i.   Perfect performance is full, not necessarily perfect performance, within the bounds of reasonable expectations.

         ii.   One party's perfect performance *satisfies the condition precedent* and triggers the other side's duty to counter-perform.

     b.   Substantial Performance

         i.   Substantial performance is slightly below reasonable expectations.

         ii.   Generally courts consider substantial performance to give rise to a non-material breach and *not to satisfy an express condition;* otherwise, the intent of the parties may be defeated.

     c.   Inferior Performance

        i.   Inferior performance is far below reasonable expectations.

        ii.   It is the equivalent of a material breach that does *not satisfy express conditions*.

3.   Constructive (Implied-in-Law) Conditions

    a.   Perfect or substantial performance satisfies the condition.

    b.   Inferior performance does not satisfy the condition.

C. EXCUSING CONDITIONS

1.   Interpretation of an Event as a Promise or Condition

    a.   When it is ambiguous whether an event is a condition or a promise, a court will interpret the event as a promise in order to avoid the forfeiture of a contract.

        i.   *See Howard v. Federal Crop Insurance Corp.*, where the court held that because the plaintiff Howard's duty to not destroy the crops before the defendant inspected them was described as a condition precedent in one place in the contract but in another place not, the event will be considered to be a promise.

    b.   Sometimes, a court will see an event as neither a condition nor a promise, but rather, as a convenient way of fulfilling a contract.

        i.   *See Chirichella v. Erwin*, where the court held that the settlement on the defendants' new home in approximately October of 1971 was *not a condition precedent* to their sale of their old home to the plaintiffs, but rather, an agreement of a convenient time to settle.

2.   Excuse to Prevent Forfeiture

    a.   When the non-occurrence of a condition would lead to a *disproportionate forfeiture*, courts often excuse a condition precedent, treating it as though it had occurred.

    b.   If a court were to strictly require the condition to be met, the counter-performing party would be unjustly enriched, since he would have received nearly full performance while being discharged from his duty to perform.

    c.   Courts tend to excuse conditions in these circumstances when their occurrence is not a material term of the contract.

        i.   *See J.N.A. Realty Corp. v. Cross Bay Chelsea*, where the plaintiff J.N.A. granted the defendant an option as an express condition to renew its lease within six months notice. The defendant failed to renew and the plaintiff's duty to continue to lease the property was discharged. The plaintiff sued to recover possession. Held: where failure of a condition is caused by a party's negligence, and that failure does not harm the other party, equity will excuse the condition. Here, the defendant invested $15,000 on the property and equity demands that the condition be excused.

3.   Divisibility of Contract

    a.   Divisibility of contract is meant to avoid the harsh effects of forfeiture when one side has substantially performed.

    b.   A contract is divisible when:

        i.   The performance of each party *may be divided* into two or more parts;

        ii.   The parties agree on the *equivalence* of one party's unit of performance in relation to that of the other party; and

        iii.   The *number of units* of each side's performance is the *same*.

    c.   The condition of complete performance is excused when one party performs some of the units of a divisible contract. That party receives compensation for the parts performed.

    d.   For example, if A agrees to mow ten lawns but only mows nine of them, he will receive the payment proportional to the work he did, even if mowing all ten lawns was a condition precedent to his being paid.

    e.   Similarly, *installment contracts*, where goods are delivered in separate lots, are divisible contracts that permit the seller to demand payment for each lot delivered.

4.   Minor Breach

    a.   When one party's performance is a condition precedent to a second party's counter-performance, the failure to meet the condition prevents the second party's duty to perform from becoming absolute.

    b.   However, when the breach is minor, the condition is excused and the duty to counter-perform becomes absolute.

        i.   Exception: when ***perfect performance*** is an ***express condition*** to the second party's counter-performance, courts will generally not excuse its occurrence.

        ii.   Exception to the exception: when enforcing the express condition of perfect performance causes ***forfeiture***, courts will generally excuse the condition.

5.   Anticipatory Repudiation

    a.   If a party whose duty to perform is contingent on the occurrence of a condition repudiates the contract, the benefit of the condition is extinguished and treated as though it has occurred.

    b.   The breaching party may not assert the failure of the condition as a reason for nonperformance.

    c.   For example, suppose that a purchaser, before he goes to the bank to get the financing to buy a computer, repudiates the purchase agreement. If the seller sues, the purchaser may not assert as a defense the non-occurrence of the condition precedent that he obtain financing. Because the purchaser anticipatorily repudiated the contract, the condition is treated as though it occurred.

6. Wrongful Interference

    a. The elements to a wrongful interference (failure to cooperate) are as follow:

        i. There must be a party whose duty to perform becomes absolute upon the occurrence of a condition.

        ii. A party must wrongly interfere with the occurrence of the condition in one of the following ways:

            1) *Passive non-cooperation* that would not have been anticipated by the other party in the contract;

            2) *Active non-cooperation*; or

            3) *Malice*/bad faith.

        iii. Finally, it must be clear that the condition would have occurred, but for the wrongful interference.

    b. When these elements are met, the duty to perform becomes absolute, even though the condition did not occur.

    c. For example, if a purchaser agrees to buy a car if he is able to get the financing, but then fails to cooperate with a lender by giving his requisite credit history, the condition precedent that he acquire financing will be treated as though it occurred.

7. Waiver and Estoppel

    a. Waiver

        i. Waiver occurs when the party having the benefit of a condition indicates by words or action that he will perform, regardless of whether the condition occurs.

        ii. Some waivers are treated as unenforceable gifts.

            1) For example, if one party waives the requirement that the other party substantially perform, in essence he is giving a gift by agreeing to pay or perform without requiring the other party to do the same.

            2) Because there is no bargained for exchange, the waiver is unenforceable.

    b. Estoppel

        i. Once a party has waived a condition, he is estopped from later raising its nonoccurrence as a defense.

            1) *See Clark v. West*, where the court held that if the defendant waived the condition that the plaintiff Clark abstain from alcohol in order to be paid $6 per page of law books written,

the non-occurrence of the condition could not be raised as a defense and the defendant would be obligated to pay $6 per page, even if Clark did not abstain from alcohol.

    ii.   Elements of estoppel:

        1)   The party benefiting from a condition indicates that he is waiving the condition; and

        2)   The other party detrimentally relies on this indication.

8.   Impossibility, Impracticability, Frustration

    a.   *See infra.*, Defenses to Contractual Obligation for rules and tests.

D.   CONSTRUCTIVE CONDITIONS

1.   Introduction

    a.   Constructive conditions have the effect of conditions but are not expressed in the contract.

    b.   Courts create them based on the facts of the case for the sake of equity.

    c.   They are not *implied* from the facts, as implied-in-fact conditions are; nonetheless; courts often refer to and treat implied-in-fact conditions as constructive contracts.

2.   The Three Classes of Contracts under the Old Common Law

    a.   Mutually Independent Covenants

        i.   One party's breach does not excuse the other party's nonperformance; each party is required to perform, regardless of the other party's failure to perform.

        ii.   Either party may recover damages from the other party for breach.

    b.   Dependent Covenants

        i.   These are covenants conditioned on the other side's performance; a party is not required to perform until a condition requiring the other side's performance is met.

        ii.   A party's duty to perform is excused if the other party does not perform.

    c.   Concurrent Covenants

        i.   In a concurrent covenant, each party has a concurrent duty to perform that is dependent on the other side's performance.

        ii.   These are therefore a kind of dependent covenant.

        iii.   An example would be a purchase where the seller is obligated to deliver the good at the same time that the purchaser is obligated to tender payment.

3.   Construing Dependency and Independency of Covenants Based on Timing (§ 234 Restatement)

a. Default rule: when both performances can be exchanged simultaneously, they are due simultaneously.

    i. A court may look to whether the performances *can be exchanged simultaneously*.

    ii. If so, a constructive condition is created whereby dependant covenants are formed and the duties to perform are concurrent.

    iii. Each side must tender performance before declaring the other side to have breached.

        1) *See Kingston v. Preston*, where the court held that, because giving sufficient security for payments was to be performed at or before the delivery of the deeds of the business, it was a condition precedent to the sale. Thus, the plaintiff Kingston must first show that he obtained the requisite security before being able to sue for SP.

    iv. Many courts further require that the parties aver in the pleadings that they tendered performance.

        1) *See Morton v. Lamb*, where the plaintiff was to pay the defendant at the time that the defendant was to deliver corn. The court concluded that the covenants were concurrent and hence dependent. However, in a suit to recover for damages for breach, the suing party must have been ***ready and willing to tender performance*** and aver the same in his pleadings. Here, the plaintiff failed to make such an averment.

b. When, however, only one party requires a period of time to perform, *that party should perform earlier*.

    i. A constructive condition is created whereby this first performance is a condition precedent to the second performance.

    ii. The first performance is thus an independent promise; the second promise is dependent on performance of the first (unless the language or circumstances require otherwise).

V. WHEN THE DUTY TO PERFORM IS DISCHARGED

A. SATISFACTION OF DUTY BY PERFORMANCE

1. Introduction

    a. Performance is the most common way of discharging a duty to perform.

    b. There are several standards through which to measure performance.

2. Standards of Performance

    a. Perfect Performance

        i. Perfect performance is full performance within the bounds of reasonable expectations.

   ii. It ***always satisfies*** the duty to perform.

  b. Inferior Performance

   i. Inferior performance is far below reasonable expectations and constitutes a material breach.

   ii. It ***always discharges*** the second party's duty to counter-perform.

  c. Substantial Performance

   i. This is performance with a minor breach that is slightly below reasonable expectations.

   ii. It generally satisfies a party's duty to perform.

   iii. However, when there is an ***express condition*** that a party's performance be perfect, courts are hesitant to allow substantial performance satisfy the condition, *unless strict adherence to the condition leads to forfeiture*, in which case the condition will be excused.

    1) *See Jacob and Young v. Kent*, where the contract expressly required Reading pipe, but the plaintiff used another kind of pipe. Held: when the breach is slight, the condition should be treated as an independent promise leading to damages rather than an express condition precedent leading to unjust forfeiture. Here, the departure from the contract was trivial and the plaintiff acted in good faith. To avoid injustice, the condition will be considered met. Thus, substantial performance of an independent covenant is satisfaction of a constructive condition and triggers the dependent covenant to make payment.

    2) *N.B.*: factors that courts look to when allowing a condition to be met through substantial performance include ***good faith*** on the part of the performer (no intent to breach) and the ***functional equivalence*** of the substantial performance.

   iv. Some contracts specifically state that if performance deviates from perfect performance, there must be replacement. Even in these circumstances, courts will only reward damages.

    1) *See Jacob and Youngs v. Kent* (N.Y. 1921) on motion for reargument, where the defendant, pointed out that a contractual provision required the plaintiff to replace all of the plumbing if he did not use the Reading pipe. Held: since substitution of the Reading pipe with another pipe is of such a trivial difference and the promise to perfectly perform is independent of the promise to pay, the plaintiff is liable only for damages in the form of ***the difference between*** the ***perfect performance*** and the ***actual performance.***

B. AGREEMENTS DISCHARGING THE DUTY TO PERFORM

1. Mutual Rescission

        a.   Mutual rescission causes the duty of each party to perform to be discharged.

        b.   The parties must expressly and mutually agree to be discharged from the agreement.

2.   Accord and Satisfaction

        a.   This applies when there is a dispute and the parties disagree on the content of the original contract (*e.g.*, the price in a sale of goods).

        b.   The parties may come to a compromise through accord and satisfaction.

        c.   An ***accord*** is an agreement that a debt obligation be settled for less than the person who is owed the debt is entitled.

        d.   ***Satisfaction*** refers to the satisfactory fulfillment of the debt obligation through the rendering of the agreed-to lesser performance.

        e.   If, in a dispute on price, one side sends partial payment in a check with "payment in full" indicated thereon, accord and satisfaction will be presumed if the receiving party cashes the check.

        f.   This is true even if the receiving party ***crosses out "payment in full"*** when cashing the check.

        g.   The obligee is thereafter barred from seeking to enforce the full contract price.

        h.   Under the UCC, however, the check can be cashed without the presumption of accord and satisfaction if the receiving party writes "without prejudice" or "cashed under protest" on the back of the check. UCC § 1-308.

3.   Novation and Substitute Agreements

        a.   Novation is the substitution of a party or parties in a contract.

        b.   The following elements are required:

                i.   A previous ***valid contract***; and

                ii.   A new ***valid contract*** that, with the agreement of all the parties:

                        1)   Revokes the former contract; and

                        2)   Names different parties.

        c.   A substitute agreement is a form of novation that requires:

                i.   A previous ***valid contract***;

                ii.   A ***valid substitute agreement*** that, with the *agreement of all the same parties*:

                        1)   Expressly or impliedly revokes the former contract; and

                              a)   If the new contract does not expressly revoke the old contract, the old contract will be impliedly revoked when the new contract contains terms that are inconsistent with the former.

2) Includes *new terms*.

C. PROSPECTIVE NONPERFORMANCE AND MATERIAL BREACH OF CONTRACT

1. Prospective Nonperformance

    a. Anticipatory Repudiation

        i. There are two interests in any contract:

            1) The actual performance;

            2) The assurance in knowing that there is a deal.

        ii. Even when a party does not breach his duty to perform, the second interest may be breached if he repudiates his promise to perform.

        iii. In such a case, the other party need not wait until the anticipated or agreed to time of performing before suing to recover damages.

            1) *See Albert Hochster v. Edgar De La Tour*, where the defendant Edgar De La Tour argued that the plaintiff should not be able to bring suit against him, since he had not yet breached his duty to hire the plaintiff, but had only repudiated the contract. The court held that a non-breaching party may *immediately sue* when the other party anticipatorily repudiates.

        iv. Repudiation must be *unequivocal*.

            1) A request or inquiry is not the same as anticipatory repudiation.

            2) *See Harrell v. Sea Colony, Inc.*, where the court held that a conditional inquiry regarding the cancellation of a contract was not enough to constitute anticipatory repudiation.

        v. Retraction of Repudiation

            1) Under the common law approach, once a party repudiates a contract, he cannot retract it; the other party is discharged of his duty.

            2) Under the UCC and Restatement approaches, a party may retract the repudiation if the following conditions are met:

                a) The retraction is done in *reasonable time* (under the circumstances);

                b) The non-breaching party has *actual notice* (through either the retracting party or another party); and

                c) The non-breaching party has *assurances* that the retracting party will perform.

        vi. Prospective Inability to Perform

            1) The anticipatory repudiation may also be by conduct.

2) This would be the case when a purchaser learns that the seller has sold the object of the sale to another party.

b. Adequate Assurances of Performance

  i. In some cases, it is not clear whether a party has repudiated.

  ii. In such situations, the second party may demand adequate assurances of performance in writing.

  iii. If the second party does not receive the assurances, he may withhold performance.

  iv. However, in sales under the UCC, the request for adequate assurances of performance *must be made in writing*.

    1) *See Scott v. Crown*, where the plaintiff Scott entered into a contract to sell the defendant wheat, and later entered into identical contracts with him. The plaintiff, later hearing about the defendant's trade practices, became worried about being paid, and demanded adequate assurances of performance. The defendant never responded but sent trucks to pick up wheat, which the plaintiff refused to load. When the defendant failed to make April payments, the plaintiff sued for breach of contract. The defendant counterclaimed, arguing the plaintiff's breach for not loading the wheat. Held: the plaintiff did not in fact have adequate assurance of performance, but because the plaintiff did not request assurances in writing as required by the UCC, the plaintiff was not discharged of his duty to deliver the wheat.

2. Material Breach (Inferior Performance)

  a. A party's **material breach** resulting from **inferior performance** discharges the other party's duty to perform.

  b. In determining whether a breach was material or immaterial, the courts will consider:

    i. Whether the breach is *intentional* or *negligent*;

    ii. Whether the breaching party *gains from the breach*;

    iii. Whether the breach was *outside of the breaching party's control*;

    iv. The extent to which the *non-breaching party will obtain substantial benefits*;

    v. The extent to which *damages make non-breaching party whole*;

    vi. The likelihood that the *breaching party will perform the remainder* of contract.

  c. Several of these factors together considered will usually shape the court's decision.

    i. *See Continental Grain Co. v. Simpson Feed Co.* (the defendant-seller), where the defendant agreed to sell 10,000 bushels of soybeans to the plaintiff. In the second shipment, the defendant did not receive the plaintiff's instructions, and, considering that to be a material breach, did not deliver the bushels. Held: a delay in sending shipping instructions is not sufficiently material to discharge the defendant of his duty to perform when *time was not of the essence*. The defendant was not materially injured by the delay and the plaintiff did not delay the instructions in intentionally.

    d.   Failure to pay only a slight percent of a contract price is not sufficiently material to discharge the non-breaching party of his duty to perform.

        i.   *See Lane Enterprises v. L.B. Foster Co.*, where the plaintiff, a general contractor, subcontracted a job to the defendant to treat bridge steel components. When the defendant's performance was inadequate, the plaintiff demanded that it be redone and requested assurance that the second batch would be done correctly. When the defendant failed to make assurances, the plaintiff sued for breach of contract. The defendant counterclaimed that the plaintiff materially breached by not giving full payment on part performance. Held: the plaintiff's withholding of 5% payment is not material breach under the Restatement § 241. The defendant's failing to give adequate assurances of performance is anticipatory repudiation and discharges the plaintiff's duty to perform.

D.   OTHER WAYS OF DISCHARGING THE DUTY TO PERFORM

    1.   Unilateral Rescission

        a.   One party may sue under equity to rescind a contract unilaterally, even when the second party does not want to rescind.

        b.   A party generally seeks unilateral rescission when he may assert a defense, such as improper obtainment of assent, or a failure of a basic assumption (*see infra.*).

    2.   Occurrence of a Condition Subsequent

        a.   When a condition subsequent occurs, the party whose duty to perform was contingent on the nonoccurrence of that condition is discharged of that duty.

    3.   Discharge by Illegality

        a.   This applies when the parties enter into a contract and the performance of a contractual obligation later becomes illegal.

        b.   *See* "Changed Circumstances," *infra.*

VI.   DEFENSES TO CONTRACTUAL OBLIGATION

A.   LEGAL INCAPACITY

    1.   Infancy

        a.   Anyone under the age of eighteen is considered by the law to be an infant.

b.   Generally, a contract between an infant and an adult is voidable by the infant, but binding on the adult.

c.   The infant may disaffirm the contract at anytime before he reaches majority (eighteen years of age).

   i.   Upon disaffirming, the infant gets restoration, not restitution.

      1)   For example, if an infant purchases a bike that he later destroys in an accident, by later disaffirming the contract, he would be entitled to a full refund, regardless of the condition of the bike.

d.   After reaching majority, he may only void the contract *after a reasonable time*.

e.   Exceptions

   i.   Misrepresentation

      1)   The infant's power to disaffirm the contract may terminate if the he lies about his age.

      2)   A clause in the contract including the minor's misrepresentation of his age could be used to prove the misrepresentation.

   ii.   Necessities

      1)   Infants are bound by contracts involving necessities and are responsible for the fair market value of the goods.

      2)   Necessities are determined relatively according to the child's economic class; rich and poor children will have different necessities.

2.   Mental Incapacity

   a.   Mental incapacity applies when a party is adjudicated as incompetent.

   b.   It serves as a defense to a contractual obligation by making the contract voidable.

   c.   If a mentally incompetent person enters into a contract, he may disaffirm it when he is lucid or have it disaffirmed by a legal representative.

   d.   He may similarly affirm the contract when lucid or when restored to normal mental capacity (with or without judicial action).

   e.   There is quasi-contractual recovery for necessities furnished during incapacity.

3.   Intoxication

   a.   Contracts entered into by intoxicated persons are voidable when a reasonable person would have known that the person was intoxicated.

b.   The intoxicated party may disaffirm the contract upon becoming sober.

c.   There is quasi-contractual recovery for necessities furnished during the intoxication.

B.   OBTAINING ASSENT BY IMPROPER MEANS

1.   Misrepresentation

   a.   A misrepresentation is any statement "not in accord with the facts." Restatement § 159.

   b.   It may be ***innocent*** or ***fraudulent***.

   c.   Misrepresentation serves as a defense to a contractual obligation that makes a contract voidable when:

      i.   The misrepresentation is *material* (it is "*likely to induce a reasonable person*" into the contract, or the maker knows that the misrepresentation would be likely to do so. Restatement § 162); and

      ii.   The victim *justifiably relies* on it.

   d.   The remedy for material misrepresentation, whether it is innocent or fraudulent, is ***rescission***.

      i.   *See Halpert* (plaintiff) *v. Rosenthal*, where the plaintiff represented that a home was termite-free and agreed to sell it to the defendant. After learning that the home was infested with termites, the defendant sought to rescind the contract and his deposit. The plaintiff sued for SP and damages. Held: even if the plaintiff's misrepresentation was innocent, it was material and rescission is therefore available to the defendant.

   e.   However, the representation must be as to present, existing ***facts***, not opinions.

      i.   *See Byers v. Federal Land Co.* (the defendant–seller), where the plaintiff entered into a contract to buy the defendant's 3,200 acres based on the defendant's promise that each acre was worth $35 and that the plaintiff would obtain immediate possession. When the plaintiff later found out that the defendant was not the actual owner and that each acre was worth substantially less, the plaintiff demanded rescission. Held: since the defendant's representation of the value of each acre was an opinion made innocently, the plaintiff was not justified in relying on it. However, the misrepresentation regarding the possession constitute a material breach, since the defendant never had possession of property.

   f.   Although generally, recipients of opinions are not justified in relying on those opinions, there are exceptions under the Restatement § 169:

      i.   When the parties are in a ***fiduciary relationship***;

      ii.   When the party receiving the opinion is ***particularly susceptible*** to misrepresentation;

   iii. When the party making the opinion has ***superior knowledge***.

     1) *See Vokes v. Arthur Murray, Inc.* (defendant), where the plaintiff claims that the defendant intentionally misrepresented the plaintiff's potential to succeed in dance in order to induce her to purchase substantial hours of dance lessons. Held: when an opinion is made by one having superior knowledge, that opinion will be treated as a fact and material misrepresentation through that opinion will allow contract rescission.

 2. Fraud

  a. Fraud in the *Factum*

   i. This occurs when one party induces a second party to sign a contract without the second party's understanding of what he is signing.

   ii. Example: an employee signs a contract when misleadingly told by his employer that it merely allows the company to publish the employee's email address on the directory. In reality, the employee transferred title to his car.

   iii. Fraud in the *factum* is a defense that voids a contract and discharges the victim of his contractual obligation to perform.

   iv. It is a defense that is rarely invoked in comparison to fraud in the inducement.

  b. Fraud in the Inducement

   i. In referring to fraud, the courts generally are making reference to fraud in the inducement, which is a misrepresentation made whenever:

     1) The maker intends his assertions to induce a second party to enter into the agreement; and

     2) The maker knows that his assertions are false or does not have the confidence that he states or implies in the truth of the assertions or knows that he does not have the basis that he states or implies for the assertion. Restatement § 162.

   ii. Fraudulent misrepresentation is a defense that voids a contract and discharges the victim's contractual obligation to perform.

 3. Duress

  a. Duress excuses contractual obligations when the following elements are met:

   i. There is a threat;

   ii. That is improper;

   iii. That induces a party to enter into a contract.

  b. A threat is improper when:

i. The threatened act is *illegal*;

ii. The threat is of *death* or *bodily harm*;

iii. The threat is of *criminal prosecution* for personal gain;

iv. The threat is a *breach of good faith* and fair dealing that hurts the victim without benefiting the party making the threat.

v. The victim is *left without a choice* in entering the contract.

    1) *See Silsbee v. Webber* (defendant), where the plaintiff entered into contract to pay a $1,500 settlement agreement to the defendant for her son who was accused of embezzling from the defendant, his employer. The plaintiff signed a settlement agreement with the defendant when he threatened to tell the plaintiff's deeply troubled and melancholy husband, who would be greatly disturbed if he found out about the accusation. The plaintiff later sued for duress to recover the money paid. Held: the defendant's acts were improper because they left the plaintiff **without the ability to exercise independent judgment**. The fact that the transaction was handled by the defendant's former attorney further supports this thesis.

c. The standard applied does not look to "a person of ordinary sensibilities"; it is subjective.

4. Undue Influence

a. Undue influence leads to rescission whenever:

i. The victim is **particularly vulnerable** at the time he is broached by the other party; and

ii. The other party exercises **unfair persuasion** over the victim through **domination**.

b. Several factors are looked at in determining whether there was undue influence:

i. Broaching a subject at an *improper time* or *place*;

ii. Placing undue pressure on the victim through *limiting the victim's time to decide*;

iii. Having *many parties* influence a sole victim at the *same time*;

iv. Giving the victim *no opportunity to consult third party advisors*.

v. *See Odorizzi v. Bloomfield School District* (defendant), where the plaintiff was charged for homosexual activity and the defendant employer, in the plaintiff's vulnerability and exhaustion, offered to not allow any publicity (and thus the possibility of another job) in exchange for the plaintiff's resignation. The plaintiff assented, but later, realizing that the offer was made with undue influence, sought to rescind his resignation. Held: because the plaintiff was *particularly vulnerable* at the time of the offer, which was made at an *improper place* and *time* (at home outside of work hours) and had *no opportunity to consult any advisors*, he pleaded sufficient facts to reverse the trial court's dismissal.

5. Unconscionability

    a. Courts consider a contract unconscionable when its terms are **shocking to the conscience**. The following factors are considered:

        i. There was **undue bargaining power** between the party that dictated the terms of the contract and the party that accepted them;

        ii. There is **unfair surprise** and the weaker party did not understand or notice some of the hidden provisions of the contract;

        iii. The terms of the contract are **oppressive***;*

        iv. The clauses are **one-sided**, deprive the party with inferior bargaining power of reasonable choice, and unduly favor the party with superior bargaining power.

            1) Example: an adhesion contract that permits a seller to repossess *all previously sold goods* if the buyer fails to make even a single payment on time. *Williams v. Walker-Thomas Furniture Co.* (1965).

    b. A contract may be:

        i. ***Procedurally unconscionable***: where unfair terms are inconspicuous (*e.g.*, in the fine print) or incomprehensible (*i.e.*, written so that an average person would not understand them); or

        ii. ***Substantively unconscionable***: the terms of the contract themselves are unfair or one sided.

    c. Price unconscionability applies to two situations:

        i. A purchaser is charged a price without being aware of the actual price he was agreeing to (courts will void the contract); or

        ii. He is charged a much higher price than other purchasers because he is in a state of particular need and is taken advantage of.

            1) Example: a driver comes to the only rest stop on a long, abandoned road. The clerk, aware of the driver's need, charges him triple the normal price of a bottle of water.

            2) Since courts are reluctant to intervene when the parties have come to an agreement, they would be unlikely to rescind the contract.

C. MISTAKES OF PRESENT EXISTING FACTS

1. Introduction

    a. This section deals with mistakes made about *basic assumptions at the time the contract was made*.

    b. Some, but *not all mistakes*, rise to the level required to *void a contract*.

2. Mutual Mistake

   a. "A mistake is a belief that is not in accord with the facts" (§ 151).

      i. A mistake cannot deal with *value judgments* or *future predictions*.

      ii. Rather, it must be about ascertainable knowledge in the present.

   b. The elements for making a *prima facie* case for mutual mistake are as follow (§ 152):

      i. Both parties must be ***mistaken***;

      ii. About a ***presently existing fact***;

      iii. That is a ***basic assumption*** going to the heart of the deal;

         1) *See Sherwood v. Walker*, where the court allowed rescision of a contract when the parties, according to the majority, mistakenly believed that the cow being traded was barren, since the cow's being barren was a *basic assumption* going to the heart of what was a "beef contract," not a "breeding cow contract."

      iv. That has a ***material effect on the agreed-to exchange*** (one of the parties is gaining more than expected and the other party less); and

      v. The adversely effected party ***did not assume the risk*** through:

         1) The *allocation of the assumption of the risk* in the contract;

         2) *Conscious ignorance* (knowing that he has limited knowledge, he treats his knowledge as sufficient); or

         3) *Allocation of the risk to him by the court* on the grounds of equity.

3. Unilateral Mistake

   a. This is the mistake of only one party.

   b. The elements of unilateral mistake are as follow:

      i. One of the parties to a contract is ***mistaken***;

      ii. As to a ***presently existing fact***;

      iii. That is a ***basic assumption*** going to the heart of the deal;

      iv. That has a ***material effect*** as to the agreed-to exchange (one of the parties is gaining more than expected and the other party less);

      v. For which he did not assume the risk through either:

         1) The *allocation of the assumption of the risk* in the contract;

         2) *Conscious ignorance* (knowing that his knowledge was limited but treating it as sufficient); or

         3) *Allocation of the risk to him by the court* because the circumstances make doing so reasonable; and

vi. The other party **had reason to know of the mistake** or was **at fault for it**, *or*, it **would be unconscionable to enforce the contract.**

    1) The other party has a duty to disclose information when she knows that the other party "is mistaken as to a basic assumption" regarding that information.

    2) This does not, however, mean that she is obligated to disclose the other party's *every mistake.*

    3) Rather, she must act "in accordance with reasonable standards of fair dealing" (§ 161, Comment *d*).

D. CHANGED CIRCUMSTANCES

1. Introduction

    a. Changed circumstances do not excuse a party's performance *unless* they render the performance **impossible** or **impracticable** or **frustrate the purpose** behind the contract.

2. Impossibility

    a. This defense applies when a *supervening event* renders a party's performance *objectively impossible.*

    b. Elements:

        i. The parties must have entered into a contract with a **basic assumption that the event would not occur;**

        ii. The event **does occur;**

        iii. The event renders performance **objectively impossible** (*i.e.*, impossible for *anyone* to perform);

        iv. The adversely affected party **is not at fault** for the event; and

        v. The adversely affected party **did not contract to perform** in case the event occurred.

    c. Subjective Impossibility

        i. For the duties to be discharged under impossibility, performance **must not be possible for anyone** (objective impossibility).

        ii. If they can be performed by *someone*, albeit not the party adversely effected, the impossibility is said to be subjective and does not discharge the duty to perform.

            1) *See Paradine v. Jane* (K.B. 1647), where a tenant was not discharged of his duty to pay rent to a landlord even though he was ousted from the property by an invading German army, preventing him from farming the land in order to pay the rent. Held: judgment for landlord affirmed because the defendant's performance is not objectively impossible (he can secure the payment using other means).

    d. Rather, the impossibility must be objective: no one would be able to perform.

        i.   *See Taylor v. Caldwell* (U.K. 1863), where the defendant lessor was excused from performance to the plaintiff lessee when his theatre was burned down. There was an implied condition that where the subject matter of a transaction was destroyed, the parties are discharged from their duties because it has become impossible to perform.

    e.   Supervening Illegality

        i.   One common category of impossibility occurs when the parties enter into a contract for the performance of an act, and that act *later becomes illegal.*

        ii.   For example, if the defendant agrees to deliver twenty bottles of French wine each week to the plaintiff's restaurant, but then an embargo is imposed against France, the defendant will have a valid defense for nonperformance.

3.   Impracticability

    a.   Impracticability is a defense when performance becomes extremely and unreasonably difficult and/or burdensome.

    b.   It represents a level of difficulty between impractical and impossible.

    c.   Elements:

        i.   The parties entered into contract with the ***basic assumption*** that a supervening event would not occur;

            1)   The event may be an act of God or of a third party.

            2)   Examples: natural disaster, war, embargo, currency devaluation, etc.

        ii.   The supervening event ***does occur;***

        iii.   The ***event*** made the performance ***impracticable;***

        iv.   The party seeking rescission is ***not at fault*** for the resulting impracticability; and

        v.   The party did ***not agree to perform*** despite the event's occurrence.

4.   Frustration of Purpose

    a.   Frustration of purpose applies when supervening events render the *value* of a contract to a party worthless or virtually worthless.

    b.   The party is *deprived of the benefit* of the contract because her *purpose* for making the contract is *"frustrated."*

    c.   The elements are virtually identical to those of impracticability:

        i.   The parties entered into contract with the ***basic assumption*** that a supervening event would not occur;

        ii.   The supervening event ***does occur;***

        iii.   The event completely or substantially ***destroys the party's primary purpose*** in entering the contract;

1)   *See Krell v. Henry* (K.B. 1903), where the defendant was discharged of his duty to pay for an apartment when Edward VII's coronation's date was rescheduled, since the central purpose behind the contract, the viewing of the coronation, was frustrated.

iv.   The party seeking rescission is **not at fault** for the supervening event; and

v.   The party **did not agree to perform despite the occurrence** of the event.

d.   Discharge of performance through impracticability and frustration of purpose

    i.   **Impracticability** generally applies to lessors, service providers, and sellers.

    ii.   **Frustration of purpose** generally applies to lessees and purchasers.

VII.   REMEDIES FOR BREACH OF CONTRACT

A.   DAMAGES FOR BREACH OF CONTRACT

1.   The Common Law

    a.   The Three Damage Interests that a Promisee may Choose Between

      i.   The Expectation Interest

       1)   The expectation interest puts the promisee back in the position that he would have been in if the promisor had not breached the contract.

       2)   The plaintiff's damages are thus equal to the value of profits he would have obtained had the promisor performed (the plaintiff's loss of value, "L") plus incidental and consequential losses and costs (spent in reliance of the contract) minus costs saved. Restatement § 347.

        a)   The formula is: $(L + I/C) - CS = EI$.

       3)   *See Hawkins v. McGee*, where the court held that the plaintiff's damage interests should be limited to the difference in value between the promised, 100% cured hand and the actual hand that the plaintiff got. Pain and suffering should *not* be taken into account.

        a)   *N.B.*: when the plaintiff enters into surgery knowing that there will be pain, this pain is part of the consideration that the plaintiff is putting up in order to get better. The plaintiff cannot collect damages on pain.

       4)   Incidentals and consequential costs may exponentially increase the plaintiff's loss in value

          a)   *See Nurse v. Barnes*, where the court allowed the jury to reward 500L of "special" damages, even though the actual damages were only 10L.

    ii.   The Reliance Interest

        1)   The reliance interest puts the ***promisee*** in the position that he would have been in had there been no contract.

        2)   The promisee is compensated for any detriment suffered in performance or preparation for performance undertaken in reliance on the breaching party's promise.

    iii.   The Restitution Interest

        1)   The restitution interest puts the ***promisor*** back into the position that he would have been in had there been no contract.

        2)   The promisor must disgorge any benefit received because of the existence of the contract.

  b.   Pain and suffering

    i.   The contract law is coldly commercial: if the plaintiff can only recover those damages that correspond to a commercial loss, *not to pain and suffering*.

    ii.   Regardless of the defendant's culpability, damages are given for economic, not emotional, losses.

    iii.   The plaintiff is also unable to recover for hassle.

2.   Sales Contracts under the UCC

  a.   Buyer's Remedies

    i.   If the seller breaches, the buyer may recover the difference in value between the market price of an item at the time that he learned of the breach and the contract price (the buyer's loss), plus incidental and consequential costs minus costs avoided (similar to the expectation interest described above).

    ii.   He may recover the difference between the amount paid for the good that he was forced to obtain from another seller and the original price he would have paid under the contract.

    iii.   This remedy is referred to as "cover." UCC § 2-712.

  b.   Seller's Remedies

    i.   General Rule

        1)   If the buyer breaches, the seller may recover the difference between the contract price and the market price at the time of the breach. UCC § 2-708.

        2)   The seller may also sell the goods to another buyer and may recover the ***difference between the contract price and the resale price*** (referred to as "Seller's Cover"). UCC § 2-706.

        ii.   Exception: the "Lost Volume" Seller

             1)   Under the "lost volume" doctrine, if the seller has a virtually unlimited supply of the goods, the court will allow him to make a double profit, awarding profit damages from first breaching buyer on top of profit received from the second buyer to whom the goods were actually sold.

   c.   When UCC Provisions Conflict

        i.   The UCC has both general and specific provisions.

        ii.   When the two seemingly conflict, the more specific provision applies. *Tongish v. Thomas.*

B.   THREE LIMITATIONS ON DAMAGES

   1.   Remoteness of Foreseeability of Harm

      a.   The defendant is liable to the plaintiff for (i) all general damages that naturally arise from the breach of contract; and (ii) any damages resulting from special circumstances **that he has reason to know about**.

      b.   This second group of damages is referred to as "consequential damages," and is limited to only those damages that are foreseeable.

      c.   If the defendant has no reason to know about special circumstances that could lead to consequential damages, he will not be held liable for consequential damages.

        i.   *See Hadley v. Baxendale* (Court of Exchequer 1854), where the plaintiff's employee brought a mill shaft to the defendant, explained that it was broken, and requested that it be repaired for the next day, without explaining that the mill would be shut down until the shaft was repaired. The defendant failed to ship the shaft overnight as agreed and as a result, the mill was shut down for five days. The plaintiff sued to recover both his **loss in value** (the difference between overnight and five day delivery) and the **consequential damages** resulting from the breach (five days of lost profits), or about 300 £. Held: the plaintiff cannot recover for the consequential damages because the defendant had no way of foreseeing the special circumstances leading to the consequential damages.

             1)   This case establishes an **objective test** for determining whether the defendant is liable for *general damages*; it does not matter whether the defendant actually foresaw the general damages.

             2)   However, with respect to the special circumstances leading to consequential damages, the court employs a partially subjective test: the special damages are equal to what one would "reasonably contemplate would be the amount of injury which would ordinarily follow from a breach of contract under these special circumstances so *known and communicated*."

a) On the one hand, the special circumstances must be "known" by the defendant (subjective prong);

b) On the other hand, the amount of damages for which the defendant is liable is equal to the injury that one would "reasonably contemplate" to follow from such special circumstances (objective prong).

d. The Restatement (Second) of Contracts § 351 establishes an objective, reasonable person test to **both general as well as special damages**.

   i. General damages: the defendant is not liable for damages (loss in value) when he "did not have reason to foresee" the damages as a result of his breach.

   ii. Special damages: the defendant is not liable for damages resulting from special circumstances that he did not have "reason to know."

e. Under the common law, when the defendant is put on notice of potential consequential and incidental damages arising out of his breach, he becomes liable.

   i. The common law duty may be modified by contract. Such agreements are usually enforced by the courts, unless they are unconscionable, illegal, or against public policy.

   ii. For example, in its contracts, FedEx puts its clients on notice that it disclaims liability for consequential damages. Clients who do not accept FedEx's terms must find other ways of sending their parcels.

2. Proving Damages with Certainty

a. The second limitation on recovering damages requires that the damages be proven with certainty.

b. In order to recover expectation, reliance, or restitution damages, there must be sufficient evidence to establish with *relative certainty* the amount of harm resulting from the defendant's breach. Restatement § 352.

c. It is especially difficult to determine expectation damages when large profits are expected from a one-time event and there are no former regular practices that could reasonably establish expected profits. In these cases, expectation damages will not be rewarded.

   i. *See Chicago Coliseum Club* (plaintiff) *v. Dempsey*, where the court held that the plaintiff could not recover for the defendant's anticipatory repudiation because there was no way of calculating lost profits with certainty. The plaintiff could, however, recover the reliance damages that were directly related to the contract.

d. Under these circumstances, non-breaching parties will often seek reliance damages.

i. Courts are divided as to whether reliance damages include only those expenditures made *after* the contract was entered into, or those preceding the contract as well.

ii. Under the ***American rule***, plaintiffs may recover reliance damages for costs incurred as a result of "preparation of performance or in performance," Restatement § 349, but these costs do not include the costs incurred from before the contract was made.

iii. Under the ***English rule***, plaintiffs may recover reliance damages for costs incurrent as a result of performance or of preparation of performance, and these costs include the costs incurred from before the contract was made *when both parties had reason to know that those damages would result* from the breach.

1) *See Anglia Television Ltd.* (plaintiff) *v. Reed*, where the plaintiff hired the defendant to act in a show. Because the defendant's agent double-booked him, he breached the contract and the plaintiff sued. The plaintiff sought reliance damages, since expectation interests could not be established with reasonable certainty. The defendant argued that the plaintiff should only be allowed to recover for expenditures made *after the contract with the defendant was formed*. Held: the plaintiff may recover for *all expenditures* made from before or after the contract was agreed to, since *both parties could have reasonably foreseen* that the breach would have led to such damages.

e. When expectation damages are uncertain (or when they are certain but the plaintiff was not expecting to turn a profit), the plaintiff will often sue for reliance damages.

i. *See Mistletoe Express Service v. Locke* (plaintiff) (Tx. Ct. App. 1988), where the defendant contracted the plaintiff to build a ramp over twelve months. At the ninth month, the defendant notified the plaintiff that it was going to breach. The plaintiff sued the defendant and opted for reliance damages (since money was being lost on the contract and there was a net loss at the time of the defendant's breach), seeking all costs expended on the project (loans taken out, vehicles purchased, etc.). The defendant argued that the plaintiff should not be entitled to all those costs, but rather, *should only be put back into position she would have been in had the contract not been breached* (which would have been at lost profits). Held: although expectation interests are the general measure of damages, the plaintiff may elect to sue for reliance damages.

3. Mitigation of Damages

a. The third limitation on damages is avoidability of harm (this is the Restatement language), commonly known as the "duty to mitigate."

b. Once the plaintiff knows that a breach of contract has occurred and nevertheless continues accruing damages, the plaintiff may not recover those damages sustained after the time the plaintiff knew of the breach. The plaintiff has a duty to mitigate.

    i.   *See Rockingham County* (defendant) *v. Luten Bridge Co.* (1929), where the defendant contracted the plaintiff to build a bridge and later notified the plaintiff that it would breach the contract, since it had no use for the bridge. The plaintiff continued to build, and at the end of the process, claimed $18,000 in damages. The defendant contended that the plaintiff should only be entitled to $1,900, which is what was spent before the plaintiff received notice of the breach. Held: according to the American rule, the plaintiff has a duty to mitigate. There is no use for a bridge built in the middle of a forest. The plaintiff cannot recover for losses accrued after receiving notice that the defendant would breach.

c.   When an employment contract is breached by an employer, the non-breaching party must mitigate by either: (i) making reasonable efforts to find new work; or (ii) accepting new work when offered by the employer.

    i.   Searching for New Work

        1)   The non-breaching party must search for new work, but if after a reasonable effort, he is unable to find comparable work, he may sue for damages equivalent to his expectation interest.

        2)   If the non-breaching party finds comparable work that pays less, he may sue for the difference.

    ii.   Accepting New Work Offered by the Employer

        1)   If new work is offered by the employer as a replacement for the work to be performed in the new contract, the non-breaching party should accept it.

        2)   However, if the new work is not substantially similar to the original work, the non-breaching party is not required to accept it. § 350.

            a)   *See Parker v. Twentieth Century-Fox Film Corp.* (defendant), where the defendant hired the plaintiff to play lead role in a musical for $750,000. The defendant breached the contract and instead offered the plaintiff the chance to play a lead role in a Western style movie to be filmed in Australia under similar terms. The plaintiff refused the new contract and sued for damages. The defendant argued that accepting the new job was required mitigation. Held: the plaintiff is not required to accept the new job as mitigation because the new job is substantially different from the old and cannot substitute it. The plaintiff is entitled to the $750,000.

            b)   *N.B.*: the court never discussed the plaintiff's duty to make reasonable efforts to find work. It may have been because these kinds of jobs come around so rarely that it may not have been practical to have required her to make such efforts.

    d.   Mitigation in the Sale of Goods under the UCC

        i.   General rule when the buyer breaches:

            1)   If the seller resells the good, he is entitled to the difference between the purchase price and the contract price.

            2)   If the seller does not resell, he is entitled to the difference between market price and contract price plus incidental and consequential damages minus costs avoided.

        ii.   If the seller withholds delivery because of the buyer's breach, he must refund the defendant all the money that the defendant gave him less either $500 or 20% of contract price, whichever is less. UCC § 2-718(2).

        iii.   However, this rule is subject to another damage-measuring formula under UCC § 2-708:

            1)   Damages for the seller are the difference between the market price and the contract price at the time and place of tender, plus incidental and consequential costs, minus costs saved.

            2)   If § 2-708(1) does not offer a reasonable result, then the seller may collect the profit (including reasonable overhead) that he would have made, plus incidentals, due allowance for costs, and due credit for payments.

C.   LIQUIDATED DAMAGES V. PENALTY CLAUSES

    1.   Introduction

        a.   Generally, damages for breach of contract are equal to expectation damages, reliance damages or restitution damages.

        b.   However, when calculating damages would be too difficult, the parties may elect to include liquidated (stipulated) damages clauses in the contract itself, to be applied in case of breach.

        c.   However, courts are hesitant in enforcing stipulated damages clauses that appear to be penalties.

            i.   Rationale: contracts must be seen in terms of economic realities. When damages could be calculated, the non-breaching party should be able to recover only monetary damages. When exorbitant damages are claimed, they are seen by the courts as penalties, which the contract law does not recognize.

    2.   Stipulated damages clauses will generally not be enforced when:

        a.   Actual damages can be calculated; and

b. The stipulated damages are significantly greater than the actual damages (this indicates that the stipulated damages are really a penalty).

    i. Courts are especially reluctant to enforce stipulated damages clauses when they apply to even immaterial breaches.

    ii. *See Kemble v. Farren* (defendant), where the defendant had a contract to be a comedian at the Royal theatre with a 1,000 £ liquidated damages clause. When the defendant breached after the second season, the plaintiff sued to recover the full 1,000 £. Held: because this contract allows the plaintiff to collect 1,000 £ in damages for even slight breach, it functions as a penalty clause and will not be enforced.

3. On the other hand, courts will enforce liquidated damage clauses when they are ***reasonable***, as determined by three factors:

a. There is *no intent to create a penalty clause.*

b. The damages *would be difficult for a court to ascertain* at the time the contract was made.

    i. *N.B.*: under the minority approach, courts look to see if the damages would be difficult to ascertain *at the time the suit is brought*.

c. The damages *accurately predict* the damages at the time they arise.

    i. *See Wassenaar* (plaintiff employee) *v. Towne Hotel*, where the plaintiff entered into an employment contract with the defendant. Under a stipulated damages clause, the defendant was responsible for its entire three year financial obligation to pay the plaintiff in the event that the defendant terminated the contract prematurely. While twenty one months remaining, the defendant terminated the contract. On the issue of whether the penalty clause was valid, the court held that the damages for breaching the employment contract comprised more than just the amount of money owed; it also included harm to reputation and other incalculable factors. The liquidated damages clause was therefore applied.

    ii. *N.B.*: this court **did not require the plaintiff to mitigate damages** because when a stipulated damages clause is found to be reasonable, the non-breaching party is not required to mitigate. However, although courts do not formally require mitigation, in practice mitigation is factored into courts' decision through courts' analysis of ***reasonableness*** *of liquidated damages clauses*. If in *Wassenaar*, the defendant was able to get information into record that the plaintiff had in fact gotten a job just after leaving the defendant's employment, the court, in evaluating the accuracy of the stipulated damages clause in predicting actual damages, would have held that this factor was not met. It would have therefore probably found the clause to be unreasonable, and would not have honored it. Instead, it would have required the plaintiff to prove expectation damages. Thus, mitigation may be indirectly factored into the analysis.

D. OTHER REMEDIES AND CAUSES OF ACTION

1. Specific Performance and Injunctions

    a. General Rule

        i. Specific performance (SP) and injunctions will not be ordered by a court unless there is *no adequate remedy at law* (*i.e.*, money damages).

        ii. It is an exceptional remedy that tends to be applied in only real estate transactions.

    b. Contracts for Land

        i. For real estate transactions, SP is granted as a matter of course.

            1) *See Loveless v. Diehl* (plaintiff), where the defendant leased his farm to the plaintiff for three years with an option to purchase for $21,000. The plaintiff found a buyer who would buy the land, allowing the plaintiff to make a $1,000 profit, but when the defendant found out about this, he repudiated the options contract. The plaintiff sued for SP. The defendant counterclaimed for a $1,440 promissory note. The courts originally held that the plaintiff was entitled to $1,000 and the defendant was entitled to the payment of the promissory note. On rehearing, it was held that there was no reason to deny SP. The general rule is that for realty, SP is granted as a matter of course. The plaintiffs spent much more on improving the property than the meager $1,000 awarded as damages. To refuse SP would be to unjustly enrich the sellers for breaching their own options contract.

        ii. But if it can be shown that there really is no difference between two pieces of real estate, then only damages will be rewarded (this would be exceptional).

    c. Contracts for Goods

        i. Under the common law, courts only order SP when the goods are scarce, rare, irreplaceable, or of sentimental value.

            1) *See Cumbest* (plaintiff) *v. Harris* (Miss. 1978), where the defendant loaned the plaintiff money and the plaintiff gave the defendant hi-fi equipment as collateral, with an option to purchase the equipment at any time before 5 pm on a specified date. When the day arrived, the plaintiff did everything he could to purchase the goods, but the defendant avoided him. The plaintiff sued for SP. The court held that the test for determining whether SP should be rewarded requires the court to consider whether damages are adequate. Here, some parts of the equipment were irreplaceable and other parts were replaceable only with much effort and time. Because the equipment was rare, unique, and difficult to acquire, SP was rewarded.

ii. UCC § 2-716 similarly awards SP when the good is unique or in other proper circumstances (*e.g.*, it is not commercially feasible for the plaintiff to obtain the good).

    1) *See Sedmak v. Charlie's Chevrolet*, where the plaintiff ordered a limited edition Corvette from the defendant for $15,000. When the time came to tender purchase, the value rose and the defendant reneged on its promise and required the plaintiff to bid on the car. The plaintiff sued for SP. Held: although this Corvette is not unique, it is so rare and finding the equivalent would be so difficult that under UCC § 2-716(1), judgment for SP is affirmed.

d. Contracts for Personal Services

i. Originally, SP was offered for contracts for personal services.

ii. However, courts later became unwilling to order SP, finding such orders impractical and unjust.

    1) *See The Case of Mary Clark, A Woman of Colour*, where Mary Clark sued to be freed from Johnston, to whom she voluntarily indentured herself. Johnston called for SP, arguing that Clark should be bound by a contract she voluntarily signed. Held: to enforce this contract and require SP would be to put Clark in a state of ***involuntary servitude***. She should be discharged.

iii. Just as courts were reluctant to enforce SP, they also were reluctant to enforce *negative injunctions*, which prohibit the breaching party from taking on similar work. Many courts consider negative injunctions to be an indirect form of SP.

    1) *See Ford v. Jermon* (defendant), where the defendant breached her contract to act in a theatre. The plaintiff sued for a negative injunction. Held: forbidding the defendant from acting in any other play would have the effect of enforcing SP through the "backdoor," which the court refused to do. SP within the context of employment contracts is a mitigated form of slavery. Judgment for the defendant was affirmed.

iv. Later, courts began allowing negative injunctions, even when they were not expressly provided for in the contract.

    1) *See Duff v. Russell* (defendant), where the plaintiff sued the defendant performer for breaching her acting contract. The court awarded a negative injunction against her, since the contract implied that she would not work for competitors.

v. Today, negative injunctions are permitted in personal service contracts for employment of unique individuals, where *the breaching party is unique* or *when finding a replacement is unusually burdensome*.

    1) Rationale: there is an implied warranty by employees offering rare or unique services not to work for competitors during the employment period.

    2) Furthermore, courts are more willing to enforce negative injunctions than SP because negative injunctions are easier to enforce.

    3) *See Dallas Cowboys Football Club* (plaintiff) *v. Harris*, where the court held that the plaintiff was entitled to a negative injunction against the defendant's working for competing football teams because the defendant's skills were sufficiently unique and exceptional, regardless of the fact that it was never shown that he was the best.

  vi. Although today, SP is not enforced in personal service contracts, this rule is limited to *personal service contracts*, not *corporate service contracts*. When there is no adequate remedy at law, corporate service contracts may be enforced through SP.

    1) Rationale: the policy of not wanting to force a defendant to work does not apply when the defendant is a large corporation with many employees working at an hourly rate.

    2) In personal services contract, then, the only SP that a party can obtain is a negative injunction in certain circumstances (the defendant has rare or unique services).

 2. Restitution – Damage Interest and Cause of Action

  a. Restitution for Breach of Contract

   i. One of the alternative damage interests that a party may seek for breach of contract is restitution.

   ii. Generally, restitution is sought by non-breaching parties to collect damages for breach of contract when expectation damages cannot be calculated.

   iii. It is available when the contract between the parties has been rescinded; however, some ***courts allow restitution even when a contract has not been rescinded***.

    1) *See Bush* (plaintiff) *v. Canfield*, where the defendant breached his contract after the plaintiff paid the first $5,000 of the $14,000 owed for a shipment of 2,000 barrels of flour. Because the price of the flour dropped between the time the contract was made and the time of the breach, the plaintiff did not seek expectation damages, which would have been negative. The court allowed the plaintiff to collect $5,000 of restitution damages without first rescinding the contract.

     a) *Dissent*: for the plaintiff to collect restitution damages, it must first rescind the contract. Here, the plaintiff did not first rescind.

        b)   *Concurring opinion responding to the dissent*: the dissent is simply dwelling on a technicality. Whether the plaintiff was to start the case all over again after rescinding the contract or pursue restitution by skipping that step, the same result will transpire.

b.   Restitution to the Party in Breach

    i.   Under the old common law, restitution was not available to the breaching party.

    ii.   Under the modern law, the breaching party is still unable to collect damages under the contract, since he breached it.

    iii.   However, in support of the ***public policy discouraging forfeiture***, the breaching party may collect restitution when the non-breaching party receives a benefit from the breaching party.

        1)   *See Britton* (plaintiff) *v. Turner*, where the defendant agreed to pay the plaintiff $120 upon the plaintiff's completing a one year labor contract. The plaintiff quit work after nine months and sued to recover the nine months of labor. Held: the plaintiff may recover *quantum meruit* ("as much as he deserves") the market value of the benefit he conferred on the defendant.

        2)   *N.B.*: it may seem unusually harsh that a person be held liable for restitution damages by a party that breaches a contract. It would seem that such a rule would discourage parties from keeping contracts and fully performing. However, most cases do not work out like *Britton*; usually, the non-breaching party's injury will be mitigated:

            a)   He can repudiate whatever benefit the breaching party has given to him, and thus not be liable for restitution damages (because he will have nothing to disgorge); and

            b)   Even if he keeps the benefit, he may be able to sue the breaching party for damages if he can prove them.

        3)   *N.B.*: breaching parties, as in this case, are not required to rescind the contract before collecting restitution, since their breach is in a sense already a rescission.

    iv.   The restitution collected is to equal ***the market value*** of the benefit that the breaching party transferred to the non-breaching party.

    v.   Thus, if the plaintiff breaches contract and then sues the defendant for restitution, and if the contract price was higher than market price, a court will only reward market price.

    vi.   However, the plaintiff is entitled only to contract price when the market value would afford him greater recovery than the contract price.

        1)   The rationale is not to encourage the plaintiffs to breach their contracts when they realize they made a bad deal.

c. A valid liquidated damages clause may prevent a breaching party from collecting restitution damages. However, if the breaching party shows that the damages clause is invalid (*i.e.*, the other party would be unjustly enriched), he may be able to collect restitution.

 i. *See Vines* (plaintiff) *v. Orchard Hills*, where the plaintiff entered into a contract with the defendant to buy a condominium. The contract had a stipulated damages clause that established the 10% down payment ($7,880) as damages in the event of the plaintiff's breach. The plaintiff informed the defendant that he would not go through with the deal, since he would be moving to NJ, and demanded the deposit. When the defendant refused, the plaintiff sued for restitution, arguing that as a result of the appreciation of the condo, the defendant benefited from the breach, since he could sell the condo for more. Held: stipulated damages clauses will not be upheld when they lead to the unjust enrichment of the non-breaching party, who **suffers no damages**. If the breaching party seeks restitution, the burden of proof is on him to show that the liquidated damages clause leads to unjust enrichment. The case is remanded with a new opportunity given to the plaintiff to bring forward evidence showing that the damages clause is unreasonable and its enforcement would lead to unjust enrichment.

d. Restitution and "Quasi Contract"

 i. **Quasi contracts** are implied contracts that are created by the courts to avoid unjust enrichment when the elements of a contract are not met.

 ii. There are two kinds:

  1) Implied in Fact Contracts

   a) Contracts may be implied by the conduct of the parties.

   b) Example: if a party finds a man mowing his lawn, goes outside, and greets him, there will be an implied-in-fact contract, even if he never contracted the man to mow his lawn.

  2) Implied in Law Contracts

   a) Implied in law contracts, also known as constructive contracts, have no basis in the facts of a case.

   b) These are created by the courts in order to avoid injustice when there is neither an express nor an implied in fact contract.

   c) Courts, in creating implied in law contracts, may order that a party that is enriched by the service of another restitute the benefit received, in order to avoid unjust enrichment.

    i) *See Cotnam v. Wisdom* (plaintiff) *(1907),* where the defendant was knocked unconscious from his street car and the plaintiff performed medical services upon him. The plaintiff sued to recover for the medical procedures performed on the defendant. Held: although no express contract was entered into, the law will construct a contract for the medical services delivered. This will encourage doctors to help those who are in need and will avoid the unjust enrichment of those receiving the benefits. The plaintiff is thus entitled to restitution equal to the value of his services.

3. Reformation

    a. When a written contract fails to reflect the meeting of the minds of the parties when they come to an agreement, the equitable remedy of reformation is used to change the document in order to reflect the agreement reached.

    b. Situations in which reformation may arise include: (i) when both parties are mistaken; and (ii) when one party is mistaken and the other acted fraudulently.

Summary Chart for Determining
When the Duty to Perform Has Become Absolute

1. Are there any conditions precedent to a party's performance?	Yes	Go to question 2
	No	The duty to perform has become absolute. Go to question 4.
2. Have the conditions been met?	Yes	The duty to perform has become absolute. Go to question 4.
	No	Go to question 3.
3. Has the condition been excused (treated as though it occurred, in order to avoid forfeiture)?	Yes	The condition to perform has become absolute.
	No	The duty to perform has become absolute. Go to question 4.
4. Has the contractual obligation been discharged through (i) substantial/perfect performance; (ii) material breach; or (iii) agreement of the parties (rescission; accord and satisfaction; novation; substitute agreement)?	Yes	There is no absolute duty to perform.
	No	Go to question 5.
5. Are there any defenses to contractual obligation (*e.g.*, legal incapacity, the improper obtainment of consent, mistake, changed future circumstances)?	Yes	The duty to perform may be voided.
	No	The party is contractually obligated to perform.

CHAPTER 2.
PROPERTY

I. THE ACQUISITION OF UNOWNED PROPERTY

A. THE ACQUISITION OF WILD ANIMALS AND UNOWNED PROPERTY

1. The Acquisition of Unowned Personal Property

   a. *Ad Coelum* Doctrine

      i. Under the *ad coelum* doctrine, for the purpose of immovable minerals, "to whomever the soil belongs, he also owns to the sky and to the depths."

      ii. *See Edwards v. Sims* (defendant judge) (1929) where the plaintiff owned and excavated a cave that Lee claimed ran under his property. The plaintiff asserted that he should be the owner because it was the result of his hard labor, he owned the entrance, he paid for it to be explored (*first occupant theory*). However, the court, applying the *ad coelum* doctrine, ordered an excavation of the plaintiff's cave to determine whether it did in fact run under Lee's property. The plaintiff sued to stop the defendant judge from enforcing the order. Judgment for the defendant: the court order is to be enforced in order to determine whether the plaintiff trespassed on Lee's property.

         1) Dissent (minority view): the *ad coelum* doctrine is an outdated theory that should not be applied; the ownership by *first occupant theory* would make more sense. The plaintiff excavated the cave through his own funds and labor; he alone is able to use and exploit it; he owns the entrance. Preventing his enjoyment of it hurts the plaintiff and does not help Lee, who cannot take dominion.

   b. *Ratione Soli* Doctrine

      i. Under the *ratione soli* doctrine, also known as "*ad coelum* minor," the owner of the soil *is the first occupant* and owner of whatever is found on the soil, including minerals and *ferae naturae*, regardless of who the finder is.

         1) *See Goddard v. Winchell*, where Winchell found a meteor on Goddard's property. Because the court applies the *ratione soli* doctrine, Goddard is able to replevin it.

      ii. This doctrine is not recognized by all states and even in those states that do recognize it, it is not always applied.

      iii. As we will explore later on, the more general rule allows finders to keep what they have found; the law grants finders better title than all the world except for the true owner, with some exceptions.

2. First Occupancy Theory

   a. Under the first occupancy theory, the first occupant becomes the owner. The doctrine applies to the acquisition of *ferae naturae* (wild animals).

b. However, the *ratione soli* doctrine continues to apply when an animal is captured and killed on someone's property.

c. When not captured and killed on another's property, *ferae naturae* belongs to the first occupant, regardless of whether the animal was originally on another's property.

d. The first occupant is the one who:

i. Intends to possess and control an animal; and

ii. Injures or traps it in a way that makes its escape either impossible or improbable, depending on the state's approach.

1) Impossible (Strict Occupancy approach under *Pierson*)

a) The animal's escape must be **impossible**.

b) *Mere pursuit* of an animal does not constitute ownership.

c) Rather, one of the following must occur:

i) The animal must b trapped *and* escape must be impossible; or

ii) The animal must be mortally wounded *and* there is continued pursuit.

d) *See Pierson v. Post*, where the defendant was charged with unlawfully killing and capturing a fox that was under pursuit by the plaintiff. Held: mere pursuit of an animal does not constitute ownership. The animal would have had to be put into a situation where escape was impossible.

2) Improbable (Law of the Chase approach under *Liesner*).

a) The animal's escape must be **improbable**.

b) If an animal is so badly wounded that escape will be made improbable, then the animal belongs to the party that wounded it.

c) *See Liesner v. Wainie*, where Liesner mortally wounded a fox, then Wainie delivered shot that killed it and took it away. The court ruled that Liesner was the first occupant and that the fox belonged to him.

B. **ACQUISITION OF VOLATILE MINERALS (OIL AND GAS)**

1. The general rule regarding minerals can be summarized by the *ad coelum* doctrine: the owner of a parcel of property has a right to the property as it extends "to the sky" and "to the depths." He becomes owner of all minerals beneath his land.

a. *See Hammonds v. Central Kentucky Natural Gas Co.*, where the court held that the defendant was not liable for using a reservoir under the plantiff's land to store gas. Once the minerals, through their natural volatile tendencies, migrate under the plaintiff's land, the defendant cannot be liable because he no longer controls and possesses them.

2. However, once volatile minerals are captured and stored, title to them is not lost, even if they migrate underneath another's land. The landowner may not exploit the stored mineral. *Lone Star Gas Co. v. Murchison.*

3. In summary, with respect to acquiring unowned property, courts apply:

    a. The *ad coelum* doctrine to the acquisition of fixed minerals and imbedded objects; and

    b. The *first occupant theory* to the acquisition of volatile minerals and *ferae naturae* (unless the *ferae naturae* is caught while on another's land).

C. ACQUISITION BY CONQUEST

1. General rule: when Europeans came to the Native Americans' land, the applicable rule was that the discoverer's government gained title to the land by conquest, despite the Native Americans' occupancy.

2. Thus, courts held that one who was granted land by a Native American does not have good title, since the Native Americans did no have good title to give.

    a. *See Johnson v. McIntosh*, where the Court held that the plaintiff, who claimed land through deeds granted to him by the Native Americans, did not in fact have title because full title was never passed on. Because the land was conquered by the early settlers, the Indians have a right to occupancy, but they do not have transferable title. Rather, transferable title belongs to the U.S. government, to which England gave title after it relinquished title after the Revolution. Because of the savage habits of the Native Americans, they have no claim to their land's title.

II. PERSONAL PROPERTY

A. BAILMENT

1. Bailment can be defined as a legally recognized property relationship between a bailor, who gives personalty to another to be held for a particular purpose, and a bailee, the party that receives the property. Bailment and bailment.

2. The agreement between the bailor and the bailee can be written or oral, gratuitous or for consideration.

3. For there to be a bailment relationship, the following five elements must be met:

    a. The object of the bailment must be ***personal property***;

b. There must be actual or constructive ***delivery*** to the bailee[4];

c. The bailee must expressly or impliedly **consent** to accepting the personal property;

d. The bailee must have the ***right of possession and actual possession***; and

e. The bailee must agree to ***return*** the personal property back to the bailor, who keeps title.

4. Conditions under which the bailee becomes liable to the bailor:

a. If he fails to return the item, he becomes strictly liable.

b. If he fails to exercise requisite care as bailee, the following standards of care apply:

    i. The Modern Law Approach

        1) An ordinary standard of care under the circumstances is *always required*.

        2) The bailee is thus liable for ordinary negligence.

    ii. The Three Approaches of the Common Law

        1) Gratuitous Bailment

            a) Gratuitous bailment is solely beneficial to the bailor.

            b) The bailee has a minimum standard of care; he is only liable for gross negligence;

        2) Mutually Beneficial Bailment

            a) When the bailment is mutually beneficial to the bailor and bailee, an ordinary standard of care is required.

            b) The bailee is liable for ordinary negligence;

            c) *See Hanes v. Shapiro and Smith*, where Shapiro is held to the ordinary standard of care for bailment of a sideboard destroyed in a fire, since both parties had a stake in the bailment.

        3) Bailment Solely Beneficial to the Bailee

            a) When the bailment only benefits the bailee, a high standard of care is required.

            b) The bailee is liable for even slight negligence.

c. Example: a store clerk finds in his store a mislaid wallet, which he intends to return to its rightful owner. If he loses the wallet, his standard of care will be:

    i. Under the common law approach, he is subject to a slight duty of care (he is liable only for gross negligence).

---

[4] An example of constructive delivery would be giving to another the keys to a car.

        ii.   Under the modern law approach, he has an ordinary standard of care under the circumstances; he is liable for ordinary negligence.

5.   In trial, the burden of proving negligence in bailment cases falls on the plaintiff bailor.

      a.   The plaintiff's *prima facie* case consists in proving: (i) he gave the personalty to the defendant in good condition; and (ii) the bailee did not return the personalty or return it back in a damaged condition.

      b.   When the problem was caused by abnormal causes, the burden is on the defendant to show that he was not at fault.

      c.   If he is able to show he was not at fault, the burden shifts back to the plaintiff to show that the defendant was negligent in exposing the personalty to the risk of harm.

B.   FINDINGS

1.   Introduction to the Findings Law

      a.   The overarching goal of findings law is to get the item back to the original owner (OO) or to preserve the rights of the OO.

      b.   At the same time, in order to promote honesty, finders are generally permitted to keep their findings. with the exceptions of the following circumstances, in which constructive possession is applied:

            i.   Mislaid, imbedded property;

            ii.   Trespass;

            iii.   In other cases where the courts reserve the right to apply constructive possession.

2.   Lost Items

      a.   The general rule of findings is that the finder obtains the right to possession against all of the world but the true owner.

      b.   *See Bridges v. Hawkesworth*, where a man found a box of bank notes on the floor of a public section of a store and told the owner to hold it for the rightful owner. When the rightful owner never showed up, the finder asked for them back. The court held that the finder had the rightful title for the bank notes, since they were found in a public part of the store.

3.   Mislaid Items

      a.   An item is mislaid when its owner intentionally places it in some place and then forgets about it.

      b.   An object will usually be considered to be mislaid when it is located on a table or a counter; it will be considered lost when found on the ground or some other area where it is unlikely to have been intentionally placed.

c. Possession of mislaid items is granted to the owner of the *locus in quo* (OLQ).

d. *See McAvoy v. Medina,* where a wallet left on a table in a store was considered mislaid, not lost. The difference is between someone deliberately placing an object on a table and saying they will come to it later, but forgetting, and dropping it on the ground without any intention. When it is the former, the owner of the OLQ, not the finder, obtains title.

4. Treasure Trove

a. Treasure trove is gold, silver, bullion, money, or coins found hidden under the ground when the true owner (TO) is unknown.

b. For the purposes of possession, treasure trove can be treated as a ***lost item***, in that the true owner keeps title, and the finder is given possession until the true owner appears. This is perhaps to encourage finders to make their findings known.

c. However, not all courts recognize treasure trove. When a state does not recognize treasure trove, it will treat the question as an ordinary ***finding***, and will determine whether the object was *lost* or *mislaid*.

   i. *See Schley v. Couch,* where workers on the plaintiff's land discovered a bottle filled with money buried in the ground. However, the court in Texas did not recognize treasure trove and simply applied the doctrine of mislaid and lost property. Because the money was buried recently (within the last few years), it was concluded that it was not lost, but rather, mislaid, and therefore belonged to the OLQ.

5. Imbedded Property

a. Imbedded property belongs to the OLQ

b. *See South Staffordshire Water Co. v. Sharman,* where the defendant, while working for the plaintiff, found rings imbedded in the plaintiff's cesspool, which the defendant surrendered to the police and then kept when the TO was not found. The plaintiff filed for detinue to recover the property or its value from the defendant. The court held that through *constructive possession,* the chattel should belong to the OLQ rather than to the finder because it was found on private property.

   i. This case makes a distinction with *Bridges*; the *Bridges* rule about lost property only applies if it is in the public or in the public part of a private store.

c. *See also Goddard v. Winchell,* where possession of a meteor imbedded in the soil is granted to the OLQ; ownership is not granted to the finder.

6. Constructive Possession

a. Constructive possession is control or dominion of property, as opposed to actual possession (physical occupancy).

b. Under the doctrine of constructive possession, control or dominion of property is granted to the owner of the OLQ, in situations in which it would otherwise go to the finder (*e.g.*, in cases of treasure trove and findings generally).

c. There are no hard, fast rules as to when courts would apply this doctrine.

    i. When an object lost in the public part of a store, a court probably *would not apply this doctrine*; the finder would obtain possession.

    ii. When an object is lost in a home or the private part of a store, a court would usually apply this doctrine; the OLQ would get possession.

7. Abandoned items

a. First occupants of abandoned items acquire *full title*, even against the TO.

    i. *See Eads v. Brazelton*, where Eads claimed that cargo of a shipwreck was rightfully his, since he found it first and laid markers around it. Held: the possession of abandoned items is like the possession of wild animals: the first occupant acquires ownership.

b. The occupant of an abandoned item must manifest the intent to exercise dominion and control and evidence that he is able to do so. In the example of *Eads v. Brazelton*, this would mean having a boat over the shipwreck that shows the intent to recover the cargo and the ability to do so.

8. Trespassing Finders

a. Trespassing finders relinquish control of found items to the OLQ.

b. *See Favorite v. Miller*, where the OLQ was able to keep the parts of a statue of King George that was found buried on his property, not only because it was imbedded in his soil, but also because it was taken by a trespasser.

Summary of Findings*

Category	Finder	OLQ	Definitions[5]
Lost	✓		The object is not intentionally set down; the TO never intends to part with the good, but is separated from it through negligence.
Mislaid		✓	The TO intends to temporarily part with the good but later forgets to retrieve it.
Treasure Trove	✓		An unknown owner intends to hide coin, money, gold, silver, plate or bullion found under the ground or otherwise hidden.
Imbedded		✓	When something is imbedded in the soil, even when the OLQ is unaware of its presence, he acquires possession.
Abandoned	✓		The relinquishing of a right or interest with the intention of never again claiming it. The TO does not transfer title to any specific third party. The finder acquires *ownership* of the article.

* However, regardless of whether an object was lost, treasure trove, etc., the OLQ will obtain possession when: (i) the court applies the doctrine of constructive possession, which deprives the finder of possession; and (ii) when the finder had been trespassing when he occupied the object.

9. Legislation Regulating Findings

    a. Many states have adopted statutes regulating findings.

    b. Generally speaking, the statutes are different from the common law in that they:

        i. Tend to lump together lost and mislaid items;

        ii. Require finders to turn in lost articles to police or face punishment; and

        iii. Give a time limit after which items are returned to finders and another limit after which finders become owners.

C. PRIOR (UNAUTHORIZED) POSSESSION

1. This relates to when a prior wrongful possessor is able to replevin against a subsequent wrongful possessor.

2. There are two approaches as to prior (unauthorized) possession:

3. Majority Approach

    a. Under the majority approach, prior wrongful possessors are always allowed to recover the property, whether it is through trover (damages) or replevin of the property.

        i. *See Anderson v. Gouldberg*, where the plaintiff sued the defendant, who took pine logs from the plaintiff, who himself wrongfully took

---

[5] Note that these often hinge on intent of TO.

the pine logs. The court held that the plaintiff was entitled to possession, even though he was a wrongful possessor, because he was a *prior* wrongful possessor.

    ii.   *See also Clark v. Maloney*, where the plaintiff found logs floating in a stream and took them up. The defendant later took possession of the logs, claiming that they had been loosened from the plaintiff's fastening and were adrift in the creek. Both the plaintiff and the defendant claimed that they had good finder's title. Held: because the plaintiff was a prior possessor, possession is given to he plaintiff. Trover (damages) is given to the plaintiff for the value of the logs that were converted by the defendant.

4.   Minority Approach

    a.   Under the minority approach, prior (unauthorized) possessors are always allowed to seek replevin of the property.

    b.   Prior possessors are also allowed to seek trover (damages) of the property as a general rule.

    c.   However, if the TO is known, the prior possessor may not seek trover (damages); he may only replevy the property.

    d.   This is because it is presumed that the TO will ultimately try to recover the property through replevy.

        i.   Thus, if the subsequent unauthorized possessor is required to pay damages to the prior unauthorized possessor, the subsequent possessor will risk a double penalty if the TO later seeks to replevy the property from him.

        ii.   He will have a double net loss, first having paid damages through trover to the prior possessor, and later giving up the property itself to the TO through replevy.

    e.   To avoid this prejudicial treatment of the subsequent possessor, the courts in the minority approach only permit the prior possessor to seek replevin of the property from the subsequent possessor.

        i.   It is presumed that if the TO later tries to recover the property, he will replevy it against the prior possessor.

        ii.   Thus, a double penalty will be imposed on neither the prior nor the subsequent possessor.

    f.   Thus, under the minority approach, the prior possessor is only allowed to obtain trover *when the TO is unknown*. Otherwise, the only possible recourse is replevin.

        i.   *See Russell v. Hill*, where the plaintiff purchased timber from McCoy, who did not have rightful title to the land because of an error in the deed. When the defendant took possession of the timber, the plaintiff brought sued for trover. The court held that because the plaintiff did not have title to the timber and the TO was known, he could not obtain trover.

D. **ADVERSE POSSESSION**

1. If a party takes possession of property of which he is not the lawful owner and maintains possession for a period prescribed by the statute of limitations in the local jurisdiction, he acquires rightful title if the lawful owner fails to oppose the wrongful possession.

    a. The statute of limitations varies between jurisdictions, but can be as little as two years.

    b. With respect to real property, the possession should be a non-permissive use of the land with a claim of right by the adverse possessor.

2. The courts incrementally established that in order for the statute of limitations to run, the possession and use of the land must be:

    a. *Open* – the possession and use must not be hidden;

    b. *Continuous* – the defendant must have continuous possession throughout the running of the statute of limitations;

    c. *Exclusive* – the defendant must not share the possession with the TO;

    d. *Adverse* – the wrongful possessor must claim and act as though he has title to the property; the claim must be adverse to the TO's rights;

    e. *Notorious* – the use must suffice to put the TO on notice that the adverse possessor is using the good and claiming title to it.

        i. This element is virtually the same as the *open* element.

        ii. To meet the open and notorious elements, one must use the chattel in a way that it is normally used.

        iii. Examples: a store will openly display a wrongfully possessed ring; however, the owner of a ring may only wear it once per year if it is of great value.

3. Meeting the Statute of Limitations

    a. Tacking

        i. Many jurisdictions permit "tacking," which allows an adverse possessor to meet an adverse possession statute of limitations by adding together the periods in which previous possessors held the chattel.

        ii. The majority approach is to allow tacking; the minority approach is to require the adverse possessor claiming title to have possessed the property throughout the statute of limitations.

    b. Tolling

        i. Tolling, on the other hand, refers to the temporary stopping of the statute of limitations whenever one of the elements of adverse possession is not met.

    c.   The Discovery Rule

        i.   Sometimes, the statute of limitations begins to run not when the TO is deprived of possession of his property, but rather, when he discovered or reasonably should have discovered the whereabouts of the chattel.

        ii.   This rule, referred to as the "discovery rule," works to the benefit of the TO.

        iii.   Courts often apply this rule when meeting the adverse possession elements, to the disadvantage of the TO, would be relatively easy for a possessor. *See O'Keeffe v. Snyder.*

4.   Two Approaches to Good Faith

    a.   Majority Approach

        i.   Under the majority approach, merely possessing the property throughout the statute of limitations will confer title to the adverse possessor, when the possession is open, continuous, exclusive, adverse, and notorious.

    b.   Minority Approach

        i.   However, under the minority approach, in addition to meeting these elements, the possession must be with *good faith.*

        ii.   *See Riesinger's Jewelers v. Roberson* (defendant), where the plaintiff lost a ring in an armed robbery. In order to determine whether or not the plaintiff had title to ring, the court applied the minority approach by requiring the previous owners to have held the ring in *good faith*, and remanded the case back to trial to determine the same.

            1)   *N.B.: Riesinger's Jewelers* also establishes that, in order for the statute to run for a stolen chattel, whether in a majority or minority jurisdiction, the good must be held *within the vicinity (i.e.,* in-state) in order to give the true owner of an opportunity to find and reclaim it. The statute of limitations is tolled anytime the item is taken out of the vicinity of the plaintiff when dispossession begins with a theft.

5.   Elements of Adverse Possession

    a.   In order for an adverse possessor to win in a claim for a good, he must prove:

        i.   His possession was open, continuous, exclusive, adverse, and continuous;

        ii.   He possessed the property throughout the statute of limitations;

            1)   In the majority of jurisdictions, he may add on the periods in which the property was held by other possessors through tacking.

        iii.   He had good faith (in minority jurisdictions);

          1)   If tacking is permitted, the other possessors similarly must have possessed in good faith.

        iv.   The possession was within the *vicinity* (in the case of stolen chattels under *Riesinger's Jewelers v. Roberson*).

    b.   When all of these elements are met, the TO loses his right to the property.

    c.   Furthermore, under the "shelter principle," if one possessor can show that he became the owner under adverse possession (or some other ownership theory), then any subsequent possessor can claim that good title was also passed to him.

E.   ACCESSION

    1.   Introduction

        a.   Accession is the acquisition of title to a thing through labor that transforms it into another thing.

        b.   General rule: an innocent trespasser does not gain title to a chattel through making improvements to it (the TO can replevy the chattel), *unless* (i) the chattel is acquired in good faith; and (ii) *substantial* improvements are made to it.

        c.   If both of these elements are met, title is transferred to the innocent trespasser and the TO cannot replevy the chattel.

    2.   Elements

        a.   The object must be taken in ***good faith*** by the later improver.

            i.   Thus, if the object is taken by a thief, no amount of improvement will cause title to transfer (this is the American approach, which follows the civil law, not the common law approach).

            ii.   This does not require that *all* prior possessors have good faith.

                1)   Example: if a good faith possessor purchases a chattel from a thief, and later makes substantial improvements to it, he may acquire title.

                2)   *See Capitol Chevrolet Co. v. Earhart*, where the court ruled that the innocent purchaser of the stripped down hull of a Corvette, who later made substantial changes to it, had good title to pass to Capitol Chevrolet, even though it was originally stolen from a previous possessor. When the stolen hull was recovered on the accessed vehicle, the TO had only the right to the value of the hull.

        b.   The chattel must be transformed into a new chattel of ***substantially greater value*** from the time it comes into the later improver's hands.

            i.   The improvements made to the chattel must not be easily separable from it.

ii. Normally, the improvements must be so substantial that the value of the chattel increases by a factor of fifteen or more (depending on what the item is).

    1) Example: a later improver will acquire title to timber that was originally valued at $25, when, with good faith, he transformed it into hoops valued at $700. *Wetherbee v. Green.*

iii. Note that this element does not require that a fifteen-factor improvement of the property is measured from the time that the property leaves the TO's hands to the time that the improvements are made; rather, it is measured from the time that the property is delivered to the later improver to the time that the improvements are made.

    1) Example: a thief steals a car valued at $15,000 and strips it down to a value of $1,000. A good faith purchaser purchases the car for $1,000 and makes improvements that bring the value of the car back up to $15,000.

    2) Although the improvements did not increase the value of the car from its *original* value, the later improver will obtain title, since substantial improvements were made from the time the car was delivered to him.

3. The True Owner's Remedies

    a. If either of the elements of accession are not met—the later improver fails to act in good faith or he fails to make *substantial* improvements to the chattel—the TO may **replevy** the chattel.

        i. When the later improver lacks good faith, the TO may replevy the chattel, no matter much labor and value the improver put into the good.

        ii. However, if he acts in good faith but fails to make *substantial* improvements, he may keep the improvements if they are separable from the original object. If they are not, the TO acquires them when he replevies the chattel.

    b. If a later improver acts in good faith *and* makes substantial improvements, although the TO may not replevy the chattel, he may obtain **damages** equal to the value of the chattel at the time that it was delivered to the later improver (*e.g.*, $25 in the case of *Wetherbee*).

F. *BONA FIDE* PURCHASE

1. We have already examined two theories of ownership in which an owner may be deprived of property without his consent—adverse possession and accession).

2. We now turn our attention to a third theory where an owner may similarly be deprived of property without his consent—*bona fide* purchase (BFP).

3. Elements of BFP:

        a.   Purchases in good faith;

        b.   Without notice of fraud;

            i.   Notice of fraud is knowledge that someone else owns a chattel.

            ii.   This element requires that the plaintiff ask questions that would give notice of fraud. *Porter v. Wertz.*

        c.   For value.

            i.   The property may not be given as a gift or at a price that is so substantially below the market value that it is considered to be a gift.

            ii.   It must be purchased at the market value or the appropriate value under the circumstances.

4.   General Principle

        a.   The general principle of BFP is *caveat emptor* ("buyer beware").

        b.   The BFP does not acquire title to a good when the seller did not have title to transfer.

        c.   A seller may not transfer better title than he has.

5.   Exceptions

        a.   The following exceptions to the *caveat emptor* ruling principle are recognized by the common law and statutes:

            i.   Under **equitable estoppel**, which is governed by the common law, there are two exceptions to *caveat emptor*:

                1)   Voidable title; and

                2)   Apparent authority.

            ii.   Under **statutory estoppel**, which applies to the sale of goods and is governed by the UCC,[6] there are two exceptions to *caveat emptor*:

                1)   Voidable title; and

                2)   Entrustment.

            iii.   All of these exceptions permit the BFP to keep title because of some action of the OO that prohibits him from later replevying the chattel.

        b.   Common Law Voidable Title

            i.   When the OO has the intent to transfer title, voidable title passes, even if title is obtained through fraud. *Phelps v. McQuade.*

                1)   Rationale: when the OO had some intent to transfer title, the result can be to some extent imputed to his neglect or other conduct.

---

[6] The Uniform Commercial Code (UCC), which is enacted with some variations in all fifty states, governs the statutory estoppel exceptions to the principle of *caveat emptor*.

2) *N.B.*: title is not passed when a party fraudulently represents himself to be an agent of another.

ii. However, when the OO had no intention of transferring title, *no title* passes.

iii. The sale must be face to face; voidable title does not pass when it is done through letter or by agent.

iv. Since there is no intent to transfer title when a chattel is stolen, thieves do not obtain voidable title or any other transferable title.

1) *See Lieber v. Mohawk Arms*, where the defendant purchased the plaintiff's Hitler uniform, which was stolen by the plaintiff's chauffeur. The defendant obtained no title, since the title that the chauffeur purported to transfer was void.

v. Even when the thief makes improvements to the stolen good, he obtain neither full nor voidable title.

1) *See National Retailers Mut. Ins. Co. v. Gambino*, where title to a stolen vehicle was held not to be transferable, even though the thief substituted the engine with one from another vehicle.

vi. Since bailors have no intent to transfer title, bailees do not obtain voidable title and therefore have no title to pass.[7] *Baehr v. Clark.*

vii. Voidable title becomes full title when it is transferred to a BFP *for value*. However, because the title of a thief is void, it remains void, even if transferred to a BFP.

c. Common Law Apparent Authority

i. Under this second exception, even if an OO has no intent to sell a good, voidable title passes if the OO, through some level of conduct, clothes the possessor with the apparent authority to sell.

ii. Under this exception, the OO's intent to sell is "imported" to the possessor.

1) *See O'Connor v. Clark* (Pa. 1895), where the OO of a wagon painted the name of his new employee. When the employee transferred the wagon to a third party, the court granted title to the defendant BFP through the employee's apparent authority to transfer title. The OO was estopped from denying that his employee was the owner.

d. Voidable Title under the UCC

i. "A purchaser of goods acquires all title that the purchaser's transferor had or had power to transfer." UCC § 2-403(1).

1) Example: if a thief steals a chattel from an OO and later sells it, the later purchaser does not receive title, since the thief had no title to transfer.

---

[7] However, under the entrustment exception of the UCC, discussed *infra.*, a merchant may pass voidable title of bailed chattel entrusted to him when he sells them to a buyer in the ordinary course of business.

      ii.   However, a seller sometimes has power to transfer more title than he actually had: holders of voidable title may transfer good title to *good faith purchasers* for *value*. UCC § 2-403(1).

      iii.   Voidable title is passed when the OO has the intention to pass title (generally, the OO owner somehow acts negligently).

      iv.   As long as goods are delivered under a transaction, voidable title passes, even if:

        1)   The purchaser *deceives the seller* as to his identity;

        2)   The goods are procured through a *bounced check*;

        3)   The transaction was by a "*cash sale*" (*e.g.*, the buyer promises to later deliver cash for a chattel that the seller immediately delivers); or

        4)   The original owner is induced to sell to a wrongful possessor through "*fraud punishable as larcenous* under the criminal law" (*e.g.*, stealing and using another's credit card, using counterfeit money, etc.). UCC § 2-403(1).

      v.   Under the UCC, voidable title may pass by letter or face to face.

    e.   **Entrustment under the UCC**

      i.   The above-mentioned voidable title and apparent authority exceptions discuss when voidable title may pass to a BFP.

      ii.   The entrustment exception under the UCC, in contrast, deals with when voidable title may pass to a buyer in ordinary course of business (BOC).

      iii.   A BOC may obtain good title from a merchant who sells bailed chattel entrusted to him for repair, improvement, etc., when the merchant deals in goods of that kind. UCC § 2-403(2).

      iv.   A BOC must:

        1)   Purchase with good faith;

        2)   Without notice of fraud;

        3)   From a business establishment in the ordinary course of business.

          a)   *N.B.*: a purchase would *not be in the ordinary course of business* if a merchant over his lunch hour takes his client to his home to sell him a chattel.

      v.   Note that, unlike the voidable title exceptions to BFP, it is not necessary to show that the purchase was "for value"; since the chattel is being purchased from a business, it is assumed that the BOC paid market value.

G.   GIFTS

    1.   A gift, or donative transfer, is a present, voluntary transfer of title without consideration.

2. Classes

    a. *Inter Vivos* Gifts

        i. *Inter vivos* gifts are given while donor is living.

        ii. They are not revocable.

    b. *Mortis Causa* Gifts

        i. *Mortis causa* gifts are given in anticipation of the donor's death.

        ii. They can be revoked if:

            1) The donee dies before the donor;

            2) The donor does not die from the anticipated illness and does not decide to give the gift *inter vivos*;

            3) The donor revokes the gift before he dies but while he is still ill.

3. Elements

    a. Donative intent

        i. The donor must *intend* to *presently transfer* title to the donee.

        ii. If the transfer will take place in the future, it is not a gift, but rather, a promise that is unenforceable if it lacks consideration.

    b. Delivery

        i. The donor must deliver the chattel.

        ii. The delivery may take on any of the following forms:

            1) *Actual delivery*: the donee physically takes possession of the chattel.

            2) *Constructive delivery*: where the donor that which is necessary for possessing the chattel (*e.g.*, the keys to a car).

            3) *Delivery by written instrument*: the instrument must show the intent to transfer, be signed by the donor, describe the subject matter of the gift, and be delivered;

            4) *Symbolic delivery*: the donor delivers some object that symbolizes the gift (*e.g.*, a cow could symbolize one's entire herd).

    c. Acceptance

        i. The donee must accept the chattel.

        ii. Acceptance is often presumed if a gift is unconditional and beneficial.

4. Courts require the best possible delivery under the circumstances.

    a. Generally, a signed, executed deed is sufficient.

        i. Some courts have held that such a document comprised delivery *even when it was not actually delivered*.

           1)   *See In re Cohn*, where the court held that a signed, executed agreement granting the decedent's wife a donative transfer of stocks was held valid, even though it was never actually delivered.

        ii.   *N.B.*: this case holding is exceptional; courts generally require actual delivery, unless precluded by the circumstances.

    b.   Symbolic delivery in the form of a written instrument has also been held to be sufficient.

    c.   Others courts have held that clear and unequivocal intent on its own is sufficient when delivery is impossible.

        i.   In *Scherer v. Hyland* (N.J. 1977), Wagner committed suicide, leaving a check and letter for Scherer to recover. Since the letter and the fact that only Wagner had access to that space gave adequate evidence that Wagner intended to give check as gift, the court "imported" delivery, even though there was no actual delivery.

III. CONVEYANCES AND ACQUIRING TITLE

A. FINANCING ARRANGEMENTS

1. Introduction

    a.   There are two ways in which a vendee may purchase land without paying at once: through mortgages and through installment land contracts.

2. Mortgages

    a.   A mortgage is essentially a security for a debt. The mortgagee, or lender, receives the mortgage, which usually looks like a deed.

    b.   If the mortgagor, or borrower, defaults on a payment, the mortgage allows the mortgagee to obtain possession of the property, usually after a hearing with proof of default in payments by the mortgagor.

    c.   Mortgages have *defeasance clauses* that recognize that, once the debt has been paid, the mortgage is no longer of any effect.

    d.   Documents involved in a deed:

        i.   The *deed of trust*, which conveys title of the property; and

        ii.   The *note*, which makes mortgagors personally liable in case a property sale or foreclosure does not raise all of the funds.

    e.   Default and Title

        i.   At common law, the mortgage operates as a conveyance of title to the mortgagee, who holds the mortgage.

            1)   However, *the title only becomes active* if the mortgagor defaults on his payments.

2)   Even a single default payment at common law allowed the mortgagee to keep all past payments, possess the land, and sell it to recover the money due.

3)   In many other states, a mortgage was not considered to grant title to the mortgagee. Rather, it is viewed as a *mere lien*.

ii.   To offset the harsh effects of the common law, the **equitable right of redemption** developed to allow the mortgagor to redeem his property (this doctrine is recognized in all states).

1)   Generally, the mortgagor may redeem the property by paying the amount due, plus interest.

2)   If he has defaulted on a mortgage note requiring the full balance in the event of a default, then he must *pay the entire balance to redeem* the property.

iii.   In about half the states, the mortgagor's right of redemption continues even **after the foreclosure** sale.

1)   The redemption period is set by statute and usually lasts from six to twelve months.

2)   The mortgagor may usually redeem the property by paying the foreclosure sale price.

iv.   Today, most states view the mortgage not as **title** to the property, but as a mere **lien**.

v.   There are two approaches to foreclosure that correspond to the views states have adopted with respect to the mortgage and the title-bearer of the mortgaged property:

1)   Foreclosure by Sale

a)   This is the approach in **lien theory states**, which treat the mortgage as a lien on the land to repay a loan.

b)   After the redemption period expires, the property is sold and the mortgagee returns to the mortgagor monies raised beyond the original debt.

c)   Today, most states view the mortgage as a lien. Foreclosure by sale is therefore the *majority approach*.

2)   Strict Foreclosure

a)   This is the approach in **title theory states**, which treat the mortgage as an instantaneous, actual transfer of title.

b)   Once an action is brought and the statutory period passes, the title actually changes hands and is transferred to the mortgagee (lender), who becomes the owner of the property.

   c)   Strict foreclosure follows the common law, which today is the minority approach.

3.   Installment Land Contracts

   a.   In installment land contracts, also known as "land contracts" or "conditional land contracts," the purchaser is granted possession, but the vendor retains title, in contrast to the mortgage, where in most states today, title passes to the mortgagor.

   b.   The purchaser pays the vendor in periodic installments and, when he completes the requisite payments, he receives title.

   c.   Installment land contracts are typically used when a buyer is unable to acquire a mortgage to purchase the land.

   d.   Traditionally, courts enforce *forfeitures* (strict foreclosures) in installment land contracts in a summary manner.

      i.   Thus, if purchaser defaults, the vendor may keep the land, as in a "summary," or "strict" foreclosure (forfeiture).

      ii.   Exception: when the forfeiture is unequivocally unjust.

   e.   Some states, however, by statute, allow the purchaser to pay off the accelerated full balance of the contract and keep the land (this parallels the equitable right of redemption for mortgages).

   f.   Some states have also passed statutes that impose grace periods, allowing the purchasers to redeem the land.

   g.   Courts consider a series of factors in determining whether to allow forfeiture in installment land contracts, including whether the purchaser has made most of the payments, whether he has made substantial improvements to the property, and whether the forfeiture provision allows the creditor to keep all monies paid as well as the defaulted land.

      i.   *See Skendzel v. Marshall* (defendant), where the plaintiff sued the defendant to enforce the forfeiture provision in an installment land contract when the defendant failed to make a payment. A liquidated damages clause allowed the plaintiff to recover possession of the land while keeping all monies paid in the event of the defendant's default. Held: this liquidated damages clause is invalid because it leads to an *unjust forfeiture*. Judgment for the plaintiff reversed.

B.   MERCHANTABLE TITLE

1.   Introduction

   a.   Merchantable title is title that is not subject to such reasonable doubt that it would create a just apprehension of its validity in the mind of a reasonable prudent person.

   b.   Title that would be subject to a substantial risk of litigation is not considered merchantable.

c.   However, merchantable title is not necessarily good title; it may have *slight defects* do not invalidate the title (*e.g.*, a missing signature in one of the preceding title holders' deeds; an unaccounted for period in the history of land ownership; etc).

2.   The Implied Warranty of Merchantable Title

a.   In every land sale contract, an implied warranty of merchantable title guarantees that the seller will present and pass merchantable title to the purchaser *at the closing* ("law day"), unless the parties have contracted otherwise.

b.   If the seller does not have merchantable title at the time that the land sale contract is formed, he may acquire it during the executory period (the period between the formation of the contract and the closing).

c.   If there are outstanding liens that would breach the warranty of merchantable title, the seller may rely on a portion of the sale proceeds in escrow to remove the liens, as long as the purchaser is assured that the escrow funds will not be released until after the removal of the liens.

d.   If the seller fails to obtain merchantable title before law day, the purchaser may rescind the contract and seek restitution.

i.   Until then, a buyer may not sue for rescission and restitution.

1)   *See Luette v. Bank of Italy Nat. Trust and Savings Association* (defendant), where the plaintiffs were to purchase a parcel of land that they later realized was claimed by a third party. The defendant refused to show good title or refund the price. The plaintiffs sued for either rescission and restitution or for an injunction preventing the defendant from canceling the contract. Held: the defendant has until law day to present merchantable title. In an installment land contract, that may mean several years after the contract was formed, when the last payment was made. Until then, rescission and restitution will not be granted. Judgment for the defendant is affirmed.

ii.   *Exception*: when property is so badly encumbered that the plaintiff may reasonably assume that the defendant will not have the merchantable title at the time that the last payment is due, the defendant may be required to offer merchantable title before law day.

e.   The parties may, however, limit the implied warranty of merchantable title. Very specific language is required.

i.   The language, "buyer agrees to purchase *all of the seller's interest in his premises*," or, "*all of the seller's interest, whether or not he has full title*," is sufficient in overcoming the implied warranty of merchantable title.

1) *N.B.*: under this contract, if the buyer later discovers that the seller did not have merchantable title, he *may not rescind* the contract before or after law day.

    ii.   However, if the contract states that the buyer "agrees to accept the land located at X location" or "all of the seller's premises," the implied warranty is not overcome. If the seller fails to present merchantable title at the closing, the buyer may rescind the contract.

    iii.   If the contract states that the buyer "agrees to accept all of the seller's premises by *quitclaim deed*," the implied warranty is not overcome, and the buyer has the right to *rescind the contract* if he finds that the seller did not have merchantable title.

1) *See Wallach v. Riverside Bank*, where the court allowed the plaintiff to rescind a land sale contract and recover his deposit when he discovered that the *seller did not have merchantable title*, even though the seller was conveying only a quitclaim deed. Rule: between the land sale contract and the closing, the buyer has the opportunity to research the seller's title. If the seller does not possess merchantable title, the buyer may rescind the contract under the ***implied warranty of merchantable title***, even if only a quitclaim deed is offered. If, however, *after the closing*, the plaintiff discovered that he does not have merchantable title, then under the quitclaim deed, he is required to accept the title "as is."

3.   Two Remedies for Breach of the Implied Warranty of Merchantable Title

    a.   Specific Performance

        i.   A court may require the seller to acquire merchantable title before law day, when doing so is practical.

        ii.   For example, if there is a lien on the property, a court may require the seller to clear it with the money received from the sale.

    b.   Rescission and Restitution

        i.   This is awarded when (i) specific performance (SP) is neither practical nor possible; or (ii) the contract does not provide for SP.

        ii.   *See Bartos v. Czerwinski* (defendant), where the plaintiff entered into a contract to purchase land from the defendant. The contract allowed the plaintiff to be released from the contract if the title was not merchantable. When the plaintiff discovered that the defendant may not have had good title to as much as half of the property, he sued for SP to force the defendant to clear title before proceeding. Held: SP will not be granted when the contract does not allow for it. The remedy would be to release the plaintiff from the contract, as provided by the contract, and to allow him to recover the monies paid.

C.   EQUITABLE CONVERSION AND RISK OF LOSS

    1.   The Doctrine of Equitable Conversion

a. There are three steps in the process of transferring title to property: (i) the *land sale contract*; (ii) the delivery of *merchantable (marketable) title*; and (iii) the *closing*.

b. There is always a question as to who "owns" the land in the period between the formation of the contract and the closing (the executory period) and who bears the risk of loss.

c. Under the ***doctrine of equitable conversion***, the purchaser is the owner of the property and bears the risk of loss from the moment the contract is executed.

d. Rationale: under equity, "what ought to be done is considered done." Since a contract ought to be followed, the buyer is considered to be the title-holder, even when he does not yet have the deed or the possession of the land.

e. However, the doctrine of equitable conversion does not apply in the following circumstances:

    i. *Contractual provisions that state otherwise* (*e.g.*, "title shall remain with the seller");

    ii. *Vendor's negligence*, where the seller damages the property during the executory period and the buyer only finds out when he takes the property;

    iii. *Misrepresentation* or *fraud* by a party;

    iv. The *inexistence of a binding contract;*

    v. The *inexistence of marketable title;* or

    vi. *Changed circumstances* that frustrate the purchaser's purpose.

        1) *See Clay* (plaintiff-seller) *v. Landreth*, where after the contract was formed, an ordinance was passed that prohibited the defendant from using the plaintiff's land for the business for which he intended to use it. When the defendant tried to get out of the contract, the plaintiff sued for SP, arguing that the defendant was already bound to the land through the doctrine of equitable conversion: from the moment the contract was signed, the seller was only a trustee of the property and the buyer was only a trustee of the money to be paid. Held: because outside circumstances frustrated the buyer's purpose, equitable conversion does not apply.

2. The Three Approaches to the Effect of the Risk of Loss

a. Majority Approach

    i. Under the majority approach, title is transferred to the buyer at the execution of the contract and the buyer bears the risks of loss during the executory period (in the absence of the above-described exceptions).

CHAPTER 2
PROPERTY

      ii.   *See Bleckley v. Langston* (defendant-vendor), where the vendee sued for rescission of a land sale contract and restitution of the deposit when a frost destroyed pecan trees on the land. Held: the equitable owner, who in this case is the plaintiff, bears the risk of loss.

    b.   Minority Approach

      i.   Under the minority approach, the seller keeps title upon execution of the contract and retains the risk of loss during the executory period; he may collect damages if, after loss, the plaintiff decides not to go forward with the closing.

      ii.   This is the approach adopted in Massachusetts.

    c.   Uniform Vendor and Purchaser Risk Act

      i.   If the Uniform Vendor and Purchaser Risk Act has been adopted, the doctrine of equitable conversion will not be applied when unanticipated damages occur.

      ii.   Instead, the contract will be rescinded and any money paid by the purchaser will be restituted to him. The vendor will not be entitled to damages.

      iii.   However, the purchaser assumes the risk of loss when either legal title or possession is transferred to him.

D.   THE MODERN DEED

    1.   Introduction

      a.   A deed has the following elements:

        i.   It must be written;

        ii.   It must contain:

          1)   The names of the parties;

          2)   A granting clause;

          3)   A legal description of the property (the subject matter conveyed); and

          4)   A signature (for the SF).

        iii.   It must be delivered.

          1)   Delivery refers to the mental state of the grantor, not to the physical custody of the deed.

          2)   Thus, even if the deed is not physically delivered to the purchaser, the deed is deemed to be delivered if the grantor evidences an intent to presently transfer title.

          3)   An undelivered deed is completely void and can pass no interest in the land, even if it is later recorded. *Stone v. French.*

      b.   Other parts of the deed

i. Some deeds also tend to include, but do not require: (i) the *stated consideration*; (ii) a *habendum clause* limiting the rights being conveyed (*e.g.*, a right to possess but not to disposed of the property); and (iii) a *redendum clause* reserving any interest in the property to the seller (*e.g.*, easements).

ii. In the old common law, a deed required a seal to be valid. In most states today, this requirement has been abolished.

2. Construing Deeds

   a. Inconsistent parts within a deed must be reconciled by the courts.

   b. When all else is equal, a **granting clause** trumps an **inconsistent habendum** *clause*.

      i. *See First Nat'l Bank of Oregon v. Townsend* (defendant), where the defendant granted a deed called a "Warranty timber and mineral deed" to the plaintiff. There was ambiguity in the interest conveyed because the *granting clause* stated "grant and convey," but the *habendum clause* transferred only limited rights, such as the "right to enter upon said land, cut and remove trees, mine and remove minerals." The plaintiff, claiming that a fee simple was transferred, sued to quiet title. Since the land would escheat to the state absent a clear deed, the State of Oregon challenged the plaintiff's claim. Held: granting clauses trump inconsistent *habendum* clauses and courts disfavor escheat, they construe ambiguities in favor of the grantee. Judgment for the plaintiff affirmed.

   c. Although the granting clause trumps the *habendum* clause, the *intent of the parties* may rebut the granting clause.

      i. *See Grayson v. Holloway*, where the intent of a land grant to the defendant and her husband trumped the granting clause, which mentioned only the husband.

E. THE RECORDING SYSTEM

1. Introduction

   a. The purpose of recording a deed is to protect present owners from subsequent BFP's.

   b. If a BFP purchases property in good faith for value without notice from a seller who is not the TO of the property being sold, he may acquire title to the land *if the TO failed to record his deed*.

   c. If, however, the TO recorded the deed, the BFP would be charged with constructive notice and no title would pass.

   d. Although recording a deed is not an essential element to the validity of the deed, recording the deed is an important step towards protecting one's property interest.

2. Four Approaches to Recordings

   a. The Common Law Approach

        i.   Under the common law, the party with the ***earlier deed*** obtains title and possession to the property conveyed.

    b.   The Three Statutory Approaches

        i.   Notice Approach

            1)   A subsequent grantee wins if he is a BFP who purchases in ***good faith*** for ***value without notice***, regardless of when he actually records.

            2)   *See Earle* (plaintiff purchaser) *v. Fiske*, where decedent Nancy Fiske conveys land to Benjamin and Elizabeth Fiske as a life estate, with the remainder to Mary Fiske, but does not record the transaction. Upon Nancy's death, her only heir Benjamin sold the land to the plaintiff, who ***purchased the property in good faith without notice for value***. The plaintiff sued for a writ of entry. Held: since Massachusetts is a notice state, the ***only requirement*** for passing title is that ***the plaintiff have no*** actual or constructive ***notice*** of the other property interest and that the plaintiff pay value. These elements are met, since the plaintiff was on neither actual nor constructive notice that Benjamin did not have fee title to transfer. Title is vested in the plaintiff.

        ii.   Race/Notice Approach

            1)   A subsequent grantee wins only if he (i) is a ***BFP***; and (ii) ***records first***.

            2)   A BPF will thus not win against another purchaser who recorded first.

                a)   *See Simmons v. Stum* (plaintiff) (Ill. 1882), where a grantor mortgaged property to the plaintiff and later granted it to a party who had notice of the mortgage. That party later conveyed it to the defendant, who claimed to have no notice of the mortgage. The plaintiff sued to foreclose the mortgage. The defendant claimed that the plaintiff should have *no property interest* since she was a BFP. Held: since the plaintiff recorded his mortgage just two days after the property was transferred to the defendant, and since the defendant has never presented evidence showing when she recorded, the mortgage stands, since the mortgagor recorded his interest before the defendant, even if the defendant was a BFP.

        iii.   Pure Race

            1)   The grantee who ***records first*** wins title.

3.   There are two systems for searching for records on one's property:

    a.   The ***grantor/grantee index***, which is a list of all previous owners of a tract; and

b. The *tract index*, which is a list of every tract and its particular owner and all recorded instruments affecting it. This index greatly facilitates the ability of prospective purchases to find if there is good title and to discover restrictions on the property.

4. Records of Easements

a. Parties are on **constructive notice** of easements on land that they are purchasing when those easements are **in the original deeds of record**.

b. **Contractors** do not have this same duty to examine those records.

    i. *See Mountain States Telephone and Telegraph Co. v. Kelton* (defendant), where the defendant contractor, while digging land, destroyed some of the plaintiff's buried cables. The plaintiff sued for damages, claiming that the defendant was on *constructive notice* of the underground cables and had a duty to examine the records. Held: contractors do not have the same duty of potential land purchasers and others with an interest in land in checking for easements in the records.

F. **TITLE ASSURANCE AND WARRANTIES**

1. The Methods of Title Assurance

a. Buyers need a way to assure that they are getting what they bargained for.

b. Although personal covenants were developed in order to promise buyers they were getting good title, they were inadequate.

c. This led to the recording system discussed above and to modern title assurance and title searches.

d. In addition, buyers may insure themselves against defective title by obtaining *covenants for title*.

2. The Six Covenants in Warranty Deeds

a. Covenant of Seisin

    i. The grantor covenants that he *owns* the estate that he purports to transfer.

b. Covenant of the Right to Convey

    i. The grantor covenants that he has the *right to convey* the estate.

c. Covenant Against Encumbrances

    i. The grantor covenants that there are *no undisclosed encumbrances*, including easements, covenants, servitudes, mortgages or liens, on the land.

    ii. If an encumbrance is open and notorious, it is not considered "undisclosed" for the purpose of the covenant against encumbrances.

iii. However, even an open, adverse, and notorious irrevocable license violates the covenant, if it is not a *permanent, public encumbrance*. If it is a permanent, public encumbrance, the covenant is not violated when it would be inconceivable that the vendor would remove it. *Leach v. Gunnarson.*

d. Covenant of Warranty of Title

i. The grantor covenants that the title is good and promises to defend the grantee against any paramount claims of title existing at the time of conveyance.

ii. If the grantee is ever evicted, the grantor may take the steps necessary to secure good title for the grantee or the grantee may claim damages from the grantor.

e. Covenant of Quiet Enjoyment

i. The grantor covenants that there is *no third party with better title* to all or part of the property who may *evict* the grantee or otherwise disturb his possession and enjoyment of the property.

f. Covenant for Further Assurances

i. The grantor agrees to perform any reasonable, necessary acts in order to perfect the grantee's title.

3. Present and Future Covenants

a. Present Covenants

i. Present covenants do not run with the land under the *majority approach* and thus may *not* be enforced by remote parties.

ii. They do, however, run with the land under the minority approach, subject to the SL.

iii. The present covenants are: (i) the covenant of seisin; (ii) the covenant of the right to convey; and (iii) the covenant against encumbrances.

iv. They may only be breached at the time of the conveyance, at which point the SL begins to run.

b. Future Covenants

i. Introduction

1) Future covenants run with the land and may thus be enforced by remote parties.

2) The future covenants are the covenant of warranty of title, the covenant of quiet enjoyment, and the covenant for further assurances.

3) A purchaser's cause of action for breach of a future covenant is not limited to the party that conveyed his deed. Rather, he may sue all the way up the chain of title, if the SL has not expired.

ii.   Breach

    1)   Future covenants may be breached any time a grantee or a remote party is evicted or disturbed in his ownership of the property.[8] The SL begins to run at that moment.

    2)   Future covenants thus allow more leeway to grantees who may have missed the SL for the present covenants.

    3)   If it becomes clear that a third party holds better title, but the grantee has not yet been evicted or disturbed in his possession, most courts will not grant damages.

        a)   *See Brown* (plaintiffs) *v. Lober*, where the plaintiffs purchased land but later discovered that they owned only a partial interest in the subsurface coal rights. They sued the seller for breach of the covenant of seisin and of the covenant of the right to convey, but since it had been more than ten years since the plaintiffs purchased the land, the SL had expired. The plaintiffs then tried to sue on a covenant of quiet enjoyment theory, which was not barred by the SL, but which was inapplicable, since the mere existence of superior title absent a disturbance of the ownership does not constitute breach.

        b)   *N.B.*: the plaintiffs' recourse would have been to grant the coal option, and if the TO sued to quiet title, to show that the covenant of quiet enjoyment was breached.

iii.   In the majority of states, damages for the breach of future covenants equal the *purchase price* at the time of the sale plus *interest* (*not* the current value of the property). *See, e.g., Davis v. Smith* (Ga. 1848).

4.   Warranty Deeds

a.   The extent of a seller's liability is covered in the ***deed***.

b.   The seller may convey any of the following:

    i.   ***General warranty deed***, where all of the warranties are included.

    ii.   ***Special warranty deed***, which includes all of the warranties, but only during the *period in which the seller was in possession*.

    iii.   ***Quitclaim deed***, where no warranty is provided.

c.   The seller may also expressly provide for some warranties or limit others in the deed.

G.   ADVERSE POSSESSION OF REALTY AND AFTER ACQUIRED TITLE

1.   Statutes of Limitation and Related Legislation as Aids to Title Assurance

---

[8] Under the old common law, only an actual eviction constituted breach of the future covenants. Today, the future covenants are also breached by "constructive eviction," (*e.g.*, a disturbance that prevents the grantee from obtaining complete possession of the property).

a.   There are three approaches to adverse possession statutes: title assurance

    i.   Objective Approach

        1)   The objective approach involves an ***exclusive claim of right***.

        2)   All that matters is that the possessor have a claim that is adverse and inconsistent with the TO's claim (*i.e.*, full title); his state of is irrelevant.

    ii.   Subjective Approach

        1)   The subjective approach takes into account the later possessor's ***state of mind*** in addition to a ***pure claim of right***.

        2)   This generally means that the possessor must have *good faith* in order for the SL to run; in some states, however, the adverse possessor must actually have *bad faith*.

        3)   In these latter states, if a person acquired possession through a mistake or good faith, the SL does not run.

    iii.   Short Term Statute Approach

        1)   While the other approaches require a SL range of about twenty years, the short term statutory approach involves a SL of as little as ***five to ten years***, when the possession is:

            a)   Under ***color of title;*** and

            b)   Including the ***payment of taxes***.

b.   For a party to successfully acquire title to land by adverse possession, the possession must be:

    i.   Open

        1)   The use of the land must be of the kind of use that the normal owner would make of the land.

        2)   It must be sufficient to put the owner on notice.

    ii.   Continuous

        1)   Continuous is *not synonymous with uninterrupted*, as long as the use is consistent with the nature of the property.

        2)   *See Howard v. Kunto*, where the court held that summer occupancy of a summer home was sufficient to meet the *continuous* element of adverse possession.

    iii.   Exclusive

        1)   The adverse possessor must not share possession with the TO.

    iv.   Adverse

        1)   Under a claim of right against the TO.

v.   Notorious

1)   This element is virtually identical to the "open" element.

c.   Tacking

i.   If the adverse possessor does not meet the statutory period, he may reach it through *tacking*, or adding periods of prior adverse possession to the period of time in which he personally was in possession.

ii.   The elements of tacking are as follow:

1)   The former possessor must have transferred the same land through either:

2)   **Deed** (sale/conveyance), **devise** (gift or will), or **inheritance** (by law).

iii.   The transfer may be oral even when the deed refers to a **different plot of land**. In meeting this **privity requirement**, a court will not elevate form over substance.

1)   *See Howard v. Kunto*, where the court allowed tacking even though there was never a transfer on the adversely possessed land from the preceding possessor, since what was transferred in the deed was an entirely different plot of land. Because both the current and previous owners thought that their deeds referred to the land they occupied, the substance of privity was met when the preceding owner transferred his interest.

d.   An owner may not claim adverse possession of subsurface minerals unless he actually exploits or occupies them, even if he possesses the surface rights.

i.   *See Failoni v. Chicago and North Western Railway Co.* (defendant), where the court held that leasing oil and gas rights to subsurface minerals was insufficient to establish the elements for adverse possession. The plaintiff failed to obtain adverse possession of the minerals because: (i) there was no color of title; (ii) she did not pay taxes on the severed minerals; and (iii) she did not try to mine or possess them. Judgment for the plaintiff reversed.

e.   For a tenant in common to claim adverse possession against another tenant in common, more than mere occupancy is required to meet the elements of adverse possession. Rather, an actual ouster must take place before the SL begins to run.

i.   *See Mercer v. Wayman* (defendants) (Ill. 1956), where property was inherited as a tenancy in common by several family members. They all (including two minors through the actions of their father) agreed to quitclaim the property to one the plaintiffs, who took possession. When one of the children reached majority, he disaffirmed his father's transfer and made a claim against the property, suggesting he was a part owner. The plaintiffs sued to quiet title under adverse possession. Held: the elements of the plaintiffs are met under neither the short term nor the long term Illinois SL. The short term SL is not met because there is no color of title, since the deed conveying property to the plaintiffs was not valid. The long term SL did not run because there was never an actual ouster of the defendants.

2. After-Acquired Title

    a. According to the ***after-acquired-title doctrine***, when a seller not having title to property purports to sell that property to a buyer, title vests in that buyer as soon as the seller acquires title.

    b. A purchaser thus acquires title when the following sequence takes place:

        i. A seller ***purports to sell*** the property;

        ii. A buyer ***purchases the property*** from the seller; and

        iii. The seller later acquires good or full title.

IV. THE INTEGRITY OF THE LAND

A. TRESPASS AND NUISANCE; SUPPORT OF LAND

1. Trespass and Nuisance

    a. A nuisance is a condition or activity on another's land that unreasonably affects the other's right to enjoy and use his land. The standard is one of a *person of ordinary sensibility*.

    b. Factors considered in determining whether a condition is a nuisance include whether:

        i. The condition begins or occurs after the plaintiff has been occupying the land;

        ii. The condition has little value to the one causing it;

        iii. The activity has little social value; and

        iv. The activity lowers the value of the owner's property.

2. Burdens of Proof

    a. If the owner of the land meets his burden of proving (i) ***causation***; and (ii) ***damages***, an injunction will be granted.

    b. However, the defendant may raise a defense and avoid an injunction by showing that either: (i) the damage is unavoidable; or (ii) the cost of avoiding the damage is so high that it would deprive the defendant of the use of the land.

        i. *See Renkin v. Harvey Aluminum* (defendant), where the plaintiff sought an injunction against the defendant, an aluminum plant that employed hundreds of workers and had a gross annual payroll of $3.5 million. There was undisputed evidence showing that the defendant's escaping fluoride caused damages to the plaintiff's apricot and peach trees. The plaintiff therefore met the burden of proving nuisance. The defendant had the burden of showing that either (i) the nuisance was *unavoidable*; or (ii) the costs of avoiding the damage would *deprive the defendant from the use of the land*. The defendant proved neither, since the problem was (i) avoidable and (ii) not cost-prohibitive. Therefore, a *future* injunction was awarded, even though the costs were substantial.

c. If either of these elements are met by the defendant, a court will **balance the equities** by looking to each side's interests in order to determine whether to award damages or an injunction.

   i. Example: if granting an injunction against the activities of a major factory would cause a substantial loss of profits and the loss of thousands of jobs, a court may instead grant money damages to the plaintiff, especially when it appears that such a remedy would make the plaintiff whole.

d. Furthermore, courts will not grant injunctions when doing so would entangle the judiciary in national policy areas generally reserved for legislatures.

   i. *See Boomer v. Atlantic Cement Co.* (defendant cement plant), where the defendant's plant caused damages to the plaintiff's land. The plaintiff sued for an injunction. Recognizing that granting an injunction would cause a commercially important business to close down, the court held that where there is much substantial benefit from an activity, as in this case, it will grant monetary damages instead of an injunction.

3. Public and Private Nuisances

   a. Private Nuisance

      i. A nuisance is private when the party whose property interest is being disturbed is one individual or a few individuals, as opposed to an entire neighborhood or community.

      ii. The owner of the land being disturbed may recover for any nuisances against the defendant when he can prove causation and damages. He will obtain at least money damages, and possibly an injunction.

      iii. However, when the nuisance existed when the owner purchased the land ("*coming to the nuisance*"), the owner will not recover, unless the nuisance has become greater in degree since the land purchase.

   b. Public Nuisance

      i. A nuisance is public when the parties whose property interest is being disturbed are large groups of individuals or an entire community.

      ii. The plaintiffs may recover from the defendant for any nuisances when they can prove causation and damages, *including when they "come to the nuisance."*

1) *See Spur Industries, Inc. v. Del E. Webb Development Co.* (plaintiff), where the plaintiff continued developing his rural housing project until it reached the defendant's feeding lot. The plaintiff sued for an injunction for flies and odors from the defendant's property. Held: because this is a public nuisance effecting not only the defendant but all of those in the defendant's housing, the injunction against the defendant is affirmed. However, the plaintiff is required to indemnify the defendant for his damages.

B. ZONING

1. Introduction

a. Zoning occurs when a legislature limits the permitted uses of the land.

i. Example: a ban on easily ignitable building materials in a part of town that is susceptible to fires.

b. Among the purposes of zoning are aesthetic values, health, safety, and welfare.

2. Constitutionality

a. All zoning laws, to be valid, must be deemed constitutional. The following two-part test is applied:

i. The law must have a ***proper purpose*** (*i.e.*, a purpose within the police power of the state (morality, health, safety, welfare);

1) A proper purpose may be aesthetic value.

2) However, the zoning standard is unconstitutional when arbitrarily applied. *Nectow v. City of Cambridge.*

ii. The law must reasonably promote that purpose.

b. When these elements are met, the law is deemed *constitutional, even if it causes a decrease in the value* of the property affected.

i. *See Village of Euclid v. Ambler Realty Co.* (1926), where an ordinance that restricted land use caused the plaintiff's parcel to significantly lose value (from $10,000 to $2,500). The plaintiff sued to enjoin enforcement of the ordinance on the basis that it was facially unconstitutional, since it substantially violated the due process ***right to property*** (loss of value) and ***right to liberty*** (use of land). Held: the fact that an ordinance causes loss of value will not on its own invalidate the ordinance, particularly when it has other beneficial effects, such as promoting health, safety, and welfare, by providing a safer environment in which to rear one's children.

C. TAKINGS

1. Introduction

a. A taking is an appropriation of private property by the state for the common good.

b.   Property is considered to be "taken" when it is *actually taken* (*i.e.,* *physically invaded* and *appropriated*) or so *heavily regulated* that the owner has been deprived of all economic use.

2.   Actual Takings

    a.   Under the Fifth Amendment Takings Clause, private property shall not "be taken for public use, without just compensation."

    b.   There are thus two requirements for valid public takings:

        i.   "Just compensation" must be paid.

            1)   Just compensation must be a "full and perfect equivalent" of the value of the property.

        ii.   They must be done for a legitimate "public use."

            1)   Today, however, the inquiry no longer looks into whether a taking is based on a legitimate public use; rather, the courts search for *any legitimate public purpose*, which may include:

                a)   Land redistribution from a small oligarchy to the general public; and

                b)   The development of a blighted sector.

            2)   The purpose need not benefit all of the public; it is sufficient if only some benefit.

            3)   Furthermore, a taking need not transfer ownership to the government; it may transfer ownership ***to private interests***.

                a)   *See Hawaii Housing Authority v. Midkiff* (plaintiff) (1984), where Hawaiian legislation that redistributed land by transferring title from lessors to lessees was held to be constitutional, since the redistribution of title that was previously predominantly held by a small oligarchy to the rest of the population was a legitimate "public purpose" affecting health, safety, and welfare.

                b)   *See also Kelo* (defendant) *v. City of New London* (Stevens, J.), where the Court held that the transfer of waterfront property to other private interests was constitutional when the purpose was to build hotels, offices, and restaurants in order to *develop the sector* and *benefit the public*.

            4)   However, where the government's transfer of interests between private interests is done *for the sole purpose of transferring ownership*, the taking is *unconstitutional*, even if just compensation is paid.

3.   Regulatory Takings

    a.   As mentioned above, property is considered to be "taken" not only when it is *actually appropriated*, but also when it is so *heavily regulated* that the owner has been deprived of all economic use of his land.

b. When property is "taken" through burdensome regulation, just compensation must be paid.

c. There are two kinds of regulatory takings that require just compensation:

    i. Physical Invasions

        1) *See, e.g., Loretto v. Teleprompter Manhattan CATV Corp.* (1982), where the installations of cables in apartment buildings constituted a taking, even though only an insignificant space in the apartments was occupied. The taking was imputed to the government, since a local law required certain property owners to permit the installations.

    ii. Regulations Denying All Economically Beneficial Use of the Land

        1) *See Lucas v. South Carolina Coastal Council*, where the Beachfront Management Act barred the plaintiff from any economically profitable use of land that he purchased for $975,000. Held (Scalia, J.): the act's effect on the plaintiff's ability to economically benefit from his land was a key factor for determining whether just compensation was required.

        2) *N.B.*: a distinction is to be made between: (i) regulatory takings, where the land is so burdened by regulations that it is deprived of all economic use, and where just compensation is required; and (ii) regulations preventing nuisances, where compensation is not required, since the government's rights are based on the common law.

V. LANDLORD / TENANT LAW

A. INTRODUCTION TO NON-FREEHOLD ESTATES

1. The Two Kinds of Estates

    a. Freehold Estates

        i. In a freehold estates, the possessor is the owner of the property (at least for a temporary period of time).

    b. Leasehold Estates

        i. A leasehold estate is one where the possessor (tenant) has only possession, and full title will spring back to the owner (landlord).

        ii. Historical origins

            1) In feudal times, the king owned all of the land. Nobles that were loyal to him were able to use parts of the land. They then were able to parcel land out to serfs and peasants.

a)   Today, this many-layered system of tenancy continues to exist. For example, in commercial shopping centers, sections of a store may be parceled out to merchants many times over.

2)   Later, leaseholds were established as collateral for loans. The tenant would "lend" the landlord the money in exchange for the use of the land. Rather than pay the loan back with interest, the landlord would simply grant the tenant use of the land.

3)   Eventually, the law began to recognize leaseholds as interests in land in and of themselves.

2.   Three Kinds of Leaseholds

a.   Tenancy for Years

     i.   Characteristics

         1)   A tenancy for years is a discreet lease with a determined beginning and end date.

         2)   If there is a provision clause in the lease, then a second, separate one-time renewal lease may be established.

         3)   When there is a renewal clause in the lease, it is evidence of a tenancy for years, since periodic tenancies and at-will tenancies require no renewal to continue.

     ii.   How It Is Created

         1)   A tenancy for years is created formally.

         2)   It requires a clear end date.

             a)   The end date need not be explicitly expressed, if the expiration of the lease could be determined.

             b)   The following clause, for example, would be sufficient: "the lease will begin on Jan 1, 2000 and will expire three years later."

         3)   According to some authorities, there must also be a set start date.

             a)   Under the majority view, however, it does not need to be fixed.

             b)   The clause "the lease begins when the construction has ended" would be sufficient.

         4)   Statute of Frauds: under the modern law, any lease for more than one year must be in writing to be enforced.

     iii.   How It Is Terminated

         1)   A tenancy for years ends automatically at the end of the term.

         2)   The lease may provide the possibility of renewal.

3)   In such a case, a court would allow the new lease.

4)   Except for when a provision of the original contract (lease) is illegal, unclear or for some other reason against public policy, the original contract controls all matters in the new lease.

b.   **Periodic Tenancy**

     i.   Characteristics

         1)   A periodic tenancy is an indefinite lease.

         2)   There is no need for renewal.

     ii.   How It Is Created

         1)   A periodic tenancy may be created by the parties in an express agreement (*e.g.*, "This lease is from month-to-month.").

         2)   In addition, it may be created by law.

             a)   If the parties attempt to create a tenancy for years, but a period is mentioned (*e.g.*, "rent will be paid each month") and no end date is determined, then a periodic tenancy is presumed.

     iii.   How It Is Terminated

         1)   Either party may end a periodic tenancy with *proper notice* (unlike tenancies at will, which do not require proper notice).

             a)   For periods of one or more years, six months of notice is usually required.

             b)   For periods of less than one year, notice equal to one full period (generally measured by payment periods) is required.

         2)   Generally, notice of termination must be in writing and delivered.

         3)   Example: the tenant rents from a landlord in a monthly periodic tenancy. The tenant gives notice to the landlord on July 15 that he wishes to leave. Until when must the tenant pay rent?

             a)   Since the tenant must have one full month of rent paid before vacating, all of August must be paid before leaving. Thus, the tenant is responsible for rent up until August 31.

c.   **Tenancy at Will**

     i.   Characteristics

         1)   A tenancy at will may be terminated at any time.

     ii.   How It Is Created

1) It is usually created by operation of law.

    a) If a tenancy for years is attempted, but there is no clear end date and no basis for ascertaining a period, then a tenancy at will is presumed.

    b) Examples of tenancies where there is no basis for ascertaining a period:

        i) The landlord agrees to allow his tenant to live on the property on the condition that the tenant keeps up the property and pays the taxes and insurance.

        ii) The tenant is an employee-at-will of a landlord who furnishes a home as part of the compensation.

    c) *See Womack v. Hyche* (1987), where the parties disputed a tenancy "for $300 per year with the option to renew so long as the camp is run as a business." The landlord argued that there was no fixed end date and that the lease was therefore a tenancy at will that would allow him to evict the defendant. The defendant argued that the end date was the end of the year. Held: a tenancy at will is created, since the end date is not clear. Remanded to determine a reasonable time required to vacate.

        i) N.B.: a court could have interpreted this to be a periodic tenancy based on the one year payment period.

  iii. How It Is Terminated

    1) Under the common law, a tenancy at will could be ended at any time.

    2) Today, many state statutes protect tenants, by requiring, for example, at least ten days of notice prior to the landlord's termination of the tenancy.

B. DISCRIMINATORY PREFERENCES AND RELIGIOUS LIBERTY ISSUES

1. The Evolution of Regulations on Landlords

  a. Under the common law, a landlord could select whichever tenants or purchasers he wanted for his housing or land.

  b. Later, statutes prohibited landlords or sellers from discriminating on the basis of race, color, religion, sex, familial status, age, handicap or national origin.

  c. One example of such a statute is the federal Fair Housing Act.

    i. The Fair Housing Act prohibits:

      1) Discrimination on the basis of race, color, religion, sex, familial status, age, handicap or national origin for the basis of choosing a tenant or buyer; and

2)   The publication or indication of a preference as to any of the above categories in choosing a buyer or tenant.

ii.   The subjective intent of the owner or landlord is irrelevant; what matters is whether a reasonable person from one of the protected groups would interpret an indication as expressing preference.

1)   *See Jancik v. Department of Housing and Urban Development* (plaintiff), where the Seventh Circuit held that the landlord violated the Fair Housing Act by indicating his preference for a "mature person," which a reasonable person would take to mean a middle-aged tenant without small children, thus violating the statute on familial status. He also violated the statute by saying that he did not want any teenagers and by inquiring as to race with a discriminatory purpose. Damages and injunction affirmed.

a)   *N.B.*: a landlord could refuse to rent on an individualized basis to persons with children who were disruptive or would damage property, but a class-based exclusion is invalid.

b)   *N.B.*: this court did not deal with the issue of whether inquiries as to race on their own are enough to violate the Fair Housing Act. The Second Circuit, however, in dicta stated that they were sufficient.

d.   Many states have adopted stricter versions of this federal act. Massachusetts, for example, has adopted statutes that also prohibit discrimination on the basis of sexual orientation.

e.   Regulations are usually more lax for the rental of rooms attached to the owner's abode (*e.g.*, he may chose a tenant based on gender).

2.   Modern Statutes and Religious Liberty

a.   Many state and federal statutes prohibit familial status discrimination.

b.   Such statutes do not necessarily prohibit landlords from discriminating against unmarried cohabitants.

i.   *See State v. French* (defendant), where a defendant religious landlord acted discriminatorily against unmarried cohabitant tenants. The Minnesota Human Rights Acts forbade the discrimination of tenants based on age, race, religion, and marital status. Because the Minnesota Constitution did not define "marital status," the court looked to the legislative history and found that the legislature excluded the language, "and other like categories" that would have protected unmarried cohabitants. Additionally, the Minnesota Constitution protects freedom of religion, with the exception of that which poses a threat to the safety of the state. Since the defendant landlord's discrimination did not threaten public safety, his right to follow his conscience outweighed the plaintiffs' right to live in his apartment.

c.   Since there is no federal law protecting against marital status discrimination, claims for marital status discrimination fall to the states, whose regulations vary widely.

   i.   Most states either have: (i) not passed statutes prohibiting discrimination based on marital status; or (ii) passed legislation prohibiting discrimination based on marital status, but explicitly exclude unmarried couples from protection.

   ii.   Other states have passed legislation protecting against marital status discrimination, but not specifically protecting unmarried cohabitants.

C.   TENANT'S RIGHTS AND REMEDIES

1.   Introduction

   a.   A tenant has four basic rights:

      i.   Legal possession;

      ii.   Actual possession;

      iii.   The covenant of quiet enjoyment / constructive eviction; and

      iv.   The implied warranty of habitability.

   b.   Furthermore, he has certain remedies if the lease violates housing regulations.

2.   Legal Possession

   a.   All states recognize tenants' right to legal possession.

   b.   The landlord must have title in order to enter into a lease.

3.   Actual Possession

   a.   The landlord has a duty to deliver the actual possession of the premises to the tenant.

   b.   This duty prevents *third parties*, such as holdover tenants, from preventing new tenants from taking actual possession of the rented property.

   c.   ***English (majority) rule****: the landlord has the duty of delivering the actual possession of the property and of preventing third parties from interfering with it.*

      i.   Some states that have adopted the English rule apply it only to *residential*, not *commercial*, leases).

      ii.   In states that have adopted the English rule, the tenant's remedy for the landlord's failure to deliver actual possession is *expectation damages*.

         1)   *See Adrian v. Rabinowitz* (defendant landlord), where the plaintiff successfully sued the defendant for failing to vacate a building to be used in a commercial lease for a shoe store

on the beginning day of the lease. Although NJ recognized the *universal rule* that *tenants are entitled to legal possession*, and though this lease imposed the *covenant of quiet enjoyment* (which otherwise would not have been recognized in NJ), the issue was whether the landlord had a *duty of delivering actual possession* to the tenant against holdover tenants. Held: NJ applies the English rule, which imposes the duty on landlords. The plaintiff is therefore awarded *expectation damages* equal to lost profits.

d. **American (minority) rule**: the *new tenant is responsible for obtaining possession* of the property and for evicting holdover tenants; the landlord is merely a title holder.

    i. In states that have adopted the American rule, the tenant has no remedy for the landlord's failure to deliver actual possession.

4. The Covenant of Quiet Enjoyment and Constructive Eviction

a. The covenant of quiet enjoyment and constructive eviction deals with the tenant's *actual and constructive continued possession* of the property after delivery.

b. It is implied in all states except NJ.

c. There are two kinds of violations:

    i. Actual (Full or Partial) Eviction

        1) There are two kinds of actual eviction:

            a) *Eviction for lack of title:* a third party with superior title evicts the tenant from the property.

            b) *Wrongful eviction:* the landlord evicts the tenant without cause.

        2) The promises in a landlord-tenant relationship are independent from one another.

            a) Thus, even if a lease is violated by a landlord, the tenant is generally not relieved of the duty to pay rent.

            b) However, a violation of the covenant of quiet enjoyment is the exception.

            c) Thus, if a tenant is evicted from the property, he is excused of the duty to pay rent.

        3) Full and Partial eviction

            a) Full eviction applies when a tenant is evicted from *all* of the property.

            b) An eviction is partial when the tenant is evicted from only *part* of the property.

            c) In either case, the covenant of quiet enjoyment protects the tenant.

d) Since the lease is seen at common law as a transfer of *all* the property, *exclusion from any of the property* is seen to be an eviction.

e) Thus, the *remedy for partial eviction is similar to that for full eviction*: the obligation to pay rent is entirely excused until the tenant's full possession is restored.

    i) *See Smith v. McEnany,* where the court held that a lessor's putting up of a wall slightly encroaching upon his lessee's property was enough of an infringement of the lessee's right to enjoy all of the land that the lessee was entirely absolved of the duty to pay rent.

f) However, the restatement and many states take a different approach: partial eviction proportionally reduces the rent that the tenant must pay, but he is still obligated to pay rent for the *portion of the land from which he has not been evicted.*

ii. Constructive Eviction

1) Some violations of the lease may be so material that the tenant can be considered to have been *constructively evicted*, even if he continues to hold actual possession of the land.

2) The elements of constructive eviction are as follow:

a) A material breach of the lease;

b) That is chargeable to the landlord;

c) Of which the landlord is given notice;

d) With the opportunity to cure; and

e) The tenant vacates the premises after a reasonable time.

3) Violations of peace and quiet can constitute violations of the covenant of quiet enjoyment.

a) Example: the landlord leases a store to one tenant who opens a bookstore. The landlord then leases adjacent space to a second tenant, who opens up a gym that is always playing loud music. If the music is so loud that it alienates all of the first tenant's clients, the first tenant may have a claim for constructive eviction.

4) Constructive eviction places a burden on the tenant to vacate the premises and then bring an action to *terminate the lease and the duty to pay*.

a) The problem with this is that it is possible that the tenant vacate the premises, sue, and lose.

b) He will then be required to pay the rent, even though he has vacated the premises.

c)   *N.B.*: in some jurisdictions, constructive eviction is an affirmative defense and the burden is on the landlord to sue the tenant.

d.   Remedies for Violations of the Covenant of Quiet Enjoyment

    i.   At common law, the tenant is *excused of the duty to pay rent* (in some states, if it is a partial eviction, he may do so while remaining in possession of the property).

    ii.   In other states, the tenant is entitled to money damages.

5.   The Implied Warranty of Habitability

a.   Because of the problems involving constructive eviction, some states have recognized the *implied warranty of habitability.*

    i.   This warranty makes it easier for the tenant to recover damages when the condition of the premises is so poor that the tenant is *virtually constructively evicted*, whether the eviction be partial or full.

    ii.   In a minority of jurisdictions, for commercial leases, some states recognize an "implied covenant of suitability" in place of an implied warranty of habitability.

b.   The implied warranty of habitability makes it possible to *recover the damages* that one would have recovered for constructive eviction (as well as other remedies, see *infra.*), but without the requirement that the tenant vacate the premises.

c.   The implied warranty of habitability is breached when there is:

    i.   A violation of a housing standard that is based on either (i) local laws providing *standards*; (ii) statutes providing *specific terms*; or (iii) statutes providing *general terms* (as in New York).

    ii.   That is chargeable to the landlord;

    iii.   With notice given to the landlord; and

    iv.   A reasonable opportunity to cure is given to the landlord.

d.   At common law, the only thing that justified not paying rent was the violation of the covenant of quiet enjoyment. It later came to be seen that some violations of the warranty of habitability could be so gross that the defendant could be considered to have been evicted.

e.   When the warranty is violated, the tenant has several possible remedies:

    i.   To move out and terminate lease;

    ii.   To abate the rent;

    iii.   To remain in possession of the property, pay rent, and sue for damages;

    iv.   To repair the property and recover the money spent; or

v. To remain on the property and withhold the rent.

    1) *See Richard Barton Enterprises, Inc. v. Tsern*, where the lease provided that the plaintiff tenant accepted the premises "as is" but that the landlord would put the elevator in good working order. Although the landlord put the elevator in working order, it failed city inspections. The tenant considered himself constructively evicted from part of complex and sued for a judgment declaring the landlord's duty to repair the elevator. Held: this lease will be considered a contract in which there is dependence of covenants. By breaching the lease, ***the landlord absolves the tenant of duty to pay full rent***.

    2) *N.B.*: many courts require the tenant to put the rent in escrow.

6. Illegal Leases

    a. The Common Law

        i. At common law, the landlord did not have the duty to maintain the property, unless specifically provided in the lease.

        ii. However, he had a duty to *make the premises safe*.

        iii. If he failed, the tenant still had the duty to pay rent, based on the independence of covenants, but he could ***recover damages***.

    b. The Modern Law

        i. Today, if a lease is invalid because of a housing law violation, the tenant's options include:

            1) Moving out of the apartment and asking that the courts declare the lease invalid, thereby absolving him of the duty to pay rent; or

            2) Remaining in the apartment and:

                a) Asking a court to order the landlord to conform the apartment to housing laws;

                b) Conforming the housing to local laws and asking the court to reward damages equal to the funds spent;

                c) Remaining in the housing with an abatement of the rent equivalent to the difference in the value between what the tenant *bargained for* (property in conformity with the law) and what he *received* (property not in conformity with the law). This is the Restatement § 6.1 approach; or

                d) Remaining in the housing rent-free (accepted in a few jurisdictions).

D. DURATION AND USE OF THE PREMISES

1. Duration of the Tenancy

a. The Holdover Tenant

    i. A holdover tenant is one who **keeps possession of the property** beyond the expiration of the lease.

    ii. Landlords have a choice as to whether to (i) declare holdover tenants to be **trespassers** (and thus evict them); or (ii) declare a **new periodic tenancy** (equal to the length of the previous term), and thus to charge them. They may do this within reasonable time.

    iii. The period between the end of a lease and the landlord's deciding as to whether he will declare the holdover tenant to be a trespasser or a periodic tenant is known as a **tenancy at sufferance**.

    iv. In order for a landlord to declare a new tenancy and to charge a tenant for another period, the holdover tenant must **voluntarily remain** on the premises.

        1) *See Commonwealth Building Corp. v. Hirschfield* (defendant tenant at sufferance), where the court held that the defendant was *not liable* to the landlord for rent for a new period, since the defendant's remaining on the premises beyond the end of the lease was *not voluntary*. Rather, he was forced to remain on the premises for one day because the building's elevator was down. When the plaintiff sued to recover double the value of the monthly rent for a one year period (as stipulated in the contract), the court held that, because it was not the defendant's voluntary act to remain on the property, and since the plaintiff had notice of this (the plaintiff's employees helped the defendant to move out), the plaintiff was only entitled to rent for the one extra day for which the defendant remained on the property.

b. The Right to the Extended Occupancy of Certain Housing

    i. Normally, a landlord has the right to terminate the tenant's right of occupancy at the expiration of the lease.

    ii. There are, however, exceptions when occupants are living in **federally subsidized housing**.

        1) In such situations, tenants are constitutionally entitled to occupancy for life.

        2) However, eviction may occur if there is good cause (*e.g.,* illegal drug use on the premises by the tenant).

    iii. Similarly, there are statutes that protect the rights of **mobile home owners**. Since the costs of relocating are relatively high compared to the cost of the mobile home, some states require park owners to extend leases of at least one-year.

    iv. There is also a law regulating **rental units** being converted into **condominiums**. The purpose of these regulations is to *protect tenants who would be unable to purchase a condominium*.

v. Finally, there is legislation, such as the Senior Citizens and Disabled Protected Tenancy Act, NJSA 2A:18-61.22 et seq., that protects the *rights of senior citizens and the disabled*.

1) If rental housing is converted into condominiums, some tenants are allowed a *forty year protected tenancy period*.

2) To qualify, one must be:

a) *Disabled* to the point of being unable to engage in gainful activity; or

b) A *senior citizen* of over sixty two years of age, or a widow of more than fifty years of age who was married to a spouse who was sixty two years of age; and

c) Must have lived in the unit continuously for at least one year.

3) When a landlord converts a housing unit to a condominium, he must inform the agency, which then contacts the tenants to inquire whether there is anyone *eligible for the protected status*.

2. Restrictions on the Uses of the Premises

a. The hallmark of a lease is the tenant's *unrestricted possession*. This does not, however, mean *unrestricted use*.

b. The uses of the property may be implied by the law or restricted by the landlord.

c. The following are the only *implied* restrictions on use:

i. Waste;

ii. Illegal or immoral uses; and

iii. Misrepresentation on the part of the lessee.

d. The landlord may also impose restrictions. He may, for example, restrict which businesses may rent the premises (*e.g.*, to avoid competitors in a strip mall).

e. In order for the landlord to restrict the tenant's use of the premises, one of following elements must be met:

i. The intentions of the parties must be clear; or

ii. Explicit restrictive language must be present in the lease, such as, "the tenant is to use the premises only as a restaurant."

1) *N.B.*: without the word "only," this phrase would be considered to be *permissive, not restrictive*.

3. The Duty of Continuous Operations

a. There is *no implied duty of continuous operations*, unless one of the following elements are met:

        i.   The lease includes a *specific provision* requiring continuous use; or

        ii.   There is an *implied covenant of continued use* based on the lease's implicit language or other circumstances.

           1)   *See Lippman v. Sears*, where the court held that there was an implied covenant of continuous use if the following three elements were met: (i) there was *no express provision* in the lease calling for continuous use; (ii) the *intention of the parties* to enter into such a lease was so *clearly in their understanding* that they did not think that it was necessary to include it in the lease (correspondence between the parties may demonstrate this); and (iii) the implied covenant of continued use is *necessary to effectuate this intent*.

   b.   To determine whether an implied covenant of continued use is applicable in a case, courts may implement a balancing test that looks to the following factors (*Thompson Dev., Inc. v. Kroger Co.*):

        i.   Whether the lease contains an *inconsistent provision*;

        ii.   Whether the lease grants *free assignability* to a tenant;

        iii.   Whether the lease was *freely negotiated* by all the parties; and

        iv.   Whether the lease contains a *non-competition provision*.

   c.   When the **base rent is token or nonexistent**, but the share of the profits is substantial, a court could infer continued operation as being within the parties' intent.

   d.   When there is a **substantial base rent**, courts usually will not recognize an implied covenant of continued use.

        i.   *See Piggly Wiggly Southern, Inc.* (defendant supermarket tenant) *v. Heard*, where the defendant was purchased by another company and moved to a new location. The property it originally occupied, which was owned by the plaintiff, was kept vacant. The original lease required the defendant to pay $29,000 per month, plus a share of any profits over $2 million. The plaintiff sued for specific performance (SP), requiring the defendant to either *occupy the property* or *rent it out*. Held: since there is a substantial base rent, and since the lease states that the premises could be used for a supermarket or "any other lawful business," and there was thus free assignability, there is a strong presumption that the lease does not create an implied covenant of continued use.

E.   FIXTURES

  1.   Common Law

   a.   At common law, fixtures remained with the landlord of the property.

  2.   Modern Law

   a.   The traditional modern law view is that fixtures remain with the landlord, but if they are installed by the tenant, they could be taken by the tenant, as long as (i) their removal would not damage the property; and (ii) they were removed *before expiration of the lease.*

b. However, the *general modern law rule* allows fixtures to be removed by tenants if the removal would not damage the property, *even if it is done after the expiration of the lease,* as long as it is done before possession of the property is yielded.

　　i. *See Handler v. Horns* (defendant lessee), where the plaintiff and the defendant were one third interest tenants in common of property. The defendant installed refrigerator units and the plaintiff later sued for partition. The defendant sought to remove the refrigerators from the property and the plaintiff objected, arguing that such fixtures form a part of the property and, since the defendant did not include a provision in the lease allowing him to take fixtures, he had forfeited the right by failing to remove them upon expiration of the first lease. The court criticized this rule and applied the *general modern law rule*: unless anything in the lease is contrary, the tenant has the right to remove trade fixtures, as long as doing so *does not damage the property* and removal is effected *before yielding possession of property.*

F. LESSOR'S REMEDIES AGAINST DEFAULTING TENANTS

1. Termination of the Lease

a. A landlord may terminate a lease against a tenant who (i) **fails to pay** rent; (ii) **wrongfully possesses** the premises after the right has terminated; or (iii) **abandons the premises** before the end of the lease.

b. However, landlords may not terminate leases for **immaterial breaches**.

　　i. *See Foundation Development Corp. v. Loehmann's, Inc.,* where the court held that it would be inequitable to allow the plaintiff to terminate a lease with the defendant, whose rent arrived three days late because of the defendant's inquiry on his bill. The plaintiff relied on a statute that gives landlords the right to terminate leases *for any reason whatsoever,* but this statute must be read by its intent, which is to create a *modern day right of lease termination* (a right not possessed at common law absent a contractual provision). Since the breach is immaterial, the lease should not be terminated, despite the fact that the lease stated that "time is of the essence."

2. Eviction

a. General rule: given adequate notice, month-to-month leases may be terminated at any time for *any reason whatsoever.*

b. Exception: when allowing landlords to evict tenants jeopardizes a public policy.

　　i. *See Edwards v. Habib* (plaintiff landlord) (D.C. Cir. 1968), where the plaintiff sued the defendant for eviction after the defendant had reported the plaintiff's violations of housing codes. Held: allowing landlords to evict tenants who report housing code violations *jeopardizes the public policy* of keeping housing safe for tenants. Judgment for the plaintiff reversed.

    c.   Retaliatory Eviction

        i.   Retaliatory eviction refers to a landlord's eviction of a tenant based on the tenant's invocation of a protected right, reporting of a housing code violation, or some other act relating to the property.

        ii.   There are three approaches to retaliatory eviction:

            1)   *Restrictive approach*: a tenant may only use the retaliatory eviction defense when the following occurs:

                a)   The property *violates housing standards;*

                b)   The tenant *reports* this to the housing authority; and

                c)   Immediately afterwards, *the landlord tries to evict* the tenant.

            2)   *Intermediate approach*: a tenant may use the retaliatory eviction defense when the landlord tries to evict the tenant for any action that the tenant takes that is *related to the property*, such as his joining of a tenants union.

            3)   *Permissive approach*: tenant may use the retaliatory eviction defense for an eviction resulting from tenant's exercise of *any legal or constitutional right*.

    3.   Damages

        a.   Expectation damages are awarded for the breach of a lease.

        b.   If the tenant leaves the property prematurely and stops paying rent, the landlord is entitled to the *difference* between what the landlord would have received under the original lease and any new lease that he obtains.

        c.   Thus, if the breached lease leads to the landlord's higher profits, he may not collect damages. *United States Nat'l Bank of Oregon v. Homeland, Inc.*

    4.   Limits on the Lessor's Actions

        a.   A landlord may not recover unpaid rents from a tenant when the lease is *illegal*.

            i.   *See Brown v. Southall Realty Co.* (plaintiff lessor) (D.C. App. 1968), where the defendant failed to make certain rental payments and quit the apartment. The plaintiff sued for *possession and termination* of the lease. The defendant argued that the lease was illegal as against hygiene regulations and if a court granted the termination of the lease, it would make the lease valid *res judicata* in a future proceeding if the plaintiff sued to recover unpaid rent. Held: the lease, being in violation of housing regulations in place *before* the execution of the lease, is invalid. It may not be terminated or used by the landlord as the grounds for collecting unpaid rent.

    ii.   *N.B.*: in order for the defendant's case to have succeeded, she had to show that laws that were violated were in place *before the lease was made*. Otherwise, the lease would have been valid. However, even if the laws were enacted after the lease was formed, the tenant could have argued that the *implied warranty of habitability*, which warrants that the leased property would continue to be fit to live in, was violated.

    iii.   *N.B.*: the court could have also ordered the plaintiff to conform the property to the required standards. The plaintiff would have then been able to evict the defendant since the contract would not have been voided. However, the defendant would have then been able to sue for damages, since the housing did not conform to the housing standards.

    b.   When a lease is invalid as against housing regulations, before evicting a tenant, a landlord may be required to either (i) make the necessary repairs and show a non-retaliatory reason to evict the defendant; or (ii) prove that he was going to take the housing off of the market.

        i.   *See also Robinson v. Diamond Housing Corp.* (D.C. Cir. 1972), where the plaintiff sought to evict the defendant, who was not paying rent. The defendant invoked the *Brown v. Southall Realty Co.* defense: the lease was illegal because it was not in conformity with housing standards. The plaintiff then tried to evict the defendant, arguing that because there was no lease, the defendant should not be on the premises. The defendant invoked the thirty day notice defense. The plaintiff then gave the defendant sufficient notice and tried to evict her. The defendant invoked the *Edwards v. Habib* defense of retaliatory discharge. Held: perhaps because the court feared that if it allowed the plaintiff to evict the defendant, the plaintiff would simply rent it out to another tenant, it required the plaintiff to first show that he had either (i) made the necessary repairs and showed a non-retaliatory reason for evicting the defendant; or (ii) not made the repairs but was going to take the housing off of the market. In retaliatory discharge cases, then, in some states, the tenant can go on living in the housing unit indefinitely until the repairs are made.

G.   ASSIGNMENTS AND SUBLEASES

    1.   Introduction

        a.   A transfer of property shifts the possession from one possessor to another.

        b.   There are two kinds of transfers:

            i.   A **sublease** grants possession of the land to a new tenant for *part of the duration of a lease period*, even if it is as little as one minute.

        ii.   An ***assignment*** grants the possession of land for the *entire period of the lease*.

           1)   By default, an assignment grants *all of the property* for the lease period.

           2)   A *partial assignment* may however, be granted for only *part of the property* for the lease period.

2.   Determining Whether a Sublease or an Assignment has been Created

    a.   Common Law

        i.   Under the common law, if the first tenant has any reversion, even for one minute, a sublease has been created.

    b.   Modern Law

        i.   Under the modern law, the ***intent*** of the parties is *dispositive*.

        ii.   *See Jaber* (defendant tenant) *v. Miller* (plaintiff second sub-lessee), where the landlord leased property to the defendant tenant, who transferred the property to a second party, who sub-leased it to the plaintiff Miller. The lease between the landlord and the defendant stipulated that *if there was a fire, the lease would be terminated*. There was a fire and the plaintiff sought cancellation of promissory notes he owed to the defendant under the agreement, arguing that his sub-lease was terminated because it was based on a sublease between the defendant and a second party, which terminated when the underlying lease between the landlord and the defendant was terminated. Held: the plaintiff's sublease was not cancelled because it is not carved out of a sublease between the defendant tenant and the second party; rather, it was carved out of an assignment. Under the modern law, we know that it is an assignment because the *intent of the parties is clear*. Thus, *the plaintiff has a continuing obligation to pay the defendant* because the assignment did not terminate, even though the lease between the landlord and the defendant expired. Judgment for the plaintiff reversed.

3.   Privity

    a.   Suppose landlord 1 (L1) is in privity with this tenant (T1). L1 then sells the property to landlord 2 (L2). According to many sources, L2 and T1 are not in *privity of contract*.

    b.   However, they are in privity of estate, since L2 owns the reversion.

    c.   To have privity of contract between T1 and L2, there must be ***attornment***, where a party to a contract recognizes a new third party as a former party's valid successor to the contract. Here: it would be the tenant's recognition of the new owner and his agreement to pay rent to him.

    d.   Examples with Explanations

        i.   L1 and T1 are in privity of contract (PK) and privity of estate (PE).

ii.   If T1 assigns his lease to T2, the resulting relationships are as follow:

1)   L1-T1: PK. L1 may look to T1 to continue to pay the rent. However, they are no longer in PE.

2)   T1-T2: PK They would no longer be in PE, since T1 no longer holds the estate.

3)   L1-T2: PE. They are not in PK, unless a lease is signed between them.

    a)   PE carries with it all of the lease provisions between L1 and T1 that *run with the land*, including the payment of rent.

    b)   As a result, L1 may look to T1 or T2 to pay rent.

iii.   In the alternative, if T1 subleases the property to S2, the following relationships result:

1)   L1-T1: PK, PE

2)   T1-S2: PK, PE

3)   L1-S2: no relationship

    a)   A sub-lessee is not liable to pay L1 for rent.

    b)   However, since S2's lease is dependant on the L1-T1 lease, *S2 may not engage in activities prohibited by that lease*.

        i)   Rationale: T1 cannot give away that which he does not have.

        ii)   Thus, if he owns only a limited possessory interest in the land, he may only give away that right to a sub-lessee.

    c)   Furthermore, when the L1-T1 lease is terminated, so too is the T1-S2 sublease, which is dependent on the former.

    d)   Thus, both T2's and S2's are obligated by at least some of the provisions in the L1-T1 lease, even though neither one is privy to it.

        i)   T2s are required in as much as those provisions *run with the land*.

        ii)   S2s are required in that they may not do that which T1 did not do.

iv.   Suppose L1 releases T1, and T2 agrees to assume T1's position with respect to L1 (this would be a case of *novation*). What are the relationships?

1)   L1-T1: no privity

2)   T1-T2: no privity

3)   T2-L1: PK, PE

      v.   Suppose L1 leases to T1 who transfers the property to T2 who transfers the property to T3. T3 defaults. Who may L1 go after?

            1)   Can go after T1 (PK);

            2)   T2 for the rent in the period in which L1 was in PE with T2; or

            3)   T3 (PE).

4.   Landlord's Rights

    a.   Restrictions of Transfers by Landlords

        i.   Provisions in which a landlord restricts transfers of the property are generally disfavored by the courts.

        ii.   For the landlord to make a restriction, it must be explicit.

        iii.   Courts will read such a restriction narrowly. For example, a *restriction on assignments does not restrict subleases*, unless the broad term "transfers" is used.

        iv.   If there is such a provision, but a tenant nonetheless assigns or subleases the property, courts treat the landlord's acceptance of rent from the transferee as a waiver of the provision.

    b.   When the landlord makes a restriction, he may limit who his tenant transfers his lease to.

        i.   When there is a clause requiring the landlord's approval before the tenant subleases or assigns the property, the landlord's approval to the first transfer **does not mean that he waives his right to disapprove future transfers**.

        ii.   According to the **Rule in Dumpor's Case**, however, once the landlord approves one transfer, he has *waived his right to disapprove others*.

        iii.   However, when the lease **makes it clear** that the landlord has the right to approve multiple transfers, the landlord retains the right, even after the first approval. *Childs v. Warner Brothers Southern Theatres*.

    c.   The landlord **may act unreasonably** (for any reason or for no reason at all) in deciding who his tenant may transfer the property to.

        i.   *See 21 Merchants Row Corp.* (plaintiff lessee) *v. Merchants Row, Inc.* (defendant landlord), where the defendant had a lease with the plaintiff lessee that prevented the lessee from assigning the lease without the defendant's consent. The plaintiff wanted to sell the business, but required the defendant's approval of the assignee. The plaintiff found an assignee that the defendant approved, but that assignee needed the plaintiff to approve an assignment to a bank that was going to finance the purchase. The defendant refused to grant it, since all the terms of the assignment would favor the bank. The plaintiff sued the defendant for breaching the contract in not allowing the assignment. Held: the court will not imply a reasonableness restriction on the defendant's right to reject potential assignees. Judgment for the defendant.

VI. EASEMENTS

A. DISTINGUISHING EASEMENTS, PROFITS À PRENDRE, AND LICENSES

1. Easements

    a. An easement is the right to use part of land owned by another for a special purpose.

    b. There are two tenements created by an easement:

        i. The *dominant tenement* refers to the estate and the tenant using the easement.

        ii. The *servient tenement* refers to the estate and tenant burdened by the easement.

    c. Easements may be positive or negative.

        i. In a *positive easement*, the grantee may use the property in a certain way.

        ii. In a *negative easement*, the grantor must *refrain* from using the property in a certain way (*e.g.*, from building a wall that blocks an ocean view from the grantee's land).

    d. Easements can be classified based on how they are *created:*

        i. *Express easements* are created and conveyed by volition in a deed;

        ii. *Implied easements* are created by legal implication. There are two kinds:

            1) Easements implied (by law) *by necessity* (*e.g.*, the grantee needs the easement in order to enter and exit his land);

            2) Easements implied (by law) *by prior use* (*e.g.*, the grantee has always used the land in a certain way).

        iii. *Prescriptive easements* are created by continual use of the property without the plaintiff's protest (analogue to adverse possession).

    e. Easements Appurtenant and Easements In Gross

        i. *Easements appurtenant* benefit the grantee's land.

            1) They may thus make the grantee's land more valuable.

            2) When there is an easement appurtenant, there are **both** *dominant* and *servient tenements.*

            3) Easements appurtenant transfer with the title, whether or not the transferor of the servient tenant mentions its existence to the transferee.

            4) The creation of easements appurtenant does not require common law words of inheritance. *Mitchell v. Castellaw.*

        ii. *Easements in gross* do not benefit the grantee's land.

          1)   Example: a utility company's right to enter the servient estate for cable work. Although this easement benefits the company, it does not benefit the company's land.

          2)   There is a servient estate, but there is no *dominant estate*.

          3)   Easements in gross do not necessarily transfer with the title.

2.   *Profits à Prendre*

    a.   A *profit à prendre* is an easement that grants the right to enter and remove timber, minerals, oil, gas, game, and other substances from another's land.

    b.   Virtually all of the law that governs profits à prendre is the same as that governing easements.

3.   Licenses

    a.   A license is a right to use another's property that is terminable at the will of the owner of the land.

        i.   Example: admission tickets to a racetrack.

    b.   However, the revocation of a license could lead to a cause of action for damages.

        i.   *See Marone* (plaintiff) *v. Washington Jockey Club*, where, although the plaintiff purchased tickets to a racetrack, he was denied entry. Held: the defendant had the full right to deny the entry, since the plaintiff's ticket represented only a license. The plaintiff may, however, sue for breach of contract.

    c.   A license can only be created by a contract. Since the SF does not apply, the contract may be oral, as long as it can be *proven*.

Summary Chart of Easements and Other Interests:

Name of Interest	*Lease*	*Easement (and most profits à prendre)*	*License*
How Created	By contract and conveyance.	Expressly by deed; also by implication or prescription.	By contract only (written or oral).
Right / Interest Possessed	Exclusive possession (the owner retains the right to enter in some circumstances).	Right to use (not to possess).	Right to use (not to possess).
Nature of Right / Interest	Estate in land.	Interest in land (but not an estate).	Mere permission.
Application of SF	SF applies.	SF applies (no parole easements).	SF does not apply.
Revocable?	Irrevocable.	Irrevocable (but it may be terminated).	Freely revocable.

B.   EXPRESS CREATION OF EASEMENTS

1.   The Two Ways that Easements May Be Expressly Created

    a.   ***Express creation by grant***: since easements are property interests, they must comply with the requirements of deeds (a delivered writing that contains the names of the parties, a granting clause, a legal description of the property; and a signature), unless they are for less than one year.

    b.   ***Express creation by reservation***: these are created when a grantor reserves an easement interest in the deed of a land conveyance (typically, in the *redendum* clause).

        i.   Under the common law and the American ***majority approach***, easements for third parties could not be reserved.

        ii.   However, under a growing **minority approach**, they could be reserved in title transfers. *Willard v. First Church of Christ, Scientist, Pacifica* (Cal. 1972).

2.   The Language Used

    a.   The language "right of way" or "right to use land" conveys no more than an easement.

    b.   However, coupled with intent, these words may create a fee simple.

        i.   *See Urbaitis v. Commonwealth Edison*, where the plaintiffs sued to quiet title on property possessed by the defendant. The plaintiffs argued that the transfer was only for an easement good for use *as long as the defendant used it as a "right of way,"* and since that use had ended, the plaintiff was entitled to the property. Held: "right of way" was the language used *merely to reference the land*, not to describe the interest created. The language *"convey and warrant"* indicates the parties' *intent to create a fee simple*. Therefore, the defendant has a right to continued possession, even though the property is no longer used as a right of way.

    c.   Such language does not, however, create a lease that entitles the holder to possession.

        i.   *See Baseball Publishing Co.* (plaintiff) *v. Bruton*, where the defendant entered into a contract to allow the plaintiff to *use the defendant's wall for advertising*. The defendant never cashed any of the plaintiff's checks, repudiated the contract, and eventually took down the plaintiff's posters. The plaintiff sued for SP. Held: the trial court erred in declaring this contract to be a license and at the same time allowing for SP, since, *under a license, revocation is always permitted*. To enforce SP would be to limit that right. However, in this case, SP is appropriate because the instrument created was an *easement* that granted the plaintiff the *exclusive right to use the defendant's wall*. The plaintiff had an *irrevocable easement*. Judgment for the plaintiff affirmed.

        ii.   *N.B.*: the court took the holding to where it wanted it, even though the facts of the case were inconsistent with that holding. ***Easements are generally created by deed***, but here, there was no deed. This interest was more likely a ***revocable license***.

    3.   The Interpretation of the Deed

        a.   According to the ***rule of reason***, when the deed for an easement is silent on a question, a court, in interpreting the deed, may import *reasonable terms*.

        b.   *See Sakansky v. Wein*, where the court refused to allow the defendant to force the plaintiff to accept a new easement in place of his old one, even though doing so would not inconvenience the plaintiff, since *the plaintiff's deed clearly laid out where the easement would be located*. However, because the height of the plaintiff's easement was not laid out, the defendant was permitted to build over the easement, leaving reasonable clearance for vehicles.

C.   **IMPLIED EASEMENTS BY NECESSITY AND PRIOR USE**

    1.   Introduction

        a.   An implied easement is a property right that is in its essentials an easement.

        b.   It may be created by necessity, by prior use, or by he creation of an irrevocable license.

    2.   Implied Easements by Necessity

        a.   The elements of an implied easement by necessity are as follow:

            i.   The ***prior common ownership*** of two parcels, which are divided when one (usually the dominant estate) is sold; and

ii. The *necessity* that results when the dominant estate becomes landlocked as a result of the severance and sale (if the only ingress and egress is a revocable license, it is considered landlocked).

b. Implied easements by necessity are created at the time of the conveyance that leads to their being landlocked.

    i. Even if at that time, the dominant tenant has other means of ingress and egress (such as a license), he still has the right to use the implied easement.

    ii. Implied easements by necessity *may lie dormant* for many years and only be exercised at the time *when the need arises* (*e.g.*, when a license that had been in use is revoked).

        1) *See Finn* (plaintiff) *v. Williams*, where the plaintiff received a land grant from several grantors, including the defendant. At the time of the grant, the plaintiff's only means of ingress and egress was through a license that was later revoked. The plaintiff sued for a judgment declaring the plaintiff's implied easement by necessity over the defendant's land in order to get to a public roadway. Held: an easement by necessity is created *at the time a conveyance depriving a parcel from ingress and egress is made*. Here, one was *created when the conveyance of land having no ingress and egress was made*. It lay dormant until actual necessity arose.

3. Implied Easements by Prior Use

a. An implied easement by prior use is an easement that comes into being when an owner of two parcels of land uses one of them, the servient estate, to benefit the other in such a way that when he sells one of them, the purchaser can *reasonably expect* that the servient estate will continue to be used in a way that is consistent with its prior use.

b. An implied easement by prior use is formed when the following elements are met:

    i. The *prior common ownership* of two parcels, which are divided when one is sold (this same element is required in implied easements by necessity);

    ii. A *reasonable, not strict, necessity* of continued use. The alternatives to the easement must either be impractical or dangerous (a higher standard is required for grantors than for grantees).

    iii. The *prior use* must be continuous, open and permanent.

c. Thus, even when the dominant tenant's use of the servient estate is *not strictly necessary*, he may be entitled to an implied easement by prior use.

    i. *See Granite Properties Limited Partnership* (plaintiff) *v. Manns*, where the plaintiff sold a parcel to the defendant, but continued using two driveways sold to the defendant, in order to access the plaintiff's apartment complex and shopping center. The plaintiff sued to enjoin interference with the purported easement. Held: the plaintiff was the common owner of the two parcels before the sale and he used the servient estate continuously, openly and permanently before the transfer. Since an alternate means of accessing to the apartment building and shopping center was dangerous or impractical, an implied easement for prior use is recognized.

4. Creation by Irrevocable License

    a. An implied easement may also be created through an ***irrevocable license***, which is created by estoppel when a licensee spends large sums of money in reliance on a license.

    b. *See Stoner v. Zucker*, where the defendant spent more than $7,000 in constructing a ditch in reliance on the plaintiff's license. The plaintiff revoked the license and sued for an injunction. Held: where a licensee expends large sums of money or labor in reliance on a license, estoppel applies and the licensor may not revoke the license; an *irrevocable license* is created.

D. PRESCRIPTIVE EASEMENTS

1. In addition to the express and implied creation of easements, easements may be created by prescription (adverse possession).

2. An easement is formed by prescription when it is held over the statutory period in an open, continuous, exclusive, adverse, notorious way.

    a. Open

        i. Any use that is consistent with the nature of the property is ***presumed to be open***, as long as it is not concealed and the owner would be able to discover it through inspection.

        ii. This requirement is therefore different from that of adverse possession of realty and personalty.

    b. Continuous

        i. The use need not be *strictly* continuous, but must be continuous in a way that is consistent with the user's requirements.

            1) Example: a path across a servient land owner's property used every summer to tow out a boat would be considered "continuous."

        ii. It is the same requirement as that for the adverse possession of *realty*.

    c. Exclusive

        i. Possession need not be *strictly* exclusive.

      ii.   The TO may share possession with the owner, as long as he does not interfere with the adverse use.

      iii.   This requirement is thus different from that of the adverse possession of personalty and realty.

d.   Adverse

    i.   Introduction

        1)   In most states, the servient tenant has the burden of rebutting the presumption that *the dominant tenant's use of the land was adverse* (in adverse states) or that it was *with the servient tenant's passive consent* (in acquiescence states).

        2)   In a few states, no presumptions are applied.

        3)   This requirement is thus different from that of the adverse possession of personalty and realty.

    ii.   Adverse Approach States

        1)   In adverse approach states, the use of the easement must be *hostile to the TO's use and enjoyment* of the property.

        2)   The possessor must claim that and act like he has title, and that claim must be adverse to the TO's rights.

        3)   The general presumption that the use of the land is adverse may be overcome by showing that the use was with either:

            a)   The express **approval** of the TO (*e.g.*, as in a license); or

            b)   There was **no interference** with the servient tenant's use.

        4)   *See Beebe* (plaintiff) *v. DeMarco* (1998), where the court held that the adverse element was met since (i) an open and notorious use during more than ten years is presumed to be adverse and (ii) the defendant failed to rebut this presumption by showing that either he granted the plaintiff express permission to use his land; or the plaintiff's use of the land did not interfere with his use of it. Judgment for the plaintiff affirmed.

    iii.   Acquiescence Approach States

        1)   In acquiescence approach states, adversity is established through the servient tenant's passive consent.

        2)   A general presumption that the dominant tenant has an easement inherited from sometime in the past is made (Lost Grant Theory).

        3)   Exceptions to this presumption:

      a)   When the servient tenant opens up access to his property allowing others to use it in a way that does not interfere with his own use

         i)   Example: the servient tenant opens up to the dominant tenant use of the servient tenant's driveway out of kindness.

         ii)   The presumption of adversity does not arise; the dominant tenant would have the burden of proving that his use was adverse to that of the servient tenant.

      b)   When the servient tenant allows use by a neighbor, a special relationship is established.

         i)   The presumption is that the use was with the servient landowner's permission.

         ii)   No presumption of adversity arises; the burden of proving that the use was adverse shifts to the dominant landowner.

   4)   The presumption of passive consent in acquiescence states is rebutted by the TO's showing of one of the following:

      a)   ***Affirmative consent***, in which case the dominant tenant is said to have had a license; or

      b)   ***Express protest***, where the servient tenant sends a letter or otherwise communicates his opposition to the dominant tenant's use of the property.

  iv.   The No Presumption States

   1)   A few states, such as California, have abolished the use of presumptions.

   2)   These states treat adversity as an *issue of fact* to which presumptions are not applied.

 e.   Notorious

  i.   This is virtually identical to the open element: the use must be sufficient in putting the servient land owner on notice that the adverse possessor is using and claiming an easement on the servient estate.

Summary chart of adverse possession and prescriptive easements

Element	Adverse Possession of Realty	Prescriptive Easements
Open	The use must be consistent with the normal use of the property and must be enough to put the owner on notice.	Any use consistent with the nature of the property is **presumed to be open**, as long as an owner would be able to discover it.
Continuous	***Need not be strictly continuous***, as long as use is consistent with nature of the property.	***Need not be strictly continuous***, as long as use is consistent with the nature of the property.

Exclusive	TO must not share in the possession of the land with the adverse possessor.	***Need not be strictly exclusive***; owner may share the land, as long as he does not interfere with the adverse use.
Adverse	- In ***objective approach*** states: an exclusive claim of right is required; - In ***subjective approach*** states: an exclusive claim of right plus good faith is required. - In ***short term statute states***: possession under color of title and the payment of taxes is required.	Use of easement is ***presumed to be adverse*** and presumption must be rebutted by the owner of the burdened land.
Notorious	*See* the open element.	*See* the open element.

E.   SCOPE

1.   The scope of an easement is limited by the nature of the easement and, in the case of an express easement, by the language of the deed defining it.

2.   The following rules apply:

    a.   Express Easements

        i.   When the use of an express easement is defined in a deed, the easement holder may only use the easement according to what is stated therein.

        ii.   If the use of the easement exceeds that scope, the servient tenant may obtain injunctive relief against the activities of the dominant tenant.

        iii.   When the use is not defined in the deed or is unclearly defined therein, the easement is subject to growth over time.

    b.   Implied Easements (by Necessity and Prior Use)

        i.   The use of implied easements may change over time, according to the circumstances.

        ii.   For example, if originally, an easement was used as a right of way to and from a farm, and the farm later grew, requiring greater traffic over the easement, the dominant tenant would acquire the right to the new, increased uses of the servient estate.

    c.   Prescriptive Easements

        i.   The holder of a prescriptive easement may only benefit from uses of the easement that gave way to the easement at its origin.

3.   Where the easement is used to benefit a dominant estate, *it may not be used to benefit extensions, expansions, or annexations* of that estate.

    a.   *S.S. Kresge* (plaintiff) *v. Winkelman Realty Co.*, where the defendant used a prescriptive easement over the plaintiff's lot to get deliveries to lot 3. The easement was later expanded to benefit lots 2 and 4 as well. The plaintiff complained over the increased traffic over its property and sued to quiet title and restrict use to the first parcel. Held: an easement holder may not use an easement to benefit non-dominant property, unless the use puts no extra burden on the servient estate. Here, this exception is not met: the burden is greater. Judgment for the plaintiff affirmed.

F. TRANSFER OF EASEMENTS

1. Easements Appurtenant

    a. The burden and benefit of easements appurtenant pass automatically to subsequent owners of the dominant (benefited) estate.

2. Easements in Gross

    a. The burden of an easement in gross passes automatically with the transfer of the servient estate.

    b. The benefit in *easements for personal benefit* is presumed not transferable, absent clear evidence to the contrary. The benefit in *easements for commercial purposes* is presumed transferable, absent clear evidence to contrary. Finally, *profits in gross* are freely alienable, absent evidence to contrary.

G. THE TERMINATION OF EASEMENTS

1. An easement may be terminated in any of the following ways:

    a. Natural Expiration

        i. An easement expires when it is for a specific use and it is *impossible for that use to continue*.

        ii. Example: an easement to mine coal expires if the coal is exhausted.

    b. Release

        i. The owner of an easement may release the servient tenant from it when both parties agree.

        ii. This is typically done through a deed granting the easement back to the servient tenant.

    c. Estoppel

        i. An easement is terminated by estoppel when the following elements are met:

            1) The servient tenant *detrimentally relies* on the dominant tenant's nonuse; and

            2) There is *no convenient way* for the servient tenant to know that the easement was not terminated and he must be ignorant if it was not terminated.

    d. Abandonment

        i. An easement is terminated by abandonment when it is: (i) no longer used; and (ii) the holder of the easement has the intent to abandon it.

ii. The servient tenant has the burden of proving both elements.

iii. Mere disuse without the intent to abandon does not bring about the termination of the easement.

       1) *See Lindsey* (plaintiff) *v. Clark*, where the plaintiff sought an injunction preventing the defendant from using an easement over the plaintiff's land, claiming that the defendant had abandoned it because of its disuse. In reality, the defendant was ignorant of the location of the easement on the southern end of the plaintiff's property, and continued to use land to the north. Held: because the defendant's disuse of the easement was not accompanied by the intent to abandon, the easement was not terminated.

e. Merger

i. An easement terminates when the dominant and servient estates come under the control of the same tenant.

f. *Bona Fide* Purchase

i. When a BFP purchases an estate and the BFP has no actual or visual notice of an unrecorded easement, the easement terminates.

g. Destruction of the Servient Estate

i. When the servient estate is a building or some other destructible property, the easement ends if the property is destroyed.

h. Prescription

i. Just as easements may be created by prescription, so too may they be terminated.

VII. REAL COVENANTS AND EQUITABLE SERVITUDES

A. COVENANTS RUNNING WITH THE LAND AT LAW

1. In general terms, a real covenant (RC) is a promise relating to land use that runs with the land at law and is enforceable at law between the original covenanting parties as a contract.

2. The four elements of RC's (assuming that they are binding between the original covenanters) are as follow:

a. A Writing

i. Although covenants need not be recorded in a deed, they must be in a writing.

ii. The writing is required for the SF.

b. Intent

i. The original parties must intend for the promise to run with the land.

ii. Usually, this intent is expressed in the writing that conveys the covenant (*e.g.*, "this covenant shall run with the land…").

iii.   The intent may also be inferred from the circumstances.

c.   Touch and Concern the Land

    i.   The RC must "touch and concern the land." That is to say, it must affect the use, enjoyment, or value of the land.

    ii.   A covenant to supply water during a portion of the year would not qualify.

        1)   *See Eagle Enterprises, Inc. v. Gross*, where the court held that a covenant to supply water failed the *Neponsit Property Owners' Association* test (see *infra.*) because: (i) a covenant does not touch and concern the land when it only applies for half of the year; and (ii) the land would have been able to supply its own water, and its legal rights were thus not affected, since the land would have been no different without the covenant in the deed.

d.   Privity of Estate

    i.   The Three Privities

        1)   Horizontal Privity

            a)   Horizontal privity is between the original parties (the covenantor and the covenantee).

            b)   Horizontal privity is created when the covenant is in the deed conveying land between covenanting parties.

        2)   Mutual Privity

            a)   Mutual privity exists between the covenantee and the party plaintiff.

            b)   When a covenantor and covenantee have a mutual and continuing interest in same land that is subject of covenant.

            c)   There must be mutual interest in burdened land.

            d)   The burdened land is the land of the covenantor who is being sued.

            e)   The mutual and continuing interest is generally an easement.

                i)   However, it can also be a leasehold, though this leads to certain complications.

                ii)   It may not be a license, because a license is not an interest, but rather, an unenforceable right.

                iii)   Note: for ownership, possession, or the right to use to be a legal interest, there should be a ***written deed***.

        3)   Vertical Privity

            a)   Vertical privity refers to the relationship between one of original covenanting parties with a subsequent owner.

    ii.   The Three Approaches to Privity

        1)   Under the **traditional approach** to privity, both *horizontal privity* between the original covenanting parties and *vertical privity* between an original party and any successor in interest are required.

        2)   Under the **minority approach** (adopted in Massachusetts), both *mutual privity* between the original covenanting parties and *vertical privity* between an original party and any successor in interest are required.

        3)   Under the **modern approach**, only vertical privity is required.

            a)   *See Gallagher v. Bell* (plaintiffs), where the court held that there was privity in a 1961 agreement between the plaintiffs and the defendants in a covenant for sharing costs for constructing a road, even though at the time that it was made, there was no property interest transfer (and thus no horizontal privity). Furthermore, there was no mutual privity, since it would be necessary that the subject of the covenant also be of mutual and continuing interest, which did not exist in the covenant of the shared costs of a road. Nevertheless, although **there was only vertical privity**, this was sufficient.

3.   Transfers and Liability

    a.   When a covenant runs with the land, the original covenanting party is not liable for its breach when he transfers the property to another party; rather, the subsequent purchaser is liable.

    b.   This is true even when the subsequent party successfully bargains for indemnity against the obligation to follow the covenant at the time that he purchased the land.

        i.   *See Gallagher v. Bell* (plaintiffs), where the plaintiffs and the defendants entered into a covenant to split the costs of a road to be built between the defendant's property and a public way. Camalier bought property from the defendants and insisted on an indemnity agreement. When she refused to contribute to the costs of the road, the plaintiffs sued the defendants. Held: because this covenant runs with the land, the defendants are absolved of liability for breach by the current owner.

    c.   The subsequent party is thus bound by covenants running with the land whenever he is in vertical privity with the original covenanting party.

i. *See Neponsit Property Owners' Association* (plaintiff) *v. Emigrant Industrial Savings Bank*, where Neponsit Realty Co., the plaintiff's assignor, conveyed lots with a RC requiring a yearly maintenance fee to be paid to the plaintiff. The defendant subsequently purchased land, but **refused to pay the maintenance fee**, claiming that the covenant was not binding. The plaintiff sued to recover the fees. Held: there is a valid real covenant that runs with the land. There is vertical privity, even though the land was never transferred to the plaintiff by the Neponsit Realty Co. This is because the plaintiff was an agent of the original owners. Thus, because the plaintiff represents all of the owners, vertical privity was established. Judgment for the plaintiff is affirmed, and the defendant is required to pay the fees in accordance with the covenant.

B. EQUITABLE SERVITUDES

1. Introduction

   a. Equitable servitudes (ES) are covenants restricting the use of land.

   b. They run with the land at equity and thus offer remedies at equity (*e.g.*, injunctions).

   c. The major difference between a RC and an ES is that while the former has remedies at law (monetary damages), the former has remedies at equity (injunctions).

2. The elements of ES's are as follow:

   a. Intent

      i. The original parties must *intend* that the promise run with the land.

      ii. This intent need not be expressed by common law words of inheritance; it may be inferred from the circumstances.

   b. Writing

      i. An original deed, or any other writing (*e.g.*, brochures) is required.

      ii. In the majority of states, no writing required when there is a common scheme of development (CSD, see *infra*.).

   c. Touch and Concern

      i. The covenant must affect:

         1) The *use or enjoyment* of both the benefited and the burdened land; and/or

         2) The *value* of both the benefited and the burdened land.

      ii. However, if there is a CSD, this rule only needs to be true of the burdened land (there need not be a benefited land within the strict meaning of the rule when a CSD exists).

   d. Privity

      i. As with RC's, only vertical privity is required.

ii. For there to be vertical privity, the party to whom the property was transferred must be in the *same chain of title* as the original covenanting party.

iii. *N.B.*: there need not be a transfer of the entire property interest.

1) Mere *possession* is sufficient (*i.e.*, a fee owner who transfers a leasehold to another party would be in vertical privity with that party).

2) Even if a holder of a fee interest in all of the land *transferred only a portion* thereof, there would still be vertical privity for the purpose of ES's.

e. Notice

i. A latter purchaser is only bound by an ES if there is:

1) *Actual notice*;

2) *Constructive notice*, where a possessor would be expected to run a title search and will be bound by any knowledge he might have; or

3) *Inquiry notice* (permitted in some jurisdictions), where notice attributed to a person when the information available to him would cause a *reasonable prudent person* to investigate further into the matter (*e.g.*, a purchaser sees a row of homes all with the same design and shape).

f. Common Scheme of Development

i. The elements of a common scheme of development (CSD) are as follow:

1) The plaintiff and the defendant must own lots within the *same scheme*; and

2) There must be *substantial similarities* in the deeds of the properties in the scheme (exact uniformity is not required).

ii. Only in Virginia is a CSD an affirmative element of ES's. *See, e.g., Sloan v. Johnson* (Virginia 1997).

3. When these elements are met, both affirmative as well as negative covenants may run at equity. *See, e.g., Tulk v. Moxhay.*

4. The Touch and Concern Requirement

a. As with RC's, the touch and concern element in ES's requires that the *covenant affect the value, use, or enjoyment* of both the benefited and the burdened land.

b. Note the similarity between RC's, ES's, and easements appurtenant: in all of these categories, there must be benefited land and burdened land, which, in the case of easements, correspond to the dominant estate and the servient estate, respectively.

        i.   *See London County Council* (plaintiff) *v. Allen*, where the plaintiff was unable to enforce an ES against the defendant because the plaintiff had no benefited land. The plaintiff would only have been able to enforce the covenant with the defendant through customary contract law, since the covenant that the plaintiff made with the defendant was a valid contract. Thus, although the covenant was written, with the intent to run with the land, and though there was privity, an ES could not be recognized.

    c.   The touch and concern element is met when a covenant establishes an anti-competition policy that limits the kinds of businesses that may be hosted on the land.

        i.   *See Whitinsville Plaza, Inc. v. Kotseas*, where an anti-competition policy was considered to run with the land because (i) the burdened land's value was affected by the restriction; and (ii) the value of the benefited shopping center increased (the shopping center businesses more harmoniously worked together and more profits were generated).

5.   Implied Equitable Servitudes Benefiting Third Parties

    a.   A court may imply an ES even if all of the ES elements are not strictly met, when there is a CSD.

    b.   The elements of a CSD are as follow:

        i.   Both the plaintiff and the defendant must own lots within a common scheme;

        ii.   The scheme must be apparent from the outset (*i.e.*, when sale of the lots begins);

        iii.   There must be *substantial uniformity* between the restrictions in the deeds of the various lots in the scheme (*exact* uniformity not required).

    c.   Majority View

        i.   If there is a common scheme of development, **it is not required that there be a writing or benefited land**.

        ii.   The benefited land is implied through the common scheme of development.

        iii.   Thus, even when the writing and benefited land (touch and concern) elements are not met, an ES may be formed through a showing of a CSD.

           1)   *See Sanborn v. McLean* (defendant), where an ES is enforced, even though it is not recorded in the defendant's chain of title, because the CSD put the defendant on inquiry notice that only residential uses of the property were permitted and the CSD did away with the writing requirement and the requirement that land be benefited (since the other properties were impliedly benefited through

the CSD). The defendant was therefore enjoined from constructing a gas station.

    d.   Minority View

        i.   Under the minority view (adopted in Massachusetts), *a writing is always required*, even if there is a common scheme of development.

        ii.   Under this view, all of the elements of ESs must be met. When a covenant is not written, or when it does not touch and concern, an ES will not be recognized. *See Sprague v. Kimball* (Mass. 1913).

        iii.   However, even if the strict requirements of touch and concern are not met (*e.g.*, there may be land by a covenant, but the covenant may not be reciprocal and there may be no benefited land), a court may imply the benefit.

            1)   *See Snow v. Van Dam* (Mass. 1935), where a covenant restricting land to residential use was created, but there was no benefited land, since it was the last piece of land to acquire such a covenant. However, because of the CSD, the court implied that the other lands would be benefited by the restriction, and the touch and concern element was met.

C.   CONSTRUCTION OF COVENANTS

    1.   In construing covenants, some states will only enforce what is *expressly written*.

    2.   Other states, however, will also consider what the actual restrictions *imply* (*i.e.*, they consider intent in addition to the writing).

        a.   *See Joslin* (plaintiff) *v. Pine River Development Corp.*, where the plaintiffs sued to enjoin the defendant from using one of its shorefront lots as a common beach area for residents of all of its 161 non-shore lots. Held: it is clear from all relevant circumstances that the defendant's shorefront lot was not intended to serve as a common recreational area, even though this restriction is not expressly in writing. Injunction affirmed.

        b.   *N.B.*: there are two inquires required when analyzing whether a covenant has been violated: (i) are all of the required elements of the covenant met; and (ii) has the covenant been violated? For the latter inquiry, both the writing as well as the parties' intent must be analyzed.

D.   MODIFICATIONS

    1.   Parties may modify covenants and servitudes by bringing all of the parties together to create a new agreements superseding previous agreements.

    2.   There may be provisions in a covenant that provide for how modifications may be made.

    3.   When a developer reserves the right to unilaterally modify a covenant, courts may find the covenant not to run with the land.

a. *See Suttle v. Bailey* (defendant), where the plaintiff sued to enforce a covenant on the defendant when, in the covenant, the grantor retained the right to modify the restriction, and did in fact modify it by excepting the defendant from a requirement. Held: because the grantor retained the right to modify the restriction, it cannot be said to run with the land, since it does not touch and concern the land. Rather, *it is a personal benefit* that the plaintiffs may not enforce. Judgment for the plaintiff reversed.

b. *N.B.*: not all courts have followed this approach. Some consider all lots to be benefited when the grantor acts reasonably.

4. When provisions in a covenant allow for modifications by an *objective standard* or a *subjective standard plus good faith* (as opposed to by the grantor's arbitrarily will), the covenant may be enforced.

a. *See Rhue* (defendant) *v. Cheyenne Homes, Inc.*, where the defendant tried to move an old-style Spanish home into a neighborhood having a covenant requiring plans for all homes to first be approved by a committee. The plaintiff sued to enjoin the defendant from moving into the neighborhood. The defendant argued that because the committee was not guided by any specific, written guidelines, its decisions were arbitrary and the restriction did not run with the land. Held: because the committee was governed by the general intent of protecting the value of the properties, the covenant is upheld, even though the criteria used were not objective.

E. TERMINATION

1. Real covenants and equitable servitudes may be terminated in any of the following manners:

a. When a promisee *releases* the promisor from a covenant or servitude through a written release;

b. Through *merger*, when a fee simple interest comes into the hands of a single owner;

c. Through *expiration*, in the case of a covenant or servitude that exists for a specific purpose, when that purpose is ended;

d. By *condemnation*, when the government acquires property by eminent domain (the government must pay damages to the owner of the benefited land that equal the difference of the land with and without the covenant or servitude);

e. When a later *BFP* buys property without notice of the property's covenants, when there is no practical way for him to find out about the covenant;

f. By *legislation*;

g. Through *estoppel* in changed conditions.

i. When changed circumstances might discharge a party from compliance with an otherwise valid covenant, a court will **balance the effects** of not enforcing the covenant on both the burdened as well as benefited land.

ii. *See Cowling* (plaintiffs) *v. Colligan*, where a covenant on the defendant's land restricted the land use to residential purposes. However, when surrounding land started to become developed and a country road became a thoroughfare, the defendant began to develop his land for commercial purposes, in violation of the covenant. The plaintiffs sued to enforce the covenant. Held: the equity of not enforcing the covenant outweighed the equity of enforcing it, since allowing the development of the property would cause the value to rise fourfold. Judgment for the defendant affirmed.

VIII. ESTATES IN LAND AND FUTURE INTERESTS

A. INTRODUCTION TO ESTATES IN LAND

1. Definitions

   a. An estate is the amount and nature of a person's present interest in land or other property.

   b. A future interest is a property interest where the possession and use of land is aimed at some future time.

2. The Five Present, Possessory Estates

   a. Fee Simple Absolute

      i. A fee simple absolute, or "fee simple" (FS), confers full title and is represented by the formula: "O → A and his heirs," where "O" represents the original owner, and "A" represents the party to whom the estate is transferred.

      ii. The grantee is entitled to possess and use the property throughout his life and his heirs may inherit it.

         1) To be fully inheritable, the word "heir" must be included in the deed.

         2) *See Cole v. Steinlauf* (Conn. 1957), where a court ruled that the formula "O → A and his assigns forever" was insufficient.

      iii. The fee simple has the following characteristics:

         1) It is *alienable*, since the grantee may sell it;

         2) It is *devisable*, since the grantee may transfer it to his non-heirs through a will;

         3) As mentioned, it is *inheritable;* and

         4) It has *no expiration;* even after direct line dies out, there is always an heir.

   b. Fee Simple Determinable

i. A fee simple determinable (FSD), or "determinable fee," is represented by the formula "O → A and his heirs if ..."

ii. It is essentially a fee simple, but with a condition, the breach of which automatically transfers the fee back to the grantor.

iii. It is *self-executing*; the statute of limitations begins once the grantee breaches the condition.

iv. It has the following characteristics:

1) It is *alienable;*

2) It is *devisable;*

3) It is *inheritable;* and

4) It is *not expirable;* however, since it terminates when the condition is breached, it is said to be "defeasible."

v. The language must be precise by including, "if," "until," "while," or a comparable equivalent. The word "only" does not suffice.

1) *See Roberts v. Rhodes*, where a deed transferring property to a local school district specified that the land was to be used "only" for school or cemetery purposes. The condition was later breached and the plaintiff, an heir to original owners, claimed he has a reversion through breach of the FSD. The court held that the necessary language for creating a FSD was deficient; the word "only" did not suffice.

c. Fee Simple on Condition Subsequent

i. A fee simple on condition subsequent (FSCS) is characterized by a condition subsequent, the breach of which allows the grantor to go on land and reclaim it.

ii. It is represented by the formula "O → A and heirs, but if [any particular condition] is not met, O and heirs may reclaim it."

iii. The statute of limitations starts only when the grantor demands the land and the grantee refuses to surrender it.

iv. A FSCS is like a FSD, except that unlike a FSD, in which the transfer is automatic when the condition is breached, in a FSCS, the grantor has the option of going on the land and reclaiming the estate (the transfer is not automatic).

1) Where there is ambiguity and it is not clear if an estate is a FSD or a FSCS, courts will prefer to interpret the estate to be a FSCS, since courts prefer not to allow for the forfeiture of estates.

2) *See Oldfield v. Stoeco Homes, Inc.* (defendant), where a plaintiff taxpayer sued to have Stoeco give title of land back to his city, since Stoeco breached the condition (filling the marshes within one year) of what the plaintiff argued was a FSD. The court held that the interpretation of the estate

should be based on more than just the language; especially when the language is ambiguous, the intent of the parties and extrinsic circumstances may be used to determine the true nature of an estate granted by a deed. Here, given that the defendant and the city agreed to an extension to the fulfilling of the condition, the court ruled that the estate was a FSCS. Since the city did not enter and reclaim the estate, the defendant was able to keep it.

    v.   The FSCS has the following characteristics:

        1)   It is *alienable;*

        2)   It is *devisable;*

        3)   It is *inheritable;* and

        4)   It is *not expirable;* however, since it terminates when the condition is breached, it is said to be "defeasible."

d.   Fee Tail

    i.   A fee tail (FT) is represented by the formula: "O → A and the heirs of his body."

    ii.   The grantee is entitled to the property his life.

    iii.   A fee tail can be modified so that only the grantee's male heirs or his bodily heirs by his wife, for example, may inherit it.

    iv.   The fee tail has the following characteristics:

        1)   The property is *not fully alienable*, although the grantee may alienate it in his lifetime;

        2)   It is *not devisable*, since the grantee may not pass it on to his non-heirs through a will;

        3)   It is *inheritable*, but only to the grantee's bodily heirs; and

        4)   The interest *expires* when the grantee's direct line is terminated.

e.   Life Estate

    i.   A life estate (LE) is represented by the formula "O → A," "O → A for life," "O → A forever," or "O → A in fee simple absolute."

        1)   *N.B.*: "O → A in fee simple absolute" does not create a fee simple interest because it fails to mention the word "heir."

    ii.   The grantee is entitled to an estate throughout his life.

        1)   A life tenant is obligated to take good care of the present estate for the holder of the future interest.

        2)   Otherwise, the future estate holder may sue the life estate holder's estate to recover damages. *Moore v. Phillips.*

    iii.   The life estate is the default estate at common law.

    iv.   It has the following characteristics:

1)   It is *alienable*, but only during the grantee's life;

         a)   If the grantee sells it to B, B inherits a life estate pur autre vie (for the life of the grantee).

         b)   For B, it is inheritable and devisable if B dies before the grantee.

2)   It is *not devisable;*

3)   It is *not inheritable;* and

4)   The interest *expires* when the grantee dies.

B.   INTRODUCTION TO FUTURE INTERESTS

1.   There are two kinds of future interests: (i) those that revert to the grantor of the estate; and (ii) those that revert to a third party, known as the "remainderman."

2.   The Future Interest of the Grantor

     a.   There are five possibilities with respect to the future interests of the grantor of an estate:

         i.   If he grants a FS, he reserves **no future interest** (the grantee receives full title);

         ii.   If he grants a FSD, he reserves the possibility of **reverter** (if the condition is breached);

         iii.   If he grants a FSCS, he reserves a **right of entry** (if the condition is breached).

         iv.   If he grants an expirable estate (a FT of LE), he reserves a **reversion**.

3.   The Future Interest of the Remainderman

     a.   Introduction

         i.   It is possible to indicate that the reversion of an expirable estate (the FT and LE) revert back not to the original grantor, but rather, to some third party.

         ii.   The third party is known as a "remainderman," and he receives a "remainder."

         iii.   Under the common law, the reversion of a defeasible estate (FSD or FSCS) could not be transferred to a third party as a remainder. However, later developments in the law made this possible in what is now termed a "fee simple in executory limitation" (*see infra.*).

     b.   Two rules are worth highlighting:

         i.   The future interest must not cut short the life of the present estate.

         1)   For example, "O → A, then to B and his heirs if B is married" would be permitted.

           2)   "O → A, but if B marries, then immediately transfer to B and his heirs" would *not* be permitted.

    ii.   The future interest must take hold immediately upon the present interest's expiration.

           1)   For example, "O → A, then to B and his heirs" would be permitted.

           2)   "O → A, then one year after the death of A, to B and his heirs" would *not* be permited.

c.   There are two kinds of interests that the remainderman may receive: the vested remainder and a contingent remainder.

d.   Vested Remainder

    i.   In order to receive a vested remainder (VR), the grantee must be born and ascertainable.

           1)   *E.g.,* "O → A, then to B."

           2)   However, the formula "O → A, then to B's oldest surviving son" would not be permitted, since it is not known who will be B's oldest surviving son at the expiration of A's interest.

    ii.   Furthermore, there must be no conditions (besides the expiration of A's estate).

           1)   Consider, for example, "O → A, then to B's children," where B has one son (S).

           2)   S has a VR in LE subject to open (it is open to members of a class, *all* of B's children, who may enter if they are born before the expiration of the LE).

           3)   There are two ways for the class to close:

               a)   A dies, which makes the VR subject to open a FS, and closes the class; or,

               b)   B dies, since B can have no more children who could enter the class.

    iii.   Example: O → A, then to B's children who reach 18. If B has two children, S1 (19) and S2 (16), what is the state of the title?

           1)   S1 has a VR in LE; S2 has an *expectancy*.

e.   Contingent Remainder

    i.   A contingent remainder (CR) arises when either:

           1)   The grantee is not ascertainable; or

           2)   There is a condition for the transfer (*e.g.,* "O → A, then to B and heirs if B is married").

    ii.   Under the ***destructibility of contingent remainders doctrine***, a CR can be destroyed if it has not vested and any of the following have occurred:

1) Expiration

    a) A's estate has expired.

2) Merger

    a) The estate has merged.

    b) Merger will occur if, for example, A sells his expirable estate (FT or LE) to O; O will then own both the present interest and the reversion, which together create a FS. The same will occur if O sells his reversion to A.

    c) In order for merger to occur, the two interests that are merged together must be consecutive (*e.g.*, if "O → A, then to B, then to C for life," if B sells his LE to O, the LE and O's reversion will not merge into a FS).

    d) However, in merger, the CR is no longer destroyed when the two consecutive estates are created by the same grant.

3) Forfeiture

    a) B forfeits his FT or LE, which means that the expirable estate, rather than expire, prematurely terminates.

    b) This can occur through B's:

        i) Commission of a felony; or

        ii) Refusal of or renunciation of the estate.

Characteristics of Future Interests

	Future interest	*Alienable*	*Devisable*	*Inheritable*
Future Interests that Revert to the Grantor	Possibility of Reverter	✓	✗*	✓
	Right of Entry	✓	✗*	✓
	Reversion	✓	✓	✓
Future Interests that Revert to a Remainderman	Vested Remainder	✓	✓	✓
	Contingent Remainder	✗	✓	✓

* This is because the Statute of Wills provided for devise of only estates "in possession, reversion or remainder."

C. EXECUTORY INTERESTS AND FEES SIMPLE ON EXECUTORY LIMITATION

1. Whereas before, strict rules applied to the granting of future interests, today, equity enters the equation.

2. A new kind of future interest in the transferee was developed: the executory interest.

3.   This is like a remainder, but it can break the rules required of remainders by cutting short the life of the present estate or failing to begin immediately upon the present interest's expiration.

4.   Classes

    a.   Shifting Executory Interests

        i.   Shifting executory interests cut back the life of the preceding estates.

        ii.   They either:

            1)   Immediately follow a defeasible fee (FSD, FSCS, FS EL);

            2)   Cut short a FS;

                a)   For example, if "O → A and his heirs, but if B marries C, to B and his bodily heirs," B has a shifting EI in FT and O has a FS EL.

            3)   Cut short an expirable estate (FT, LE) or VR.

                a)   For example, if "O → A, but if B marries C, to B and his heirs," then B has a shifting executory interest in fee simple (EI FS).

    b.   Springing Executory Interests

        i.   Springing executory interests do not begin immediately after the preceding estate's expiration.

        ii.   They either:

            1)   Follow expirable estates (FT, LE) but do not become immediately possessory.

                a)   For example, if "O → A, then one year after A's death, to B and his heirs," then B has a springing EI FS.

            2)   Are created by the grantor to take effect in the future, with no other interest given to any other grantee.

                a)   For example, if "O → A and his heirs upon his marriage," then A has a springing EI FS and O has a fee simple on executory limitation (FS EL).

5.   After the Statute of Uses, a VR can become lost in two ways:

    a.   Possession of the VR can become lost *after* the grantee has been granted possession (he therefore has a ***VR on executory limitation***).

    b.   The remainder can be cut off *before the grantee acquires possession*.

        i.   He therefore has a ***VR subject to divestment***.

        ii.   For example, if "O → A and his heirs, then to B and heirs, but if A farms land, to C and his heirs," then B has a VR subject to divestment in FS (VR SD FS).

        iii.   Distinguishing VR's Subject to Divestment from CR's

1) If the condition is a condition subsequent, it is a VR SD; if it is a precondition, it is a CR.

2) Preconditions tend to begin with "if."

3) Conditions subsequent tend to have the following characteristics:

   a) The language "but if" is indicated;

   b) The clause introducing the condition is separated by commas; and

   c) The condition follows a grant.

4) If the condition is a condition subsequent, you must decide if the condition can be met before or only after B gets possession.

   a) If the condition can be met *before* B gets possession, then it is **subject to divestment**.

      i) For example, if "O → A, then to B and his heirs, but if B gets married, then to C and his heirs,"

      ii) B has a VR SD FS.

   b) If the condition *must happen after* B's possession, then it is on **executory limitation**.

      i) For example, if "O → A, then to B and his heirs, but if B farms the land, then to C and his heirs."

      ii) B has a VR FS EL.

D. THE RULE AGAINST PERPETUITIES

1. As earlier mentioned, CR's are destructible through expiration, merger, or forfeiture.

2. In the early days of EI's, courts were not certain whether they were destructible.

   a. In *Pells v. Brown* (1620), the court held that they *were indestructible*.

   b. *Purefoy v. Rogers* (1670) held that, in cases where there is ambiguity, a future interest will be construed as an EI, not a CR.

   c. In *Duke of Norfolk* (1682), the courts eventually decided that EIs are in fact destrictible.

3. The Rule Against Perpetuities

   a. Under the Rule Against Perpetuities (RAP), "no executory interest is good unless it must vest, if ever, within 21 years following the lives in being at the time of the creation of the interest."

   b. In other words, no EI is valid if it is possible that it may vest more than twenty one years after the last "life in being." A "life in being" is any person mentioned in the grant who was living at the time of the grant.

c.   Thus, the rule requires both that the interest vest and that it vest soon enough (within twenty one years of the lives in being at the time of the creation of the interest).

d.   For our purposes, all present interests and future interests are vested, with the exception of only EI's and CR's. The RAP therefore applies only to EI's and CR's.

e.   A CR becomes vested if the condition is fulfilled or if the grantee becomes born or ascertainable. An EI vests by becoming possessory.

f.   Examples:

   i.   O → A, then to B and his heirs, but if the well on Blackacre ever runs dry, then to C and his heirs.

      1)   B acquires a VR FS.

      2)   C does not have a valid EI under the grant because the well may go dry more than twenty one years after the last life in being.

   ii.   O → A and the heirs of his body, then if the well on Blackacre runs dry, to B and his heirs.

      1)   B has an invalid CR FS, since it is possible that the well run dry twenty one years after the last life in being.

      2)   Thus, A has a FT and O has a reversion.

   iii.   O → A for life, then if prayer has returned to the schools, to B and his heirs.

      1)   A acquires a LE.

      2)   B acquires a valid CR FS, since, if the CR were ever to vest, it would have to vest within twenty one years of A's life (since A has a LE).

      3)   O has a reversion.

   iv.   O → A for life, then if prayer returns to the schools, to B and his heirs.

      1)   Under the common law, this scenario would have the same result as above.

      2)   However, under the modern law, because of the RAP; B would not acquire a valid CR. Since the condition is within the present tense "*returns*," it is implied that there can be a gap between A's death and the vesting of B's interest. Therefore, B is granted a springing EI. However, because it is possible that prayer return to the schools more than twenty one years after the lives in being, the EI is invalid. B receives nothing.

E.   DEFEASIBLE LIFE ESTATES

1.   Life Estate Determinable

a.   The following are examples of life estates determinable (LED):

i.   "O → A, as long as the land is farmed."

1)   O has a reversion and a PR, but the PR is "swallowed" by the reversion.

2)   O thus simply has a reversion.

ii.   "O → A, as long as the land is farmed, then to B and heirs."

1)   It is not clear that O wanted to keep the reversion, so it is presumed he did not.

2)   B thus receives the reversion and the PR.

3)   The PR is swallowed by the remainder, giving B a VR FS.

iii.   "O → A, as long as the land is farmed, then to B upon A's death."

1)   A has a LED.

2)   B has a VR.

3)   O has a PR.

2.   Life Estate on Executory Limitation

a.   "O → A, but if the land is farmed, then to B and heirs."

i.   A as a LE EL, since his interest is followed by an EI (it is an EI because it uses "but if" language).

ii.   O keeps the reversion; B gets only a PR.

3.   There are five different scenarios that come out of *defeasible life estates*:

	Who takes at expiration	Who takes on breach of condition	Name of present estate	Name of future interest
(i) O → A as long as A remains unmarried	O	O	LED	Remainder
(ii) O → A as long as A remains unmarried, then to B	B	B	LED	VR
(iii) O → A, but if A marries, then to B	O	B	LE EL	Shifting EI (B) Rev. FS EL (O)
(iv) O → A as long as A remains unmarried, then to B upon A's death	B	O	LED	VR (B) PR (O)
(v) O → A, then to B, but	B	C	LE EL	VR (B)

| if A marries, then to C | | | | EI (C) |
| | | | | Rev. FS EL (O) |

4. When the future interest is split, and a grantee takes a PR (EI), then it is a LE EL, or another way of saying it:

    a. The only time when there is a LE EL is when the reversion is split from the EI, and the grantee takes only the EI, or

    b. The only time a defeasible LE is a LE EL is when an EI is formed.

F. MODERN LEGAL APPROACHES

1. Life Estates

    a. Under the common law, "O → A" and "O → A in fee," like all estate transfers that did not include the word "heirs," were presumed to be LE's.

    b. Modern American statutes have changed this, and presume that O meant to transfer as much as he could to his grantees. The fee simple is thus default estate under the modern law.

        i. Thus, "O → A" and "O → A in fee" are seen as fees simple.

    c. The rule for creating LEs is now constructive, whereas earlier, it operated under a system of law. Now, an estate is seen to be a fee simple, unless otherwise indicated.

        i. *See Lewis v. Searles*, where the court read an estate that did not mention the words "heirs" as being a FS, since state statute eliminated the required words, and held that absent some evidence or indication showing otherwise (such as the mention of a remainderman), an estate will be read and considered to be a FS.

2. Fee Tails

    a. Many states have abolished FT's or changed their application.

    b. The California rule is exemplary:

        i. The FT is abolished.

            1) The formula "O → A and his bodily heirs" is equivalent to a FS.

        ii. However, where there is a remainder, the FT operates in a special way.

            1) The formula "O → A and his bodily heirs, then to B and his heirs" = is the equivalent of "O → A and his heirs as long as A dies with a bodily heir, then to B and heirs."

            2) In this case, A acquires a FS EL;

            3) B acquires a shifting EI FS.

            4) O reserves no interest.

3. Fees Simple Determinable and Fees Simple on Condition Subsequent

    a. These defeasible estates place two new conditions on the PR and right of entry:

        i. Many were given a statute of limitations (typically thirty years), after which the estate could no longer become terminated;

        ii. For the right of entry, there was a limit put upon O from the time that the condition was breached to the time that he could exercise his right of entry.

4. Inalienable or Undevisable Interests

    a. Interests that were inalienable or not devisable (such as CR's or EI's) became fully alienable and devisable.

    b. However, one still could not pass on more than what he had.

5. Destructibility of Contingent Remainders

    a. Under the majority approach of the modern law, CR's remain even if preceding estates have expired, merged, or been forfeited before the CRs have vested.

    b. The CR's continue and become possessory when they vest.

    c. Consider, for example, "O → A for life, then to B in fee simple if B marries C," and B is unmarried when A dies.

        i. Under the common law, B's CR terminates and O acquires a reversion.

        ii. Under modern law, however, O acquires has a reversion in FS EL, but B's CR continues to exist. If and when B marries C, B's CR vests, granting B a FS, and terminating O's reversion. B therefore is said to have a springing EI FS.

6. The Rule Against Perpetuities

    a. The RAP continues to apply to unvested interests (CR's and EI's), just as it did under the common law, by requiring them to vest within twenty one years of the lives in being at the time of the creation of the interest.

IX. CONCURRENT ESTATES

A. TENANCY IN COMMON

1. Introduction

    a. A tenancy in common is an estate conveyed to two grantees and to their heirs as co-tenants.

    b. Each co-tenant has a right to possess all of the property and to share in the rents.

c. However, each co-tenant's share of the property is separate and distinct. Thus, each co-tenant may dispose of his undivided share, by deed or by will.

2. Creation

a. Under the modern law, the tenancy in common is the presumed estate.

b. Therefore, under the formula "O → A and B and their heirs," A and B hold a tenancy in common (under the common law, they held a JT).

3. Right of Survivorship

a. Unlike joint tenancies, the tenancy in common does not carry a *right of survivorship*; a co-tenant's share passes on to his devisees and heirs at his death, *not to his co-tenant(s)*.

b. The tenancy in common, unlike joint tenancies, is thus both devisable and inheritable.

4. A tenancy in common is terminated when either of the following occur:

a. The interests *merge* in one person; or

b. One of the joint tenants files for a *partition*, where the court physically divides the estate among the owners (*partition in kind*) or sells the interest and divides the profits (*partition by sale*).

i. This usually occurs when the co-tenants cannot agree on how to share or split their interests.

ii. *N.B.*: the concurrent owners may limit their ability to seek a partition if they sign an agreement that they will not partition the estate (this applies in joint tenancies and tenancies by the entirety as well).

B. JOINT TENANCY

1. Introduction

a. In a joint tenancy (JT), an estate is conveyed to grantees and their heirs as co-tenants.

b. Each co-tenant owns an undivided share in all of the property.

2. Classes

a. A joint tenancy can be made in FS or in LE.

b. What the joint tenancy is based on will affect what interests the joint tenants may transfer.

c. Note the difference between:

i. "O → A and B for their joint lives, remainder to the survivor and his heirs."

1) A and B each acquire a joint LE with a CR FS.

        a)   A's remainder is contingent on B's dying before him; B's remainder is contingent on A's dying before him.

    2)   O will acquire a reversion if the CR does not vest within twenty one years of the lives in being at the creation of the interest, as required by the RAP.

    ii.   "O → A and B as joint tenants, with a right of survivorship, and not as tenants in common."

        1)   A and B each acquire a JT FS with a right of survivorship.

        2)   O will retain no interest in the estate.

3.   Creation

    a.   As we have seen, the formula "O → A and B and their heirs" creates not a tenancy in common, but rather, a joint tenancy under the common law and under the modern law.

    b.   However, under the modern law, this formula constitutes a *joint tenancy* under the following circumstances:

        i.   Under the majority approach, the four unities (***time***, ***title***, ***interest***, and ***possession***) *and* clear intent are required.

            1)   *N.B.*: under this approach, if A had a FS in land that he wanted to share with B in JT, he would need to go convey the estate to a strawman, who would reconvey the property to A and B, in order to assure that the conveyance satisfied the time unity.

        ii.   Under the minority approach, *clear intent on its own* is sufficient to overcome the presumption of a tenancy in common.

            1)   *N.B.*: under this approach, the intervention of a strawman would be unnecessary.

        iii.   In some states, such as Texas, the JT is abolished, and language creating a JT (*e.g.*, "to A and B as joint tenants, and not as tenants in common, with the right of survivorship") is construed as a tenancy in common in LE with an indestructible CR to the survivor.

    c.   When there is ambiguity, courts will sometimes overlook common law rules of construction and look to the grantor's ***intent***. *Palmer v. Flint.*

        i.   *See Miller v. Riegler* (Ark. 1967), where Mrs. Wager, before her death, devised her property to her two nieces. She left $45,000 worth of stocks to her niece, Mary Riegler, with whom she lived, through a right of survivorship of a joint tenancy. The other niece, the plaintiff, initiated a suit to set aside the joint tenancy, arguing that (i) there was no ***unity of time*** in the conveyance of the stocks, since Mrs. Wagar held the stocks before she granted them to her daughter; (ii) there was *no **unity of title***, since Mary received the stocks from a grant from her aunt and Mrs. Reigler had possession from an earlier title; and (iii) there was no ***joint possession***, since all of the dividends of the stocks continued to go to Mrs. Riegler throughout her life. The court placed heavier weight on Mrs. Riegler's intent than on the common law rules, holding that joint tenants may come to agree upon how revenues and possession would be split and shared; it is important only that the joint tenants would have a right to evenly split revenues.

d. Language such as, "to A and B as joint tenants, with a right of survivorship and not as tenants in common" is ideal in creating a joint tenancy.

e. In most states, including the word "survivor" simply clarifies the JT. In fact, in Virginia, not mentioning "survivor" creates the presumption of a tenancy in common and prevents the creating of a JT. *Hoover v. Smith*.

f. However, in some states, mentioning the word "survivor" prevents A and B from partitioning the land or severing the interest.

    i. *See Jones v. Green* (Mich. Ct. App. 1983), where the court held that the language, "joint tenants with full rights of survivorship" automatically precluded the right of partition, since a Michigan law stated that mentioning the word "survivor" indicates the grantor's intent to give the survivor an indestructible CR FS. Thus, while mentioning "survivor" is required in some states to create a JT FS, mentioning it in Michigan creates a joint LE with an indestructible CR FS to the survivor.

4. Right of Survivorship

a. Each joint tenant holds a *right of survivorship*; if one of the joint tenants die, the other tenant or tenants receive his share of the property.

b. Nothing passes on to the decedent's devisees or heirs; the joint tenancy is neither devisable nor inheritable.

5. Termination

a. A joint tenancy is terminated when one joint tenant *conveys* his interest to a third party.

    i. Suppose for example, the formula "O → A and B and their heirs," where the four unities and clear intent to create a joint tenancy are present.

    ii. If A transferred his interest to C, then B and C would own the estate as tenants in common.

    iii. However, if A alienated merely a portion of his undivided interest to C, the conveyance would destroy the joint tenancy only with respect to the portion conveyed.

    iv. In this same manner, if A is a joint tenant with two other co-tenants, the transfer of A's interest does not destroy the entire joint tenancy. Rather, B and C continue to hold a joint tenancy with a right of survivorship with one another. The grantee of A's interest would thereafter hold a tenancy in common with B and C. *See, e.g., Jackson v. O'Connell.*

b.   A joint tenancy is similarly terminated when one of the joint tenants files for a ***partition***.

c.   Termination also occurs if the joint tenants enter into an ***agreement*** to permit one join tenant to devise his share. The agreement, not the devise, is what severs the joint tenancy.

d.   Normally, a divorce does not destroy a JT, but the parties, through manifesting clear intent, may convert a JT into a tenancy in common.

    i.   *See Mann v. Bradley*, where the defendant divorced his wife, and in the divorce decree, they agreed that, upon the wife's remarriage or the couple's oldest child's turning twenty one years of age, the property would be sold and the interest split between them. Mrs. Mann died and the defendant, claimed that none of the four unities were destroyed, that there was a JT, and he had full title through his right of survivorship. The children sued for one half of the interest, claiming that the interest was a tenancy in common. The court held that it was not necessary to destroy any of the 4 unities or sever the interest and convert it to a tenancy in common; it became a tenancy in common as soon as intent to end the right of survivorship was manifested through the JTs' plans to sell the property and split the proceeds. Therefore, a tenancy in common was created, and the children were entitled to one half of the interest.

e.   Finally, joint tenancies are terminated at the death of the joint tenant(s), leaving one joint tenant, whose right of survivorship is activated.

    i.   Many states have adopted Slayer Statutes, which deal with the result on a joint tenancy when one joint tenant murders another.

    ii.   States have adopted varying approaches:

        1)   The murderer acquires nothing and the murdered joint tenant's heirs or devisees acquire the property;

        2)   The murderer acquires everything through his right of survivorship;

        3)   The murderer gets a LE, with the remainder to the heirs of the murdered joint tenant;

        4)   The joint tenancy becomes a tenancy in common, one half of which is taken by the murderer, and the other half of which is passed to the murdered joint tenant's heirs and devisees.

C.   TENANCY BY THE ENTIRETY

1.   Introduction

        a.   The tenancy by the entirety (TE), which is recognized in only twenty states, is essentially a JT that includes a fifth unity: marriage.

        b.   It is thus typically only used when there is an interest in land shared by a married couple.

2.   Right of Survivorship

        a.   Tenancies by the entirety, like joint tenancies, grant each tenant a right of survivorship.

        b.   Tenancies by the entirety are therefore neither devisable nor inheritable; the survivor spouse takes the decedent's entire share of the property.

3.   Termination

        a.   Like a joint tenancy, a tenancy by the entirety gives way to a tenancy in common when it is severed.

        b.   A tenancy by the entirety is severed when any of the following occur:

            i.   The spouses *agree to jointly convey* a share of the property (one spouse may not do so without the agreement of the other);

           ii.   The spouses jointly *agree to destroy* the tenancy;

          iii.   The spouses *agree to partition* the tenancy (the agreement is essential; involuntary partition is not possible);

           iv.   The spouses *divorce*; or

           v.   Either *spouse dies*.

Summary Chart of the Concurrent Estates

	Tenancy in Common	*Joint Tenancy*	*Tenancy by the Entirety*
Alienable	✓	✓	✓*
Devisable	✓	✗	✗
Inheritable	✓	✗	✗

* A tenancy by the entirety is only alienable when jointly transferred by both spouses.

D.   **FIDUCIARY DUTIES**

1.   Accounting

        a.   An accounting is a detailed statement of the debits and credits between parties to a contract.

        b.   If one tenant in common rents out part of the estate and makes rental income, he is required to make an accounting and to distribute the profit to the other tenant in common, absent an agreement stating otherwise.

2.   Contribution

a.   When one concurrent owner spends money on the property, he is doing it on behalf of all of the concurrent owners, and is thus entitled to contribution.

b.   However, if the funds are spent on something unnecessary, such as a swimming pool, the concurrent owner is only entitled to what would be the increased added value at the time of a sale.

c.   On the contrary, when one tenant in common spends money to save a property, the other tenants in common must contribute to his costs or lose their title.

E.   **ADVERSE POSSESSION**

1.   One concurrent tenant may obtain full ownership of an estate through adverse possession when the following elements are met:

a.   The concurrent owner exclusively possesses the estate; and

b.   He makes an open claim to full ownership (*i.e.*, makes an "ouster").

CHAPTER 3.
TORTS

I. INTRODUCTION TO TORT LAW

A. INTRODUCTION

1. Definition

   a. A tort a civil wrong, other than a breach of contract, for which the law provides a remedy.

2. General Overview

   a. Seventy to eighty percent of torts fall under the classification of "negligence torts," a group of torts in which the civil wrong was not intentional.[9]

   b. The other torts fall into a smaller group known as "intentional torts," where the requisite *mens rea* is intent.

3. Purpose of the Tort System

   a. While the criminal law seeks as its principle objective the punishment of the offender, in the civil law, of which the tort law is one branch, restitution to the victim is the primary objective.

      i. In the civil law, retribution also plays a limited role, since courts will at times award punitive damages, which are based on a theory of retribution.

      ii. The restitution in the tort law aims to return innocent parties back to their original position through compensation.

      iii. This is done through awarding them money damages, which the tortfeasor is required to pay.

      iv. In the criminal law, in contrast, the criminal pays his debt to society through paying fines to the government or through serving prison sentences.

   b. Among the other purposes of the tort system are as follow:

      i. To discourage negligence and civil wrongs;

      ii. To protect innocent victims; and

      iii. To avoid private revenge.

4. Sources

   a. The tort law is derived from the common law.

   b. However, in some states, the tort law is, to a certain extent, based on statute.

   c. In other states, such as California, it has been largely codified.

---

[9] The majority of these torts are automobile-related.

B. **DEVELOPMENT OF LIABILITY BASED ON FAULT**

1. Traditional approach: the "strict liability rule."

   a. There was a time when fault was not even considered for the purpose of ascertaining liability.

   b. Determining liability was *only about asking whether the defendant cause the injury.*

      i. If so, the defendant was liable.

      ii. If not, he was not liable.

   c. Intent, recklessness and negligence were not a part of the analysis.

2. Later developments

   a. Later, the idea of fault began to creep into the system.

   b. Under the earliest fault rule, the defendant was liable, *unless he was able to prove that he was **utterly without fault**.*

      i. *See Weaver v. Ward* (1616), where the plaintiff sued the defendant for an injury caused by the defendant when his musket accidentally discharged during a military exercise. The court held that the defendant was liable when he was unable to prove that he was utterly without fault. He would not have been liable if, for example, the plaintiff ran into the traveling bullet after the defendant pulled the trigger.

      ii. *N.B.*: this is perhaps the earliest case where fault was discussed.

   c. Eventually, the common law developed the notion that the burden was on the plaintiff to prove fault (intent for intentional torts, recklessness or intent for IIED, breach of duty for negligence), *not* on the defendant to prove that he acted with care. *See, e.g., Brown v. Kendall* (1850).

   d. There is no fault when injury is caused by sudden, unforeseeable illness.

      i. *See Cohen v. Petty* (1933), where the defendant caused a car crash when, while driving, he suddenly passed out. Since his passing out was unforeseeable and it was the first time it had happened, he was not held liable.

   e. Nevertheless, the traditional common law rule of strict liability still applies to some situations.

      i. *See Spano v. Perini* (1969), where the defendant's blasting caused damages on the plaintiff's land. Held: unless the plaintiff was trespassing or there was contributory negligence, the defendant is strictly liable. The plaintiff is therefore required to prove only causation, not fault (intent, recklessness, or negligence).

II.   STRICT LIABILITY

A.   INTRODUCTION AND BACKGROUND

1. Strict liability (SL) applies in cases involving: (i) *animals;* (ii) *abnormally dangerous activities;* and (iii) *products liability*.

2. Unlike negligence, the plaintiff must not prove that the defendant violated a *duty to exercise reasonable care*.

3. Elements of a *prima facie* case:

   a. An absolute duty to protect the plaintiff from risks associated with the act;

   b. The breach of this duty;

   c. Causation in fact and proximate cause;

      i. Causation in fact is actual causation (*e.g.*, "but for X, Y would not have occurred").

      ii. Proximate cause is legal causation.

         1) This serves as a limitation on actual cause.

         2) All acts can be connected to a result; the law draws a limit with those acts which are closely enough connected to the consequence that the law will impose liability in a particular case.

         3) Proximate cause is the legal principle that courts apply in determining where to draw the line.

   d. Damage to the plaintiff's person or property.

B.   ANIMALS

1. Wild Animals

   a. There is no-fault liability for injuries caused by wild animals with vicious temperaments.

   b. One keeps such animals "at his peril."

2. Domestic Animals

   a. Under the common law, a domestic animal is entitled to one bite free of liability.

   b. However, if the domestic animal has a dangerous propensity known by the owner, he would not be entitled to any bites free of liability.

   c. The statutory approach in most states imposes *strict liability* for dog bites.

   d. Exception: there is no liability when the plaintiff was trespassing or committing some tort.

e.   Other states create other exceptions, such as when a sign is posted warning of a dangerous dog.

f.   Many states have passed statutes requiring muzzles or leashes.

         i.   If a person is injured due to the violation of such a statute, he will be held guilty of negligence *per se* (negligence as a matter of law), such that breach of duty is not a jury question; the plaintiff only needs to prove that the violation of the statute caused damages.

         ii.   However, if the violation of the statute was not the cause of the injury (*e.g.*, in the case of a statute requiring the use of a muzzle, abiding by the statute would not have prevented the dog from knocking over a child), the burden is on the plaintiff to prove the violation of a duty owed by the defendant.

C.   ABNORMALLY DANGEROUS ACTIVITIES

1.   There is strict liability for damages arising out of abnormally dangerous activities. To prove SL, the plaintiff must prove both of the following elements:

     a.   The activity was abnormally dangerous.

         i.   A weighing test that balances the following factors is used to determine whether an activity is abnormally dangerous:

             1)   Whether the activity carries a high risk of serious injury;

             2)   Whether the activity is infrequently engaged in within the community and whether it is inappropriate there;

             3)   Whether it is impossible to perform the activity in a way that eliminates the risk, no matter how great the burden; and

             4)   Whether the activity's social utility outweigh the risks. § 520 Restatement.

         ii.   Activities that have been held to be abnormally dangerous include: blasting, the testing of rockets, the storage of water and of toxic chemicals, fireworks displays, and oil drilling.

         iii.   Among the activities that have been held *not* to be abnormally dangerous include: the use of firearms and the use of fire.

     b.   The abnormal activity was the actual and proximate cause of the plaintiff's damages.

2.   The care exercised is immaterial in determining SL.

     a.   *See Rylands v. Fletcher* (plaintiff) (1868), where the defendant constructed a reservoir on his land, which burst and caused damage on the neighbor's land. The court held that when the defendant brings unnatural substances on land (here, the unnatural substance being the great amount of water), he does so at his own peril; regarding of the amount of care he exercises, he will be liable for damages caused by his act. Judgment for the plaintiff.

3.   There is no strict liability for activities that are not abnormally dangerous. The duty to exercise reasonable care is applied.

    a.   *See Miller v. Civil Constructors, Inc.*, where a court held that the discharge of firearms was not an abnormally dangerous activity, but rather, the duty was of reasonable care under the circumstances.

D.   LIMITATIONS (DEFENSES)

1.   Superseding Cause

    a.   The defendant will not be held guilty if the damage arose not from that which made the activity abnormally dangerous, but rather, from a superseding cause.

    b.   *See Foster v. Preston Mill*, where the plaintiff sued the defendant for blasting that caused the plaintiff's mink to kill its young. Held: what makes blasting dangerous is the damage it may cause to persons or property. The plaintiff's damages arose not from this dangerous quality, but rather, from the minks' nervous disposition, a superseding intervening cause that caused the mink to kill their young. The defendant is not strictly liable.

2.   Unforeseeable Intervening Cause

    a.   An intervening cause is an act that intervenes in the series of events after an act, such that it alters the resulting consequence.

    b.   When an intervening cause is strong enough to relieve a wrongdoer of liability, it becomes a superseding cause.

    c.   However, the defendant will not be liable when the intervening cause is unforeseeable.

        i.   *See Golden v. Amory* (1952), where the plaintiff, relying on *Rylands v. Fletcher* (1868), sought compensation when water being stored in a dike on the defendant's property caused damage on the plaintiff's property as a result of an unforeseeable act of God—a hurricane. Held: the defendant is not liable, since the intervening cause was unforeseeable.

        ii.   *N.B.:* the defendant would have been strictly liable if he had reason to believe that an act of God would come to bear.

3.   Contributory Negligence

    a.   Contributory negligence is generally not a defense when a defendant is strictly liable.

    b.   However, knowing contributory negligence may be a defense.

4.   Assumption of the Risk

    a.   Assumption of the risk is an affirmative defense for strict liability.

    b.   *See Sandy v. Bushy*, where the plaintiff was injured by the defendant's horse and sued. The defendant argued that the injury was caused by *contributory negligence*. Held: when the owner of an animal is aware of the animal's vicious propensity, the owner is strictly liable for injuries caused by the animal, regardless of whether there was contributory negligence. However, assumption of the risk *is* an affirmative defense. If the plaintiff unnecessarily puts himself in a situation where he knows of the probability of injury, the defendant is not liable. However, the facts in the present case do not support such a conclusion. Judgment for the plaintiff affirmed.

    i.   *N.B*: assumption of the risk *and* contributory negligence are defenses in ordinary negligence cases, but only assumption of the risk is a defense in SL cases.

III.   INTENTIONAL TORTS

A.   INTRODUCTION

1.   Characteristics

    a.   Intentional torts (IT's) are those that involve the most fault.

    b.   They require actual intent, or, in the case of the intentional infliction of emotional distress (IIED), recklessness.

2.   Elements of the Plaintiff's *Prima Facie* Case

    a.   A Volitional Act

        i.   A volitional act, or an external manifestation of the inner will, is always required.

        ii.   Volition is an act of the will that indicates that a tortfeasor's action resulted from a conscious choice.

        iii.   An action lacks volition if it was committed while the actor was sleepwalking or forced by some outside compelling force or circumstance (*i.e.*, *force majeure*).

        iv.   If the plaintiff wants something to come about, his omission to make it materialize cannot constitute an IT, since such an omission would not be a volitional act.

    b.   Intent

        i.   All of the IT's require intent.

        ii.   Intent is formed when the defendant possesses either:

            1)   Purpose (a wanting or desiring) that a certain result come about; or

            2)   Knowledge to a substantial certainty (KSC) of an extremely high risk that a particular consequence will materialize as a result of one's act (based on knowledge or belief).

                a)   *See Garratt v. Dailey*, where an infant was held liable for battery when, with knowledge to a substantial certainty that the plaintiff would try to sit in a chair, he moved it, causing the plaintiff to fall when she attempted to sit on it. Although the defendant did not have purpose, his KSC provided the requisite intent.[10]

    c.   The Resulting Tort

        i.   Finally, the plaintiff must prove that a resulting tort (assault, false imprisonment, etc.) came about.

B.   **THE SEVEN INTENTIONAL TORTS**

    1.   Assault

        a.   The elements of assault are as follow:

            i.   A volitional act (an act of the will; see definition, *supra.*, for fuller treatment);

            ii.   With the intent (purpose or KSC) to cause an *offensive or harmful contact* or a *reasonable fear* of an immediate offensive or harmful contact; and

            iii.   A resulting immediate fear of imminent offensive or harmful contact.

        b.   Words alone, no matter how threatening, do not constitute assault.

        c.   If the defendant unsuccessfully attempts battery on the plaintiff, he may be liable for assault.

            i.   *See I de S et ux. v. W de S,* where the defendant came to the plaintiff's home to buy wine, but the door was shut. The defendant banged the door with a hatchet and when the plaintiff looked out the window to tell him to stop, the defendant threw the hatchet at her and missed. Held: the intent to offensively or harmfully contact the plaintiff is transferred to the intent to cause an immediate fear of an offensive or harmful contact. The defendant is liable for assault.

            ii.   *N.B.*: this may be the first case that has come to recognize assault as a tort.

        d.   Present ability to carry out offensive or harmful contact *not* necessary to establish assault, as long as there is an intent to cause an offensive or harmful contact and this causes the fear of such a contact.

            i.   *See Western Union Telegraph Co. v. Hill,* where the plaintiff sued the defendant for assault when he attempted to offensively contact her by reaching across a counter and telling her he wanted to "love and pet" her. The defendant argued that he lacked the ability to reach across the table and touch the plaintiff. Held: the ability to make an offensive or harmful contact is unnecessary, as long as the defendant intends to effect the contact and he has the apparent ability to do so.

    2.   Battery

---

[10] Infants are liable for their torts, just as adults (although in negligence cases, they are held to a different standard of care).

a.   The elements of battery are as follow:

    i.   Volition (an act of the will, as in all intentional torts);

    ii.   Intent (purpose or KSC);

        1)   In some states, there must be intent to cause an *offensive or harmful contact;*

        2)   In other states, the intent to cause *any contact at all* suffices.

            a)   Example: tortfeasor innocently intends to pat V on the shoulder, but, not realizing that V recently underwent surgery on her shoulder, he causes a harmful contact. The requisite intent would be met and the tortfeasor would be liable for battery.

    iii.   A resulting offensive or harmful contact.

        1)   The test for determining whether a contact is offensive or harmful is an objective test based on what a *reasonable person not unduly sensitive as to his personal dignity* would find harmful or offensive.

        2)   However, there is an exception to the objective test when the defendant knows that the plaintiff would or would *not* find a contact offensive, based on past history, special sensitivities, or their relationship.

            a)   For example, if the plaintiff was the defendant's old wrestling partner, the defendant could reasonably expect a bear hug not to be offensive to the plaintiff, given their relationship.

b.   The victim need not be aware of the offensive or harmful contact at the time that it is done.

    i.   Example: the tortfeasor, in a voluntary act, kisses a girl while she is sleeping. When the girl later finds out what happened, is is offended. If only the intent to cause *any contact at all* is necessary, the defendant will be held liable for battery.

c.   An offensive or harmful contact on the plaintiff's person need not transpire in order for there to be a battery; a rude or offensive contact with any object connected to the plaintiff's person suffices in establishing battery.

    i.   *See Fisher v. Carousel Motor Hotel, Inc.* (1967), where the defendant snatched the plaintiff's plate and yelled that "Negroes can't eat here!" Held: the intent to cause offensive contact not only with the plaintiff's person, but to the plaintiff's clothing or objects attached to the his person, is sufficient in establishing battery. The defendant is liable.

d.   Proving insanity does not exculpate tortfeasors from their batteries or other IT's.

      i.   *See McGuire v. Almy* (defendant), where the tortfeasor battered a nurse with a furniture leg, while having a psychological episode. Held: the tortfeasor is liable for battery because she *intended* to batter the nurse. Rationale: public policy seeks to make the insane liable for their actions (even though they cannot be at fault when there is no volition) in order to (i) give those responsible for the insane incentive to be more watchful; (ii) discourage tortfeasors from claiming insanity and (iii) to restitute the innocent, who should be allowed recovery for damages.

      ii.   Exception: when the insanity precludes the requisite intent.

          1)   Example: the tortfeasor thought that it was a disappearing furniture leg that could cause no contact. There would be no liability.

          2)   Example: the tortfeasor, believing a nurse to be an alien trying to kidnap him, battered her in self-defense. There would be liability because *he had the intent to batter her*.

3.   **False Imprisonment**

  a.   Several acts can give rise to false imprisonment (FI), including: confining the plaintiff to a space; taking possession of the plaintiff's chattel such that the plaintiff will not leave until it is released; placing the plaintiff in a room where the only escape risks life or limb; or confining the plaintiff to a space where the exit is hidden.

  b.   The elements of FI are as follow:

      i.   A ***volitional act*** (an act of the will, as in all intentional torts);

      ii.   Executed with ***intent*** (purpose or KSC) to confine the victim;

      iii.   In an ***unlawful manner*** (not under the authority of a law permitting confinement);

          1)   *See Enright v. Grove*, where the plaintiff sued the defendant for FI when the defendant arrested the plaintiff after the plaintiff refused to show him her drivers license after he interrogated her about a dog in violation of a dog-lease ordinance. Held: since no law permitted the arrest of a citizen for violation of the dog lease ordinance, or for the refusal of a citizen to hand over her license while in a non-moving vehicle, the defendant's confinement of the plaintiff was unlawful.

      iv.   With the ***victim's consciousness*** of the confinement, or, if this is lacking, with a resulting harm. *Parvi v. City of Kingston* (police would not be liable for FI if the plaintiff were not conscious of the confinement);

      v.   ***Against the plaintiff's will***. *Hardy v. LaBelle's Distrib. Co.* (there is no FI when the plaintiff implies consent to an interrogation and states that she wants to stay to clear up a problem); and

        vi.   A ***resulting confinement*** within boundaries (a room, moving car, city, state, etc.).

            1)   This confinement requires that the plaintiff be deprived of the means to exit a space; it does not require the defendant to lay a hand on the plaintiff.

            2)   *See, e.g., Whittaker v. Sandford*, where the plaintiff was falsely imprisoned on a boat when the defendant refused to allow the plaintiff to use the rowboat to get to shore.

4.   Intentional Infliction of Emotional Distress

    a.   The elements for the intentional infliction of emotional distress (IIED) are as follow:

        i.   A ***volitional act*** (an act of the will, as in all intentional torts);

        ii.   Extreme and ***outrageous conduct***;

            1)   The conduct must be shocking to the community.

            2)   Under the Restatement, it must be "atrocious and intolerable in a civilized society."

            3)   The test for the IIED, like that of battery, is based on an objective reasonable person of ordinary sensibilities standard.

               a)   *See Slocum v. Food Fair Stores of Florida*, where the plaintiff suffered a heart attack after an employee insulted her. Since a person of *normal sensibilities* would not have been so offended by the comment ("you stink to me") that he would have suffered a heart attack. The plaintiff's shock and outrage is not enough to establish that the conduct was extreme and outrageous, since the plaintiff may have been unduly sensitive. Since the conduct would not have been shocking to the community as a whole, the defendant is not liable.

               b)   *Compare State Rubbish Collectors Association v. Siliznoff*, where the court held that words threatening physical injury, and the destruction of one's property and business were sufficiently extreme.

        iii.   A ***causal connection*** between the conduct and the emotional harm;

            1)   *N.B.*: as in all the intentional torts, when we refer to the "resulting" harm, we are implying the causal relationship.

        iv.   A resulting ***severe and disabling emotional distress*** that, in some jurisdictions, must be accompanied by bodily harm.

            1)   *See State Rubbish Collectors Association v. Siliznoff*, where physical threats that lead to emotional distress, vomiting, and sleeping problems met this requirement.

2)   *Compare Harris v. Jones*, where the exacerbation of one's speech impediment and increased nervousness failed this element.

5.   Trespass to Land

    a.   The elements of trespass to land are as follow:

        i.   A volitional act (an act of the will, as in all intentional torts);

        ii.   Intent (purpose or KSC) to enter a plot of land;

        iii.   A resulting trespass.

    b.   Neither knowledge of trespass nor damage to the land are necessary elements of trespass. If there is no damage, a court may infer nominal damages.

    c.   The plaintiff may win damages if the defendant merely possesses the intent to enter the plaintiff's land, whether or not he knows that he is trespassing.

        i.   *See Dougherty v. Stepp*, where the plaintiff sued the defendant for trespass to land and the defendant had no knowledge that the land belonged to the plaintiff, and did not intend to trespass or cause any damage to the land. Held: subjective intent to trespass is not necessary in establishing trespass, as long as there was an intention to enter the land; damages are not required.

    d.   Failure to remove objects from the plaintiff's land after the plaintiff's consent has expired also constitutes trespass.

        i.   *See Rogers v. Board of Road Commissioners*, where the plaintiff agreed to allow the defendant to put up a snow fence on the plaintiff's property with the understanding that the defendant would later remove it. The defendant failed to remove one post, which led to an accident in which the plaintiff's husband was killed. Held: trespass is the presence of a person *or* object on the plaintiff's land without the plaintiff's consent. If the plaintiff consents to presence of object for a limited period, and that period has passed, then the object is in trespass of the plaintiff's land and the defendant is liable for any damages arising out of the trespass.

    e.   Trespass may occur without the defendant's actual setting foot on property; the defendant only needs to threaten the plaintiff's right to enjoy the property or violate the space above or below the surface of the property.

        i.   *See Herrin v. Sutherland* (1925), where the defendant was firing shots above the plaintiff's land from other property. The plaintiff claimed that this violated his right to enjoy the property. Held: the defendant is liable for trespass because his acts violate the integrity of the air space above the plaintiff's land.

6.   Trespass to Chattels

a. Trespass to chattels is defined as an act, without justification, of physical interference with a chattel that belongs to another person.

b. The elements of trespass to chattels are as follow:

    i. A volitional act (an act of the will, as in all intentional torts);

    ii. The intent to physically interfere with a chattel belonging to another person; and

    iii. An act whereby the defendant either:

        1) *Dispossesses the possessor* of the chattel;

        2) *Impairs* the condition or value of the chattel;

        3) *Deprives the possessor of the use* of the chattel for a substantial period of time (can be through dispossessing him, impairing the value of the chattel, etc.); or

        4) *Causes bodily harm* to the possessor or harm to persons or property in which the possessor has a legally protected interest.

c. Damages for harmless intermeddling are not rewarded.

    i. *See Glidden v. Syzbiak*, where court held that a girl who played on a dog's back and pulled his ears was not liable for trespass to chattels, since she did not *impair* the dog's condition or value or *deprive the owner of use* of the dog for a substantial period of time.

d. Damages *are* rewarded for *impairing the value of a chattel* or *causing harm to persons* in whom the owner has a legally protected interest, even when no dispossession takes place.

    i. *See CompuServe Inc. v. Cyber Promotions, Inc.*, where the defendant was found liable for trespass to chattels in sending spam through the plaintiff's server, since he (i) impaired the value of the services provided by the plaintiff to its clients; and (ii) harmed the plaintiff's clients, in whom the plaintiff had a legally protected interest.

7. Conversion

a. Conversion is an act of willful interference with the property of another without lawful justification, in a way that *deprives the owner of the use of his property*.

b. Examples of conversion include illegal takings, the assumption of ownership, and the destruction of the property of another.

c. The elements of conversion are as follow (Restatement § 222A):

    i. A volitional act (an act of the will, as in all intentional torts);

    ii. The intent to exercise dominion over a chattel;

1)   In so doing, the interferer need not know that he is interfering with a chattel of another (the BFP of a stolen vehicle, for example, could be liable for conversion).

iii.   That results in such a serious interference with the true owner's right to control the chattel that the defendant may be required to pay the true owner the full value of the chattel.

     1)   In determining whether the interference was sufficiently serious, the following factors are considered:

         a)   The intent to assert a dominion control incompatible with that of the true owner;

         b)   The duration of the dominion control;

         c)   Bad faith;

         d)   Harm to the chattel; and

         e)   Inconvenience to the owner.

     2)   Use of a chattel for a short period is not considered sufficiently serious to meet the interference element.

         a)   *See Pearson v. Dodd*, where the plaintiff sued for conversion when the defendant broke into the plaintiff's office, took some documents, photocopied them, and returned them unharmed. Held: there is no conversion when the defendant has not been deprived of the documents for a substantial period and when the documents have not been substantially harmed.

d.   Damages for Conversion

i.   The plaintiff may ask the court to treat the conversion as a sale of the chattel to the defendant, and thus require the defendant to pay the full value of the chattel to the plaintiff.

ii.   Compare with damages in trespass to chattels, where the plaintiff is entitled only to damages equal to the diminished value of the chattel resulting from the trespass.

8.   Person-to-Person Transferred Intent

a.   A tortfeasor intends to batter B, but instead, batters C.

b.   The tortfeasor will be liable for the battery of C; although he did not intend to cause an offensive or harmful contact with him, his intent to batter B is transferred to his battery against C.

9.   Tort to Tort Transferred Intent

a.   Five of the IT's arose from the old common law tort of trespass: assault, battery, false imprisonment, trespass to land, and trespass to chattels.

b.   In all of these torts, the tortfeasor trespasses on the victim's *person* (assault, battery, false imprisonment), *land* (trespass to land), or *chattels* (trespass to chattels).

      c.   Accordingly, these five torts all allow for what is called, "tort to tort transferred intent": if one tort is intended, but another results, the tortfeasor will be liable for the resulting tort, regardless if he did not intend it.

      d.   This principle can be combined with the effects of person-to-person transferred intent, transforming the nature of a tortfeasor's act.

          i.   Example: a tortfeasor intends to assault B, but instead, batters C. The tortfeasor will be liable for the assault of B (and possibly of C, if he caused C a fear of proximate harm) and the battery of C. The fact that there was intent to batter neither B nor C is immaterial; the tortfeasor will be liable for battery.

C. PRIVILEGES (DEFENSES)

1. Introduction

      a.   A privilege is a legal right, immunity, or exemption to a duty.

      b.   Privileges are affirmative defenses where the defendant is not liable, even if the plaintiff's *prima facie* case is met.

2. Consensual Privilege: Consent

      a.   There is no liability for IT's if the plaintiff consents.

      b.   There are two kinds of consent: (i) express (actual) consent; and (ii) implied consent.

          i.   Consent is express when a party declares orally or in writing that the defendant may engage in some act.

          ii.   Implied Consent may be implied-in-law or implied-in-fact (apparent consent).

      c.   Implied-In-Law

          i.   The law "constructs," or "imports" the consent of certain actors when the following elements are met:

              1)   The actor is in an emergency situation (the threat of life or limb);

              2)   The actor is unable to consent (*e.g.*, because he is unconscious);

              3)   A reasonable person would consent under similar circumstances; and

              4)   There is no indication that the patient would *not* consent if he could.

          ii.   The key is that there be a threat to life or limb, and, unless acts are taken to save the patient, substantial damage would result;

          iii.   In non-emergency situations, doctors do not have implied-in-law consent to perform elective surgeries.

iv. A doctor who performs surgery on a patient without his express or implied-by-law consent, or who performs surgery in a way that is contrary to the patient's consent, can be held liable for battery.

1) *See Mohr v. Williams* (1905), where a doctor, having the patient's consent to perform surgery on one ear, was liable when he performed surgery on the other ear without patient's consent.

v. If the patient is mentally incapacitated, and tells the doctor that he does not want him to perform a procedure that doctor believes is necessary for preservation of the patient's life or limb, the law will construct the patient's consent.

d. Implied-in-Fact (Apparent) Consent

i. When the circumstances would lead the defendant to believe that the plaintiff has consented, the defendant is said to have the plaintiff's "implied-in-fact" consent.

ii. The plaintiff's subjective state of mind is immaterial; what matters is whether a *reasonable person* would consider the plaintiff's conduct to imply consent.

1) *See O'Brien v. Cunard Steamship Co.* (1891), where the plaintiff sued a ship's physician for battery when he administered a vaccination to her. Held: the doctor is not liable, since the context (a boat where a sign was posted everywhere stating that all passengers needed a shot before disembarking) coupled with the plaintiff's waiting on line and holding out her arm would cause a *reasonable person* to believe that she had consented.

e. Consent is invalid under the following circumstances:

i. When obtained through duress;

ii. When obtained through fraud or mistake induced by fraud;

1) *See De May v. Roberts* (1881), where an obstetrician/gynecologist was found liable for assault, battery, and deceit when he brought a non-physician into a delivery room and introduced him to a patient as his "assistant." Held: there is no consent when it is based on the consenter's mistake obtained through the defendant's fraud.

iii. When the person consenting lacks capacity (*e.g.*, infants, the mentally insane, etc.);

1) When the subject lacks capacity, a parent, caretaker, or guardian must give consent on his behalf.

iv. When consent is given to an activity prohibited by statute (*e.g.*, consenting to a statutorily-prohibited fistfight).

1) Many courts will not allow the defense of consent under this circumstance.

3. Non-Consensual Privilege

    a. Introduction

        i. Non-consensual privilege is similarly an affirmative defense, but it is not based on the plaintiff's consent.

        ii. Examples of non-consensual privilege include: self-defense, defense of others, defense of property, and shopkeeper's privilege.

    b. Self Defense

        i. One is privileged to use reasonable force in defending himself if it *appears reasonable* that such force is necessary to protect himself. The privilege applies even when there is in fact no such necessity.

        ii. Two Approaches

            1) Majority View

                a) One may use reasonable force in defending himself and standing his ground in *any situation*.

                b) He may only use deadly (likely to cause death or serious bodily harm) force when threatened with the same.

            2) Minority View

                a) Under the minority view, which is embraced by the Model Penal Code and the Restatement (Second) of Torts, one may stand his ground and defend himself using reasonable force.

                b) However, when required to use deadly force, he first must "flee to the wall," *unless*:

                    i) There is the *slightest* reason to believe that he cannot make a safe retreat (*e.g.*, he is threatened with a firearm at close range); or

                    ii) When he is threatened in his home, he may use deadly force when threatened with deadly force (the *"Castle" Exception*).

            3) Because guns have made much of retreat impractical, the distinction between the majority and minority (Restatement) views has decreased, since the plaintiffs will not be required to retreat when threatened with a gun under either approach.

        iii. Self-defense applies only to *threats to one's physical safety*, not to mere insults. The privilege expires when the threat retreats; it does not apply to retaliation.

    c. Defense of Others

        i. The self-defense privilege to use *reasonable force* when doing so appears necessary (or, in some states, *is* necessary) extends to defending others, including family and servants.

        ii. Reasonable Mistake

1) Minority (Restatement) Approach

    a) Under the minority approach, which is embraced by the Restatement, .one is privileged to use reasonable force when a *reasonable person would have concluded that such force was necessary* to defend others

    b) *Reasonable mistake* applies in the same way that it applies under *self defense*: the privilege applies even if the actor is reasonably mistaken as to the threat.

2) Majority Approach

    a) Under the majority approach, the defendant is *only entitled to use reasonable force when **the party he is defending would have had that privilege***.

    b) Thus, if the party being defended is in fact under no threat, the defendant would be liable for his tort, even if the mistake was reasonable.

    c) Under the majority approach, one therefore must be *certain* that there is a threat to the third party before intervening.

3) Example

    a) B perceives that his family member C is being threatened by D. In the interests of defending C, B batters D, but later finds out that C and D were only rehearsing for a play.

    b) Under the minority approach, B would not be liable if the court concludes that his mistake was reasonable.

    c) Under the majority approach, B would be liable, since C did not have the privilege to act in self defense.

d. Defense of Property

i. General Overview

1) The owner of property is privileged to use *reasonable force* in defending this property when it appears that such force is necessary for the protection of his property.

2) The *reasonable force* standard of self-defense and defense of others applies to the defense of property; the force employed must be proportionate to the threat detected.

3) The defense of property privilege does not permit the defendant to use *deadly force* in protecting a home that is not a dwelling.

    a) *See Katko v. Briney* (Iowa 1971), where the court held that the blowing off of a petty thief's leg with a shotgun when the petty thief posed no threat to anyone's life in an abandoned home was *not* a reasonable use of force. The dignity of life outweighs the right to protect property.

4) Under a traditional common law doctrine, the defendant may, however, use deadly force in his own home against trespassers based on the reasonable belief that such force is necessary to prevent certain felonies.

5) A minority of jurisdictions have even gone as far as permitting defendants to use deadly force against trespassers *who do not commit felonies* within the home but who the occupant believes may use *even slight physical force* against the occupant (*see, e.g., Colorado Revised Statutes*).

6) Other states have limited this use of deadly force, requiring, for example, that deadly force be used only against trespassers who threaten the occupant's *life or limb*.

ii. Recovery of Property

1) One is granted privilege of using reasonable force in recovering a chattel taken from him through fraud if (Restatement §§ 101-106):

a) He is entitled to the immediate recovery of the property;

b) He has demanded for the chattel to be returned and the other party has refused;

c) The force is proportionate to the threat;

d) There has been reasonable diligence in discovering the loss and attempting recovery;

e) The party against whom force is being exercised is a wrongdoer, not one who purchased in good faith from a wrongdoer;

f) He has not breached the peace.

2) *See Hodgeden v. Hubburd*, where the plaintiff accused the defendant of using force in recovering a stove that the plaintiff had fraudulently induced the defendant to sell. Held: because the defendant used proportionate and reasonable force that was necessary (since the plaintiff drew a knife), the defendant is not liable.

iii. Shopkeeper's Privilege

1) A storeowner is entitled to detain shoppers in potential cases of shoplifting when the following elements are met:

a) The storeowner has a *reasonable belief* that the shopper is a shoplifter;

b) The detention is *in the store or within the immediate vicinity*;

        c)   The detention is conducted in a *reasonable manner* (the storeowner may not publicly embarrass the shopper) and over a reasonable *period of time* (generally, no more than ten to fifteen minutes); and

        d)   Reasonable, non-deadly force is used.

    2)   *See Bonkowski v. Arlan's Dept. Store*, where a store owner was held not to be liable for false arrest and slander against a customer, since the store owner's detention of the customer was based on a reasonable belief of the shoplifting of costume jewelry and was reasonable in duration.

e.   Necessity

    i.   Public Necessity

        1)   Trespass is privileged as a public necessity when the actor **reasonably believes** it to be necessary to avoid an imminent public disaster.

        2)   The defendant not only has a privilege for his trespass, but he is also *not liable* for any damage to property incurred during the trespass.

        3)   Example: A breaks into a private building in order to defuse a bomb that he has been informed is about to go off.

    ii.   Private Necessity

        1)   Trespass is privileged as a private necessity when the actor **reasonably believes** it to be necessary to avoid a grave risk of harm to his person, land, or chattels.

        2)   Although the trespass is privileged, the trespasser is liable for any damage to property incurred during the trespass.

        3)   Example: A is wandering about a forest when a lion spies him. A may break into B's log cabin to take shelter until the threat retreats.

        4)   *N.B.*: the privilege of necessity does *not* permit one to trespass on another's land in order to recover a domestic animal that strayed off due to the owner's own negligence.

IV. NEGLIGENCE

A. INTRODUCTION

1.   Negligence (N) arose as a tort of its own in the 1800s, as distinct from intentional torts (IT's), in that it does *not* require a volitional act; an **omission** would be sufficient in proving the plaintiff's *prima facie* case.[11]

2.   The elements of the plaintiff's *prima facie* negligence case are as follow:

    a.   The duty to protect persons and property from foreseeable, unreasonable risks;

---

[11] However, as we will see, some N cases also involve a volitional act.

b.   A breach of this duty;

c.   Actual and proximate cause; and

d.   Damages to a third party's person or property interests.

B.   THE DUTY TO EXERCISE REASONABLE CARE

1.   Introduction

      a.   One has a duty to protect third parties from foreseeable, unreasonable risks.

      b.   When an act is either unforeseeable or reasonable, the defendant does not have a duty to protect the plaintiff from the associated risks of the act.

2.   Unforeseeability

      a.   A defendant is liable for failing to protect others from *foreseeable risks*.

            i.   *See Gulf Refining Co. v. Williams* (plaintiff), where the plaintiff sued the defendant for giving him a gas drum whose bung cap was jagged, causing a spark when being opened that lead to a fire and injury to the plaintiff. The defendant's witnesses testified that the possibility of a fire was so unlikely that it was unforeseeable. The defendant therefore testified that he did not have a duty to prevent unforeseeable risks. The court, however, held that the defendant was liable because the condition of the bung attracted the attention of one of the defendant's employees and would have notified a reasonable prudent person of the foreseeable danger.

      b.   He is not liable for failing to prevent damages resulting from unforeseeable risks.

            i.   *See Lubitz v. Wells*, where the plaintiff sued the defendant for negligently leaving a golf club lying in his back yard, allowing the defendant's son to pick it up and hurt the plaintiff. Held: although there is a duty to exercise reasonable care and to prevent unreasonable risks, the risk of one's son's picking up a club lying in the yard and injuring a person is so slight that a reasonable person would not have taken actions to prevent it. The defendant is not liable.

            ii.   *See also Blythe v. Birmingham Waterworks Co.*, where a company took measures to prevent damages resulting from foreseeable storms. However, when one highly unusual frost came to past, a fire hydrant burst, causing damages. Since the frost was so extraordinary, it was not foreseeable and the defendant was held not to be liable.

3.   Unreasonable Risks

      a.   Introduction to Risk-Utility Analysis

        i.   One has a duty to protect third parties not from *all* foreseeable risks, but from all *unreasonable* foreseeable risks.

        ii.   When a risk is reasonable, the defendant is not necessarily held liable for all resulting injuries.

        iii.   Determining whether a risk is reasonable requires applying risk-utility analysis.

        iv.   When the activity is of great public utility (*e.g.*, railroads, roads, shipping), society must be prepared to tolerate some degree of unreasonable risk in order to be productive.

        v.   In these cases, defendants are less likely to be held liable for the resulting risks.

b.   When the burden of reducing unreasonable risks costs less than the damages that may otherwise result, there is a duty to protect others.

c.   However, when the burden is cost-prohibitive, no such duty exists.

        i.   *See Davison v. Snohomish County*, where the court held that the defendant was not liable for not making stronger guard rails in order to prevent injuries on the roads, since making all roads safe would be cost-prohibitive.

d.   When the burden to prevent damage to third persons is low, there is liability despite an activity's high utility

        i.   *See Chicago, B. and Q.R. Co v. Krayenbuhl* (plaintiff), where the plaintiff sued the defendant for negligence when his foot was severed while she was playing on a turntable. Held: society tolerates some of the unreasonable risks associated with trains because of the high utility of trains. However, *when the burden of prevention* is much *slighter than the risk of damage*, there is liability. Here, the burden of putting a padlock on the turntable is much slighter than the risk of injury to children. The defendant is therefore liable.

e.   The Learned Hand Formula

        i.   According to Judge Learned Hand, one is negligent when the probability of **damage** (P), multiplied by the **magnitude of the potential damage** (L) is greater than the **burden** (B) of preventing the risk.

        ii.   There is thus negligence when $(P)(L) > B$

        iii.   *See United States v. Carroll Towing Co.*, where the plaintiff sued the defendant for negligently allowing the plaintiff's barge to sink. Because the probability of harm multiplied by the magnitude of potential harm being was greater than the burden of prevention (having an attendee on board), the defendant was held to be liable.

f.   Traditional Common Law View

        i.   Judge Learned Hand's formula ignores an important factor that most courts include in their analysis: the degree to which an activity is useful to society (utility).

      ii.   Under the traditional common law view, there is thus negligence when the *risk* (R) is greater than the *utility* (U) plus the *burden* (B).

      iii.   There is thus negligence when R > U + B.

      iv.   When the risk is great and unreasonable, there is negligence, unless the utility and the burden are very high and outweigh the risk (*e.g.*, *Davison v. Snohomish County*).

      v.   When there is great risk, but greater utility, there will generally not be negligence, unless the burden is slight.

    g.   The View of the Restatement of the Law (Second) of Torts

      i.   The Restatement view summarizes the common law view and add precisions to the definitions of risk and utility.

      ii.   Factors determining risk include the probability of the harm, the magnitude of the harm, and the number of people who would be harmed.

      iii.   Factors determining utility include the social value of the activity and the extent to which this value can be met with other, less dangerous activities.

      iv.   Under the Restatement, there is unreasonableness from which the defendant has a duty to protect third parties when:

         1)   The *risk* (the probability of damage times the magnitude of the potential damage times the number of people (N) who would be harmed) is greater than the *social utility* plus the *burden*.

         2)   There is thus negligence when R (P x L x N) > U + B.

C.   THE STANDARD OF CARE

    1.   The Standard Objective Test

      a.   In negligence cases, tortfeasors are generally held to an objective, reasonable prudent person standard.[12]

      b.   It is an objective standard that does not take into consideration a party's lack of skill, thoughtfulness, or intelligence.

        i.   *See Vaughan v. Menlove*, where the court applied an objective standard when it held the defendant liable for stacking hay in a way that caught fire, even though he sincerely believed that there was no such risk. The defendant's intelligence was not taken into account.

    2.   An Amalgam Subjective/Objective Test

      a.   Under certain circumstances, a person will be held to an amalgam subjective/objective test that looks to a reasonable prudent person *in that person's position*.

---

[12] Although custom may provide evidence as to what the reasonable prudent person standard is, custom is *not* dispositive, since an entire society can breach its duty of care.

b. For example, in emergency situations, an actor is held to the standard of a reasonable prudent person *in an emergency situation;* the actor must exercise reasonable care *under the circumstances.*

   i. *See Cordas v. Peerless Transportation Co.,* where the defendant jumped out of his cab while it was still running, injuring a woman and her children, after a robber came into the car and, with a gun pointed at his head, commanded him to drive. Held: the defendant is not negligent, since a reasonable prudent person would have acted similarly in like circumstances and quick decision-making was necessary.

c. The disabled are held to a "reasonable prudent person of like disability" standard. *Roberts v. State of La.* (applying the standard of a "reasonable prudent blind person").

d. Those with a diagnosable impairment (*e.g.,* retardation) are generally held to a subjective standard.

e. Similarly, those who are subjected to a sudden and unforeseeable mental illness will be held to a subjective standard, as long as he has no prior history of the potential impairment that would make injury to third persons a foreseeable risk.

   i. If an actor has a history of mental illness or some other warning of a potentially dangerous mental condition, he will be held to an objective, reasonable prudent person standard in most states.

   ii. *See Breunig v. American Family Ins. Co.,* where the plaintiff sued the tortfeasor's insurance company for negligence when the tortfeasor, in a psychotic episode, believed God had been driving her car and slammed into the plaintiff's truck. The tortfeasor was held to a reasonable prudent person standard, and, given her history of mental illness, she failed.

f. Children are held to a subjective standard that looks not only at the "reasonable prudent child," but rather, to a reasonable prudent child of "similar age, ability and intelligence."

   i. Some states have established a minimum age (*e.g.,* seven years old) under which children are not capable of negligence.

   ii. However, if the child, regardless of his age, is engaged in some highly dangerous (adult) activity, he will in most states be held to the reasonable prudent person standard as though he were an adult.

      1) *See Robinson v. Lindsay,* where the plaintiff brought suit against the defendant, a child who was operating a snowmobile when the plaintiff was injured. The defendant argued that a subjective standard based on a reasonable child of like age, ability, and intelligence should be applied. However, the court held that when a child is engaged in adult activities, the reasonable prudent adult standard is applied.

3.   The Standard for Professionals

    a.   Introduction

        i.   With respect to professionals, a standard that looks to the reasonable prudent *professional*, not *person*, is applied.

        ii.   A doctor or a lawyer is therefore not held to a duty commensurate with that of ordinary reasonable persons, or even a duty according to his own experience and training.

        iii.   Rather, he is held to an industry-wide standard, a duty commensurate with that of *other professionals within his profession*. *Heath v. Swift Wings* (applying a standard of care based on a reasonable prudent pilot).

        iv.   While custom normally serves as *evidence* of a standard of care, it is generally dispositive in establishing malpractice in cases involving professionals.

        v.   The plaintiff does not, however, need to prove breach of a standard of care based on custom when an act or omission is so negligent that the duty of care is considered to be breached as a matter of law (*prima facie* negligence, *e.g.*, a scalpel left in a patient's wound).

    b.   Standard of Care in the Legal Profession

        i.   A lawyer has the duty perform services with the care, diligence, and prudence of an ordinary and reasonable attorney under similar circumstances.

            1)   *See Hodges v. Carter*, where the plaintiff sued his attorney, who served an insurance company improperly the first time and then failed to serve the company the second time before the SL expired. The court ruled for the defendant, since he performed his services with the care, diligence and prudence of an ordinary lawyer, who similarly would have concluded that the service was proper, given the statute in the case and a twenty-year custom.

            2)   *N.B.*: if the court held that the defendant failed to meet the reasonable prudent attorney standard, he would have had a second defense if he had proven that there was less than a fifty percent chance that the plaintiff would have won the case.

    c.   Standard of Care in the Medical Profession

        i.   The standard of care in the medical profession is that of an ordinary and reasonable doctor *from within the community* under similar circumstances.

            1)   *See Boyce v. Brown*, where the defendant performed surgery on the plaintiff many years earlier. When the plaintiff later returned to the defendant and complained of pain, the defendant did nothing. The plaintiff went to another doctor, who took X-rays and found and removed a screw that had

been causing the plaintiff's pain. The plaintiff sued for malpractice, alleging that the defendant should have taken an X-ray. Held: the standard to be used is not that another doctor would have taken steps contrary to those of the defendant, but rather, that the defendant's actions were contrary to the standard of medical practice *within the community*. Judgment for the defendant.

ii. The rule that a doctor be held to the standard of the care, diligence, and prudence of a doctor *from within the community* is not strictly applied. Sometimes, the courts hold a doctor to a standard of acting with the care of a doctor from *outside* of the community.

    1) *See Morrison v. MacNamara*, where the plaintiff brought suit against the defendant for negligently requiring the plaintiff to stand during a urethral smear test, leading to the plaintiff's dizziness and fainting. The plaintiff brought in an out-of-state expert who testified that the standard in the medical community was to allow patients to sit or lie down during such tests. The trial court held that the testimony was inadmissible, since the expert was not from *within the community*. The appeals court reversed, holding that the origins of the locality rule are outdated in an age of greater mobility and communication. A national standard was adopted.

iii. Today, most jurisdictions require doctors to perform services with the care of an ordinary and reasonable physician from a similar community under similar circumstances.

    1) Thus, a doctor from in a small, rural town in Ohio may testify in an action against a doctor in a small, rural town in Indiana, as to what he would do in similar circumstances.

    2) The benefit is that a doctor from a small, rural town will not be held to the standard of a doctor from an urban teaching hospital. Furthermore, plaintiffs are not limited in their selection of experts to bring in.

iv. Some states have gone as far as adopting a national custom standard.

v. In some cases, however, custom—within the community or otherwise—has not been dispositive. Although it is rare, risk-utility analysis has been applied in a malpractice cases.

    1) *See Helling v. Carey*, where the plaintiff sued the defendant for failing to screen the plaintiff for glaucoma. The defendant argued that it was not custom within the community to screen patients under forty years of age for glaucoma. Held: the defendant is liable, since the magnitude of the potential harm far outweighs the slight burden of the screening.

D.   **CAUSES OF ACTION BASED ON NEGLIGENCE**

1.   **Informed Consent**

a.   Introduction

i.   Informed consent, despite its misleading name, is not a defense to negligence, but rather, a cause of action relating to medical malpractice.

ii.   The tort arises when a physician fails to disclose the *risks*, *benefits*, and *alternatives* to a procedure, drug, etc.

b.   Elements

i.   Duty

1)   The duty is to disclose the *material risks, benefits and alternatives* to a procedure, a drug, or other medically-related practice.

2)   Generally, the standard for malpractice is custom (what other doctors do); here, the standard is based on what *other reasonable patients would expect and wish to know*.

a)   *See Scott v. Bradford* (defendant), where the plaintiff was not informed of the risks associated with a hysterectomy that a *reasonable patient* would wish to know. She would not have gone forward with the procedure had she known of the risks, which materialized and led to further surgeries. The defendant was liable for failing to disclose these risks.

3)   "Material" information includes a doctor's personal interests.

a)   *See Moore v. The Regents of the University of California*, where the court held that a doctor breached his fiduciary duty and his duty to disclose material information by not disclosing to a patient that he would profit from a strain of cells he would create from cells removed from the plaintiff during surgery.

ii.   Breach

1)   Failure to disclose material information constitutes breach of the duty.

2)   As exceptions, failure to disclose material information does not constitute breach of the duty when:

a)   The disclosure would cause an overly sensitive patient *undue alarm;*

b)   The risks are widely known and of *common knowledge;* or

c)   The patient's judgment is impaired by an *emergency*.

iii.   Causation

1) There are two approaches to causation in informed consent:

    a) The *subjective* approach:

        i) The plaintiff must testify that he would have acted differently if informed of the risks;

        ii) The plaintiff's credibility is subject to jury's scrutiny.

    b) The *subjective/objective* combined approach:

        i) The plaintiff must testify that he would have acted differently if informed of the risks;

        ii) The plaintiff's credibility is subject to jury's scrutiny; and

        iii) The jury must conclude that a reasonable prudent patient would not have gone forward with the procedure if properly informed.

iv. Damages

    1) With respect to the injuries, the plaintiff must testify that he suffered injuries whose risks he did not know of.

2. Negligent Infliction of Emotional Distress

    a. Evolution

        i. Under the common law, the negligent infliction of emotional distress (NIED) was a cause of action when there was a physical impact as well as an injury (***parasitic damages***).

        ii. Under the intermediate impact rule, any ***impact*** was both sufficient and required.

        iii. Under the modern approach in many states, an impact is no longer required, but some states require a physical manifestation of the emotional distress (ED).

            1) *See Daley v. LaCroix* (Mich. 1979), where the defendant's airborne car caused an explosion in the plaintiff's home. Because the crash caused the plaintiff to suffer nervousness and weight loss, there was enough evidence to support a jury finding for NIED, even though the plaintiff was neither physically impacted nor injured.

    b. The Three Approaches

        i. ***Zone of danger rule***: one can recover for the NIED only if:

            1) He was so close to the danger that he could have been injured; and

            2) He witnessed the accident.

        ii. ***Dillon v. Legg rule***: one can recover for the NIED according to the following *factors*:

            1) Proximity to the scene of the accident;

2) The witnessing of the accident; and

3) A close relation to the victim.

iii. ***Heightened requirements rule*** (used in California): one can recover for the NIED if the following *elements* are met:

1) *Presence* at the scene of accident;

2) Awareness that it is causing injury to victim; and

3) A close relation to victim;

a) *See Thing v. La Chusa* (Cal.), where the plaintiff, who was later informed of the accident by a third party, could not recover for NIED because she was not present at the scene of the accident and did not have awareness of the accident as it was happening.

V.   THE DUTY OF CARE

A.   STATUTORY STANDARDS OF CARE

1. Introduction

a. As we have seen, in establishing a defendant's duties owed, plaintiffs often look to custom (especially in cases involving professionals) or risk-utility analysis.

b. A third tool that plaintiffs may use in establishing the duty owed is the violation of statutes (negligence *per se*), including civil, criminal, and regulatory statutes.

c. The violation of a statute often establishes negligence *per se*, or negligence as a matter of law, without the need to prove to a jury the duty owed and the breach of that duty.

2. Statutes Establishing Negligence *Per Se*

a. The violation of a statute may give rise to: (i) *negligence per se* (a dispositive finding of negligence, regardless of the care taken); (ii) a *rebuttable inference* of negligence; or (iii) mere *evidence* of negligence.

b. State vary widely in how they treat statutes for the purpose of establishing a duty. One important factor that is considered is whether the statute is civil, criminal, or regulatory in nature.

c. Plaintiffs may combine various classes of statutes when establishing a duty.

i. *See Stachniewicz v. Mar-Cam Corp.*, where the plaintiff sued the defendant for breach of a duty based on (i) a statute prohibiting giving alcohol to those visibly intoxicated; and (ii) a regulation prohibiting allowing disorderly or intoxicated persons to remain on the premises. The first theory failed because it was virtually impossible to prove that the plaintiff would have not been injured but for the extra drinks served to the already intoxicated the defendants; the second theory succeeded since, but for the violation of the regulation, the plaintiff would not have been injured.

3. Classes of Statutes

    a. Civil Statutes

        i. Civil tort statutes create a duty and a cause of action. The violation of such a statute establishes *negligence per se*.

            1) Because negligence is established as a matter of law, breach of duty is not a jury question.

            2) Example: a state adopts a statute requiring all people to sweep their driveways after a snowstorm. The legislature expresses in the statute that reasonable people would do so in order to avoid the hazard of a slippery driveway. If A slips on B's driveway as a result of B's failure to sweep his driveway, A will have a cause of action for negligence and will not need to establish duty or breach.

        ii. However, if a legislature adopts a civil statute without explicitly creating a cause of action or defining a reasonable person as one who would abide by that statute, most courts would adopt the statute as establishing a *rebuttable presumption* or *mere evidence* of negligence.

    b. Criminal Statutes

        i. Most states, based on the rationale that the purpose of criminal statutes is to punish wrongdoers, not to restitute victims, have not instituted the violation of a statute as negligence *per se*.

        ii. Some of these states have deemed the violation of a criminal statute to constitute a *rebuttable presumption* of negligence that can be rebutted with a valid excuse.

        iii. In other states, the violation of a criminal statute constitutes *mere evidence* of negligence.

        iv. In still other states, the violation of a criminal statute is considered negligence *per se*; it is dispositive in establishing negligence.

    c. Regulatory Statutes

        i. Regulatory statutes are passed not by legislatures, but by legislatively created agencies (*e.g.*, the FCC).

        ii. Regulatory laws, unlike civil laws, do not restitute victims, and unlike criminal laws, do not punish wrongdoers. They may, however, *revoke licenses*.

        iii. Violation of regulatory statutes, like custom, is **evidence of negligence**, but it is *not dispositive*.

4. The Applicability of a Statute

a. Courts only adopt statutes for the purpose of establishing a duty and breach when doing so is "fair, workable and wise." The following factors are considered:

i. Whether the **duty** was recognized in the common law;

1) When a statute creates a new duty that did not exist in the common law, courts will rarely hold non-compliant citizens liable for tort damages, unless it is a tort statute allowing for such recovery.

2) Courts tend only to adopt regulatory or criminal statutes as standards of care when these statutes *clarify* already existing common law duties.

ii. Whether the statute is clear as to what constitutes a **breach** or violation;

iii. Whether the **causal** link between the violation and the injury is clear; and

iv. Whether **damages** for the tort liability eclipse the civil fine.

1) *See Perry v. S.N. and S.N.* (plaintiffs), where the defendants did not report the Kellers' sexual abuse of the plaintiffs' children. They were held not to be liable because: (i) the common law recognizes no duty to rescue (*see infra.*); (ii) the statute is not clear in defining the forbidden behavior, since it does not state at which point in their suspicions must the defendants report the abuse; (iii) the non-reporting of the abuse and the actual harm in this case are very indirect; and (iv) adopting the statute as a tort duty of care could lead to significantly higher civil liability than envisioned by the statute.

b. If a court decides that adopting a statute as a duty of care is fair, the statute will only be applied to a case in particular if the party establishing negligence proves that:

i. The *victim* is part of the class that the *legislature intended to protect* through the statute; and

ii. The *injury* is of the kind that the *legislature wanted to prevent.*

5. Effects of Statutes Adopted as Standards of Care

a. Statutes imposing a duty on citizens may be **used by defendants** in the affirmative defense of **contributory negligence**.

b. Defendants must show that (i) the plaintiff violated a statute that represents a duty of care owed to the defendant; and (ii) violation of the statute contributed to the plaintiff's injury.

i. *See Martin v. Herzog* (defendant), where the plaintiff sued for negligence when the defendant violated a statute by crossing the white line while turning in his car, hitting the plaintiff's buggy and causing the plaintiff's husband's death. The defendant argued and the court agreed that the plaintiff was contributorily negligent *per se* by violating a statute that required him to keep his lights on.

    ii.   *N.B.*: the court expressed the need to show that the violation of the statute was what caused the injury: had it not been for the plaintiff's not having lights on, the accident would not have occurred.

  c.   When the violation of a statute creates a rebuttable presumption of negligence, the presumption may be rebutted by the following valid excuses (§ 288A Restatement):

    i.   The actor *lacks capacity* (*e.g.*, he is an infant, is mentally insane, etc.);

    ii.   The actor has *no knowledge of the violation*;

    iii.   The *impracticability* of compliance (*e.g.*, violation would be safer than compliance);

        1)   *See Zeni* (plaintiff) *v. Anderson*, where the plaintiff was held not to be contributorily negligent for violating a statute requiring pedestrians to walk on the sidewalk facing traffic, since the sidewalk was covered in snow and it would have been more dangerous for the plaintiff to walk on it than on the highway.

    iv.   The *impossibility* of compliance; or

    v.   An *emergency* renders compliance outside of the actor's control.

B.   DUTY TO RESCUE

  1.   The Common Law Approach

    a.   The common law never recognized a duty to intervene or to rescue.

      i.   *See Hegel* (plaintiff) *v. Langsam*, where the court held that universities have no duty to monitor the lives of their students, and the defendant was accordingly not liable when the plaintiff's child became involved with drug criminals and missed classes.

    b.   Rather, the common law imposed liability on a rescuer who undertook to act and exacerbated a victim's condition through his negligence or other torts.

    c.   Naturally, this creates a disincentive to rescue. To offset the disincentive of potential liability, many states have passed ***Good Samaritan statutes*** that protect rescuers from liability.

      i.   What is protected:

        1)   *Majority approach*: negligence only.

        2)   *Minority approach* (*e.g.*, California): *all* torts.

      ii.   Who is protected:

        1)   *Majority approach*: any rescuer.

        2)   *Minority approach*: licensees (*e.g.*, doctors) only.

2.   Exceptions to the Common Law "No Duty to Rescue" Rule

    a.   The general common law rule is that there is no duty to intervene or to rescue.

    b.   However, under certain circumstances, the common law imposed liability on a defendant for an omission to act. The duty to rescue was recognized by the common law when:

        i.   The defendant undertook to act by: (i) promising to act; or (ii) beginning to undertake a rescue by giving assistance.

        ii.   The defendant caused the victim's peril or left him in greater peril than he found him, whether or not he acted with intent or negligence.

        iii.   The instrumentality is within the defendant's control (especially when the plaintiff is an invitee).

            1)   *See L.S. Ayres and Co.* (defendant) *v. Hicks*, where a child was injured when his fingers were caught in the defendant's escalator. Since the escalator was an instrumentality within the defendant's control, the defendant had a duty to rescue. Because he was not being attentive in shutting it down rapidly enough, the defendant is liable for the aggravation of the injury resulting from the delay.

        iv.   There is a special relationship with the victim (*e.g.*, relationships between spouses; employers and employees; parents and children; inviters and invitees; innkeepers and guests; common carriers and passengers, etc.).

        v.   Other circumstances based on: (i) the *foreseeability* of the harm; (ii) the *societal interest* in recognizing the duty; and (iii) the *opportunity to avoid risk.*

            1)   *See Tarasoff* (plaintiff) *v. Regents of University of California,* where the defendant was liable for failure to rescue when it was *foreseeable* that the a patient of the defendant university's psychologist would murder another patient, since the former confessed his intention to do so. The plaintiff's duty was to do more than merely temporarily detain the patient.

            2)   *See also J.S. and M.S. v. R.T.H,* where the defendant was sued for not reporting her husband's sexual abuse of the plaintiffs' children, who frequented the defendant's home to play with the defendant's horses. Held: because the defendant had known or should have known about her husband's propensities, she owed a duty to rescue the children.

                a)   *N.B.*: because the defendant was the abuser's spouse, the foreseeability of sexual abuse was much higher, causing the court to impose a duty to rescue.

C. Premises Liability

1. In the majority of states, the duty owed in premises liability varies according to whether the person on one's land is an invitee (highest duty of care owed), a licensee, or a trespasser (lowest duty of care owed).

    a. Invitees

        i.   An invitee is a person who is conferring a business or pecuniary benefit on the owner or occupier of the premises.

        ii. The standard of care owed to invitees is one of **reasonable care** in all circumstances. This includes the duty to **inspect** the property at reasonable intervals, to **warn** invitees of potential hazards, and possibly to **repair** such hazards.

        iii. The pecuniary benefit may have been conferred at regular intervals in the past; the fact that the invitee did not confer a pecuniary benefit on the day that the negligence arose does not change his status.

             1) *See Campbell v. Weathers* (defendant), where the plaintiff fell through a trap door in the defendant's restaurant's toilet facility. The defendant argued that the plaintiff was not an invitee, since the plaintiff had only loitered at the counter and did not purchase food on that day. Held: because the plaintiff was a regular customer who intended to purchase something on that day or in the future, he is considered an invitee, and a *standard duty of care* is imposed on the defendant. Judgment for the defendant reversed.

    b. Licensees

        i.   When a person is on the owner's premises with the owner's permission, but is not conferring a pecuniary benefit to the owner (*e.g.*, an invited social guest), he is a licensee.

        ii. States are divided on the duty of care owed to licensees.

             1) Under the majority approach, which is the approach adopted by the Restatement, there is a duty to warn licensees of *dangers known* by the owner and *dangers that should be known* by the owner.

                 a) *See Barmore v. Elmore* (defendant) (Ill. App. Ct. 1980), where the plaintiff sued the defendant for failing to protect him when the defendant's son stabbed him while he was in the defendant's home. Held: since the plaintiff was not on the premises to discuss business directly benefiting the defendant, he was a mere licensee. Therefore, the defendant owed him *only a duty to warn of reasonable dangers*. Since the defendant had *no reasonable basis* to suspect his son was a threat, he did not breach this duty.

             2) Under the minority approach, the duty is to warn licensees only of *dangers known* by the owner.

        iii.   However, an owner has no duty to warn licensees of dangers that are:

            1)   Open and in the obvious; or

            2)   The cause of natural weather patterns.

        iv.   A person's status from invitee to licensee (and vice versa) may change under the circumstances.

            1)   *See Whelan v. Van Natta*, where an invitee who bought cigarettes from a store became a licensee when he went into a back room to retrieve a box.

    c.   Trespassers

        i.   Trespassers constitute the last category in premises liability.

        ii.   Owners owe ***no duty of care*** to unknown trespassers.

        iii.   However, owners have a duty to warn ***known trespassers*** of *hidden dangers* on the property of which the owner is aware or has reason to be aware (under the majority approach) or, under the minority approach, only of which he *knows*.

            1)   *See Sheehan v. St. Paul and Duluth Railway Co.* (defendant), where the plaintiff's foot was run over by a train when he was trespassing near train tracks and got stuck when a train was passing. Held: since the defendant did not know of the trespasser's presence, no duty of care was owed.

        iv.   A trespasser is known by the owner if he directly eye witnesses the trespasser if he becomes aware of the trespasser through an indirect third source.

        v.   If the owner knows or reasonably should know that part of his property is frequently trespassed, an unknown trespasser using that part of the land will be treated as a known trespasser.

2.   Distinction merged

    a.   California has led a minority of states in merging the distinction between invitees, licensees, and trespassers.

    b.   In such states, juries are instructed that the defendant owed the plaintiff a *duty of reasonable care under the circumstances* (informed by foreseeability).

    c.   The jury may consider whether the plaintiff was a trespasser, licensee or invitee in determining whether there was a breach of duty.

    d.   Other states have merged the difference between licensees and invitees only, but have continued imposing no duty of care towards unknown trespassers.

VI. PROVING BREACH

A. INTRODUCTION

1. In examining standards of care, we have reviewed the three tests that are used in establishing duties owed: (i) the reasonable prudent person test; (ii) custom; and (iii) statutory standards of care.

2. Now, we move on to breach, which, unlike duty, is always *heavily factual*.

3. It is generally obvious when a duty has been breached, but when direct evidence does not prove the breach, the analysis can be complex.

4. In such cases, fact finders are permitted to draw inferences based on circumstantial evidence.

5. The following is a general framework for analyzing breach:

   a. Look to direct evidence (99% of breach analyses end here);

   b. If there is no direct evidence, use *circumstantial evidence* – secondary facts and other evidence that lead to primary fact inferences;

   c. If there is no probative evidence, *res ipsa loquitur* may be used (*see infra.*).

B. CIRCUMSTANTIAL EVIDENCE

1. In making a *prima facie* case for negligence, the burden is on the plaintiff to produce evidence that proves the defendant's negligence by a *preponderance of the evidence*.

2. When the plaintiff fails to meet this burden, a directed verdict is ordered in favor of the defendant.

   a. *See Goddard* (plaintiff) *v. Boston and Maine R.R. Co.*, where the plaintiff failed introduced neither direct nor indirect evidence of the plaintiff's *actual notice* or *constructive notice* (legal notice derived from the circumstances) of a banana peel's being on the ground. Failing to prove breach, the plaintiff's *prima facie* case was not made. The directed verdict for the defendant was affirmed.

   b. *Compare Anjou v. Boston Elevated Railray Co.*, where the plaintiff proved **constructive notice** by a preponderance of the evidence. Using circumstantial evidence, the plaintiff showed that a peel had been on the ground for a substantial period, since it was black, dry, and gritty.

3. This burden may be met through the use of either circumstantial or direct evidence. Circumstantial evidence is often used in establishing constructive notice of an unreasonable harm from which the defendant has a duty to protect third parties.

   a. *See Joye v. Great Atlantic and Pacific Tea Co.*, where the plaintiff introduced evidence in court showing that the defendant should have known about the banana peel on the ground, since it had been there for thirty five minutes or more. The plaintiff won and the defendant made a motion for a judgment *non obstante veredicto*. Held: the plaintiff failed to bring in clear evidence that established whether the banana peel had been on the ground for three minutes or three days. The defendant's motion for a judgment *non obstante veredicto* is granted.

4.   Normally, there is a burden on the plaintiff to produce evidence that gives rise to either a **conclusion**, or, when there is no direct evidence, an **inference of negligence** (*exception*: when the facts so strongly create an inference of negligence that probative evidence is not required—see *res ipsa loquitur, infra.*).

    a.   In either case, the burden is on the plaintiff to prove the breach.

    b.   However, some courts have been sloppy about this and have ruled for the plaintiff *even when he has failed* to furnish the evidence that proves breach as a part of his *prima facie* case.

        i.   *See Ortega* (plaintiff) *v. Kmart Corp.*, where the plaintiff failed to show with a preponderance of the evidence that Kmart had either actual or constructive notice of a puddle of milk that the plaintiff slipped on. Furthermore, the defendant testified that it was highly unlikely that milk would be on floor for more than fifteen to thirty minutes, and the plaintiff did not establish that it was on the floor for longer. The court nevertheless ruled in favor of the plaintiff

5.   However, for certain activities, the plaintiff is not required to introduce evidence of the defendant's breach. Rather, certain activities ("mode of operation") are given strict liability treatment.

    a.   *See Jasko* (plaintiff) *v. F.W. Woolworth Co.*, where the defendant was liable to the plaintiff for a slip on a slice of pizza because of the *mode of operation* (a self service pizza parlor with pizza served on wax paper). Thus, despite the defendant's normal precautions (regular sweepers, etc.), he is on constant constructive notice of hazards and is liable for injuries.

C.   *RES IPSA LOQUITUR*

1.   Introduction

    a.   *Res ipsa loquitur* (RIL) is a negligence circumstantial evidence doctrine.

    b.   It is invoked when the facts create such a strong presumption of negligence that "the thing speaks for itself" (*Lat.*). The plaintiff is not required to introduce evidence.

        i.   *See Byrne v. Boadle*, where the plaintiff was walking when a barrel rolled out of the defendant's warehouse, striking him. The plaintiff sued for negligence, but had no evidence to prove a breach of duty. Held: it would be preposterous to require the plaintiff to produce evidence proving breach. The accident *would not have happened* but for the defendant's negligence. Judgment for the plaintiff.

c. Two elements must be satisfied before RIL may be successfully invoked:

   i. The instrument must be in the defendant's exclusive control; and

   ii. The event must normally not occur absent someone's negligence.

   1) *See Larson v. St. Francis Hotel*, where the plaintiff was injured by a chair that was thrown out of the defendant's hotel window. The threshold test was not met when the plaintiff failed to show that (i) the defendant had exclusive control over the instrumentality, since guests at the defendant's hotel could have thrown the chair out of the window; and (ii) that absent the defendant's negligence, the event normally would not occur, since the event could occur even if the defendant exercised all reasonable care, besides posting a security guard in each room.

d. In meeting the threshold test, the plaintiff may invoke common sense and experience.

   i. *See McDougald* (plaintiff) *v. Perry*, where common sense dictated that but for the defendant's negligence, a tire from his truck would not have come loose, striking the plaintiff's windshield.

e. Once successfully invoked, the plaintiff's burden of proving breach is significantly lightened. However, the defendant may still rebut the presumption of negligence.

2. The Three Approaches to RIL

   a. *Permissive inference approach:* the jury may accept or reject the RIL inference.

   b. *Presumption and shift of the ultimate burden of proof approach:* this approach requires the defendant to prove by a preponderance of all of the evidence that the injury not caused by his negligence.

   c. *Mandatory presumption approach:* raises a presumption that a jury *must accept*, unless the defendant proves otherwise.

3. Group *Res Ipsa Loquitur*

   a. In some jurisdictions, where group RIL is accepted, when the plaintiff knows that one of a group of the defendants was responsible for an injury, but is not certain which one, the plaintiff may sue all the defendants jointly.

   b. *See Ybarra v. Spangard* (Cal. 1944), where the plaintiff, unaware of who caused an injury during surgery that lead to pain in the plaintiff's shoulder upon his awaking, sued all of the doctors. The plaintiff invoked RIL and the defendants plead that RIL may not be applied, since the harm could not have arisen from the act of any single the defendant. Held: RIL applies because the injury was in the defendants' *exclusive collective control* and such injury does not normally arise absent negligence.

D. SUMMARY FOR PROVING BREACH

1. The plaintiff must:

   a. Offer *direct evidence;*

   b. If direct evidence is lacking, offer *indirect (circumstantial) evidence;*

   c. If there is no probative evidence, *res ipsa loquitur* may be invoked in certain cases (*see infra.*).

2. In *slip and fall cases*, there are four ways of proving breach:

   a. By proving that *the defendant's employee caused the hazard*;

   b. By showing that the defendant had *actual notice* of a hazard (usually with direct evidence);

   c. By show that the defendant had *constructive notice* (usually with circumstantial evidence); or

   d. By proving a dangerous *mode of operation.*

VII. CAUSATION

A. CAUSE-IN-FACT

1. *Sine Qua Non*

   a. In order for a defendant to be held liable in tort, the plaintiff must prove causation.

   b. First, cause-in-fact (*sine qua non* causation) must be established. The test is whether the plaintiff would have been injured had the defendant not done the negligent act.

      i. *See Perkins v. Texas and New Orleans Railway Co.*, where the plaintiff was unable to recover for her husband's death, since she was unable to prove that: (i) the train's violation of the speed limit was the *sine qua non* cause of his death; (ii) the train's speeding prevented it from stopping in time, because even if it had been going twelve miles per hour slower, the 1,250 foot long train still would have been unable to stop; and (iii) the train's speeding deprived the defendant's car from the extra moment to cross the tracks, since the car may have been going anywhere between three to twenty five miles per hour, rendering this theory pure speculation.

2. Proof of Causation

   a. Causation must be proven with the ***preponderance of the evidence***.

      i. *See Reynolds* (plaintiff) *v. Texas and Pac. Railway Co.*, where the plaintiff was injured while rushing up the stairs of the defendant's unlit railroad platform. Held: the defendant was liable for not having the stairs lit at the platform, even though the plaintiff's negligence in rushing up the stairs could have been the but-for cause of the injury, since not having the stairs lit greatly multiplied the chances of injury. The defendant's negligence was more than fifty percent likely to have caused the plaintiff's injury.

b. The subsequent timing between one factor and another is not enough to establish the requisite proof of causation.

 i. *See Kramer Service, Inc. v. Wilkins* (plaintiff), where the fact that cancer subsequently appeared in an area cut by glass due to the defendant's negligence was too attenuated to prove causation, particularly since even the plaintiff's experts said that the chances that a cut could cause cancer were one in one hundred.

3. Concurrent Causes

a. When there is more than one cause of an injury, the agent of either cause is fully responsible for the injury.

b. This is true even when the defendant's actions on their own would not have passed the "but-for" test. *See Hill v. Edmonds* (plaintiff's contributory negligence does not bar him from recovery).

c. When the defendant's breach of duty was a concurrent cause of the plaintiff's harm, and when this cause fails the *but-for test*, courts may find causation-in-fact satisfied if the factor was a **substantial and material cause**.

 i. *See Anderson v. Minneapolis R.R.* (defendant), where a fire that was sparked by the defendant's breach of duty merged with another fire of unknown cause, damaging the plaintiff's home. The plaintiff sued for negligence and the defendant argued that because the other fire would have burned down the plaintiff's home anyway, but-for cause was not satisfied. Held: because the defendant's breach of duty was a **substantive factor** in bringing about the plaintiff's harm, the cause-in-fact test is satisfied.

 ii. *N.B.*: the *substantial factor test* would release a defendant from liability when his act only slightly contributes to the damage (*e.g.*, throwing a lit match into an already raging forest fire).

B. PROXIMATE CAUSE

1. Unforeseeable Consequences

a. Because so many causes may be considered causes-in-fact, public policy must draw a line somewhere. *Atlantic Coast Line Railroad Co. v. Daniels.*

b. Thus, even when the defendant is negligent, he is not liable for damages caused to another's property when those damages were **unforeseeable**.

 i. *See Ryan v. New York Central R.R. Co.*, where the defendant's negligence led to a fire on his property that eventually spread to and damaged the plaintiff's property. Because the wind, heat, and other circumstances leading to the spreading were so unusual, the defendant was not liable for negligence.

ii.   *N.B.*: today, plaintiffs in NY have a cause of action when the damage comes from neighboring property.

c.   Under the ***thin skull rule***, a defendant is liable for *all* personal bodily injuries resulting from his negligence, including injuries due to a plaintiff's *unforeseeable sensitivity*, when at least *some* of that injury was foreseeable.

d.   Some jurisdictions apply the ***thin skull property rule***, or the Polemis *rule*, where the defendant is liable not only for all bodily injuries, but also, for all damages to property, when (i) at least some damage was *foreseeable;* and (ii) there was a *direct chain of events*, without superseding causes.

    i.   *See In re Arbitration Between Polemis and Furness Withy and Co., Ltd.*, where the defendants were held liable for *all damages* directly resulting from the defendants' dropping of a plank on a ship, including the damages resulting when a spark *unforeseeably* ignited a fire due to petrol vapors, since (i) there was some foreseeable damage (*i.e.*, a broken plank) and (ii) the unforeseeable damages resulted from an uninterrupted chain of events.

e.   Other jurisdictions have repudiated the Polemis *approach*, and have adopted the "*Wagon Mound* approach," which allows for liability for *foreseeable property damage only*.

    i.   *See Overseas Tankship (UK) Ltd.* (plaintiff) *v. Morts Dock and Engineering Co., Ltd.*, where the plaintiff's wharf was ***foreseeably and nominally damaged*** by the defendant's freighter's oil discharge and later ***unforeseeably destroyed*** when cotton floating in the water caught fire. Under *Polemis*, the foreseeable initial damage would be enough to establish liability for the later unforeseen damages. Held: the *Polemis* rule is "inherently unjust" and the defendant is not liable; judgment for the plaintiff is reversed.

f.   Under the *Palsgraf* foreseeable plaintiff rule, foreseeability also factors into *who* may sue.

    i.   *See Palsgraf* (plaintiff) *v. Long Island R.R. Co.* (Cardozo, J.) where the defendant's employees, helping a passenger onto a train, caused a package to fall, leading to the explosion of fireworks. This caused a scale to fall on and injure the plaintiff, who was standing at the other end of a platform. Held: because the employees had no way of knowing that the package contained explosives, the explosion was unforeseeable. Furthermore, the plaintiff was an unforeseeable plaintiff, since no risk of injuring her was foreseeable. The defendant could not have had a duty to prevent an unforeseeable injury to an unforeseeable plaintiff. Judgment for the plaintiff is reversed.

ii. *Andrews dissent*: all people have a duty to protect all other people all of the time. Here, the defendant had a duty to protect the plaintiff and all of the passengers. Thus, the duty element is met, and it was breached. In analyzing proximate cause, the following factors must be considered: foreseeability, proximity in time and space, attenuation, the directness of cause and effect, the possibility of too many intervening acts, and superseding causes.

g. Today, the defendants are held liable for injuries and damages that are proximately caused by their negligence, and the main factor used in determining proximate cause is *foreseeability*: defendants are liable for *foreseeable risks* when the burden of eliminating the risk is outweighed by the risk and its magnitude.

2. Intervening Acts and Superseding Causes

a. An *intervening act* is an act that falls in the line of events between an event and an injury, altering the chain of events that might have connected wrongful conduct to an injury.

b. When an intervening act is sufficiently unusual and unforeseeable, it becomes a *superseding cause*. When intervening acts, such as the plaintiff's own conduct, become superseding causes, the defendant is exonerated of liability. *See Yun v. Ford Motor Co.*

c. However, when an intervening act is foreseeable, is it not a superseding cause and the actor is liable.

d. One relatively dispositive test in measuring whether an intervening act is foreseeable is when rules and customs are established to prevent the act from occurring.

i. *See Derdiarian* (plaintiff) *v. Felix Contracting Corp.*, where the defendant, a general contractor, was liable for injuries to the plaintiff, his employee, when the defendant failed to erect a safety barricade around the plaintiff's work station to protect him from oncoming traffic. When a nearby driver had an epileptic seizure, his car hit the site, causing sealing material to burn the plaintiff. The defendant's defense—the driver's epileptic seizure was an unforeseeable superseding cause—was without merit, since the barricades, as *required by custom*, were designed to protect against this very kind of car accident.

e. Generally, because criminal and malicious acts are considered to be unforeseeable, intervening malicious acts are superseding causes.

i. *See Watson* (plaintiff) *v. Kentucky and Indiana Bridge and R.R. Co.*, where the court held that maliciously dropping a match over gas spilled when a train derailed would be a superseding act that would render the defendant not liable.

3. Rescue Doctrine

a. Under the rescue doctrine, a party that negligently places another in peril is deemed to owe a duty of care to anyone who may attempt to rescue the imperiled party.

b. The doctrine lightens rescuers' burden of proving negligence.

c. For an actor to fit within the categories covered by the "rescue doctrine," he must show the following elements:

   i. Negligence *caused peril* to the person rescued;

   ii. The peril was *imminent;*

   iii. A reasonable prudent person would have concluded that there was *danger present;* and

   iv. The rescuer was *not grossly negligent.*

d. Once these elements are met, the rescue doctrine applies and the following occurs:

   i. The plaintiff rescuer is permitted to sue the defendant whose breach of duty towards the injured party is transferred to the plaintiff;

   ii. The defendant may not raise A/R; and

   iii. The defendant may not argue that the rescue was a superseding cause. Rather, it is considered foreseeable.[13]

e. Once the rescue doctrine applies, the plaintiff must prove:

   i. Duty towards the original party;

   ii. Breach of that duty;

   iii. Causation (proving the rescue doctrine substitutes here); and

   iv. Damages.

f. *See McCoy* (plaintiff) *v. American Suzuki Motor Corp.*, where a car manufactured by the defendant flipped over on a highway and the plaintiff, while rescuing the driver, was struck and injured by a car. The plaintiff sued the defendant for negligence, invoking the duty to rescue. The defendant argued that the duty to rescue may not be invoked in products liability law, since that area of the law has been codified by statute, which has not included the doctrine. Held: even when the rescue doctrine is invoked, proximate cause must be proved. Since the plaintiff could prove that a rescuer's injury while rescuing the driver of a car that flipped over was foreseeable, this question needs to go to a jury. Reversed and remanded.

   i. *N.B.*: note the similar underlying public policy in the **rescue doctrine** and the **Good Samaritan doctrine**. In the rescue doctrine, the defendant is unable to invoke assumption of the risk as a defense to his injury to a rescuer; in the Good Samaritan doctrine, the injured cannot sue the rescuer for negligence.

---

[13] According to Justice Cardozo, "Danger invites rescue."

4.   Public Policy: the Dram Shop Acts

    a.   Many states have passed Dram Shop Acts, which make a host liable for injuries caused by his guests if the host serves alcohol to the guests when the guest is visibly intoxicated.

        i.   Some Dram Shop Acts limit the liability of the host to only when the host knows that the guest will be driving.

        ii.   Others allow for liability for *any* injury caused by a guest's intoxication.

    b.   *Majority approach*: commercial hosts are liable for serving alcohol to *all guests*; social hosts are liable for serving alcohol *only to minors*.

    c.   *Minority approach*: both social and commercial hosts are liable for serving alcohol to all guests.

        i.   This is the approach adopted in NJ.

        ii.   *See Kelly* (plaintiff) *v. Gwinnell* (N.J. 1984), where the court held that social hosts are henceforth liable to parties injured by their visibly intoxicated guests, whether they are majors or minors, when the host served the guest alcohol knowing that the guest would be driving.

VIII.   DAMAGES

A.   DAMAGES FROM PERSONAL INJURIES AND MITIGATION

1.   Introduction

    a.   To win a judgment, the plaintiffs must prove both **damage** (some kind of injury or harm) and **damages** (the amount of money they are entitled to receive from the defendant).

    b.   There are two kinds of damages that accrue both before and after trial:

        i.   **General damages**: physical pain and emotional suffering.

        ii.   **Special (consequential) damages**: lost wages and medical bills.

    c.   In the appropriate case, there is also **property damage**.

    d.   Because plaintiffs must prove future damages in order to receive them, they often wait until just before the SL expires before filing suit in order to have more evidence for determining damages with certainty.

2.   Personal Injuries

    a.   **Remittitur** is the power of the judge to force the plaintiff to accept an award less than that awarded by the jury when the judge considers the jury award to be excessive.

    b.   Remittitur is not necessary when the jury awards damages within what it is permitted to find, even when those damages may seem excessive.

        i.   *See Anderson* (plaintiff) *v. Sears, Roebuck and Co.*, where the defendant's heater malfunctioned, injuring the plaintiffs and burning their home. The jury awarded over $2 million to husband, wife and daughter. The defendant moved for remittitur. Held: because the damages were within what the jury was allowed to find, and because the injuries, especially those sustained by the daughter, were severe, leading to emotional and physical pain for the rest of her life, the damages were not excessive. Motion for remittitur denied.

3.   Collateral Source Rule

    a.   When the plaintiff receives collateral sources to cover his costs or damages, the damages awarded are not to be reduced.

    b.   Rationale: the defendant should not benefit from the plaintiff's foresight and industry.

        i.   *See Montgomery Ward and Co., Inc. v. Anderson* (plaintiff), where the plaintiff received a 50 % discount from the hospital following her injury. Nevertheless, her damages were not reduced: collateral sources do not affect the judgment awarded.

    c.   The collateral source rule is the majority approach today.

4.   Mitigation of Damages

    a.   Mitigation of damages is required when an ordinary, prudent person would mitigate in like circumstances.

    b.   This does not always mean undergoing surgery to mitigate otherwise permanent injuries, especially when the surgery implicates high risks or costs. *Zimmerman v. Ausland.*

    c.   If a party fails to mitigate, he may not recover the difference between the present injury and its mitigation (through having either avoided aggravation or reduced overall injury).

B.   **PUNITIVE DAMAGES**

1.   Introduction

    a.   The purposes of punitive damages are as follow:

        i.   The *punishment of the tortfeasor*;

        ii.   *Specific deterrence* (deterrence of the particular tortfeasor); and

        iii.   *General deterrence* (deterrence of other potential tortfeasors).

    b.   Punitive damages are applied to aggravated forms of misconduct. The plaintiff must prove *recklessness* or *intent.*

        i.   Generally, gross negligence does not warrant punitive damages.

        ii.   Thus, some lawyers will deliberately frame causes of action as based on intentional torts, rather than on negligence.

c. Punitive damages are usually paid directly to plaintiffs. However, some states require all or a portion of punitive damages to be paid directly to the state or to some fund.

    i. *See Cheatham v. Pohle*, where the court held that funneling 75 % of punitive damages to a state fund was not unconstitutional, since the purpose of punitive damages was to punish the defendant, not to compensate the plaintiff.

2. Due Process

a. Punitive damages are often criticized for having the same effects of criminal statutory fines, but without having the same safeguards.

b. The Supreme Court, in *BMW v. Gore* (1996), has therefore developed a three-prong test that assures the constitutionality of punitives, which must not significantly eclipse:

    i. Civil fines imposed in like circumstances;

    ii. The reprehensibility of the defendant's act; and

    iii. Compensatory damages.

c. The Supreme Court has refined this test by holding that no more than a one-to-nine ratio of compensatory to punitive damages may be awarded.

    i. *See State Farm Mutual Automobile Ins. Co.* (defendant) *v. Campbell* (U.S. 2003), where the Court held that the $2.6 million compensatory to $145 million punitives against State Farm was unconstitutionally excessive. Reversed and remanded.

IX. DEFENSES

A. CONTRIBUTORY AND COMPARATIVE NEGLIGENCE

1. Introduction

a. As we have already examined, the defenses to the IT's include consent and the non-consensual privileges (self-defense, defense of others, and the defense and recovery of property).

b. The defenses to negligence include: contributory and comparative negligence and the assumption of the risk (A/R).

2. Contributory Negligence

a. Contributory negligence refers to a plaintiff's failure to exercise ordinary care over himself. The same negligence elements against the defendant are applied to the plaintiff.

b. If the defendant successfully proves all of the elements of contributory negligence, then this affirmative defense bars the plaintiff from recovery.

        i.   *See Butterfield v. Forrester* (King's Bench 1809), where the plaintiff, by riding his horse too fast, was contributorily negligent when trying to go around an obstruction negligently left in the road by the defendant. Held: because the plaintiff's contributory negligence was a factor bringing about his harm, he may not recover.

    c.   Over the years, the courts have become more flexible and have developed the following tests:

        i.   ***Substantial factor test***: the jury will not find contributory negligence if it finds that the plaintiff's negligence was not a substantial factor in bringing about his harm.

        ii.   ***Last clear chance doctrine***: the plaintiff may recover, even when he was contributorily negligent, when he can show that the defendant: (i) had the *last clear chance*, or opportunity to prevent the harm from coming about; but he (ii) failed to use reasonable care in doing so.

            1)   *See Davies v. Mann*, where the plaintiff, steering his fettered donkey onto a road, was struck by the defendant's wagon, killing the donkey. Held: because the defendant could have avoided the accident upon seeing the plaintiff, he had the *last clear chance* and the plaintiff may therefore recover.

3.   Comparative Negligence

    a.   Many states have completely replaced contributory negligence with comparative negligence, which allows the plaintiff to recover proportionately according to the degree of his negligence.

    b.   There are two approaches to comparative negligence against a single the defendant:

        i.   ***Pure comparative negligence***. The plaintiff may always recover the percentage of his damages corresponding to the defendant's fault.

        ii.   ***Modified comparative negligence***

            1)   There are two approaches to modified comparative damages:

                a)   The plaintiff may only recover when the defendant's fault was greater than or equal to the plaintiff's fault (*i.e.*, when the defendant's share of the fault was 50 % or more);

                b)   The plaintiff may only recover when the defendant's fault was greater than the plaintiff's fault (*i.e.*, when the defendant's share of the fault was *greater* than 50%).

            2)   Unless the defendant's fault is greater than (or equal to) 50 %, the plaintiff may recover nothing (it has the same effect as contributory negligence).

c. Similarly, there are two approaches to comparative negligence against multiple the defendants:

    i. ***Pure comparative negligence*** states

        1) The plaintiff may always recover the percentage of his damages that corresponds to the defendants' fault, even if that percentage is less than 50 %.

        2) Example: if the plaintiff was 40 % at fault, and the first defendant and his codefendant were each 30 % at fault, the plaintiff may collect 60 % of his damages.

    ii. ***Modified comparative negligence*** states

        1) Cumulative approach:

           a) The plaintiff may only recover if his negligence was less than (or, in some states, less than or equal to) the defendants' combined negligence (*i.e.*, less than (or less than or equal to) 50 %).

           b) Example: if the plaintiff was 40 % at fault, and the first defendant and his codefendant were each 30 % at fault, the plaintiff may collect 60 % of his damages, since his 40 % fault is less than that of the cumulative 60 % of the defendants. .

        2) Non-cumulative approach:

           a) The plaintiff may only recover against defendants whose negligence is greater than (or, in some states, greater than or equal to) the plaintiff's negligence.

           b) Example: if the plaintiff was 40 % at fault, and the first defendant and his codefendant were each 30 % at fault, the plaintiff would collect nothing, since his 40 % share of the fault is greater than either defendant's 30 % share.

d. Forty six states have replaced contributory negligence with comparative negligence through statutes and through judicial decisions. *See, e.g., McIntyre v. Balentine* (adopting comparative negligence and abandoning the last clear chance doctrine and J/SL for Tennessee).

e. Effects of the Adoption of Comparative Negligence on Other Doctrines

    i. Last Clear Chance Doctrine

        1) Since this rebuttal to contributory negligence is no longer needed, the last clear doctrine has been abolished in many states.

        2) However, the tests used in determining whether the defendant had the last clear chance continue to be used in apportioning his degree of fault.

    ii. Joint and Several Liability (J/SL*)*

      1) Many states that have adopted comparative negligence have abolished J/SL.

      2) Instead, they use the same tests in determining the plaintiff's comparative negligence in also determining each defendant's particular share of the fault.

B. **ASSUMPTION OF RISK (A/R)**

  1. Express Assumption of the Risk

    a. When a party assumes the risk through signing a contract, he is precluded from later suing a defendant if the risk materializes, *unless*:

      i. The contract where he assumed the risk resulted from ***unequal bargaining power***;

      ii. The defendant acted with ***wanton*** or ***reckless negligence***; or

      iii. An area of the ***public interest*** (common carriers, hospitals, and other essential services) was involved.

    b. *See Seigneur v. National Fitness Institute, Inc.* (defendant), where the plaintiff was unable to recover against the defendant when her shoulder muscle was torn at the defendant's fitness facility, since (i) her exculpatory clause was not the result of unequal bargaining power; (ii) the defendant was not grossly, wantonly, or recklessly negligent; and (iii) fitness institutes are not core institutions of the public interest.

  2. Implied Assumption of the Risk

    a. A/R may be implied when the following three-part test is met:

      i. The plaintiff ***knew of the risk*** involved;

        1) This is a subjective element that is not concerned with the reasonable, prudent person; the plaintiff must have *actually known* of the risk.

        2) The best way to establish this is through the plaintiff's *admission*.

      ii. The plaintiff ***appreciated the magnitude*** of the risk; and

      iii. The plaintiff ***voluntarily assumed the risk***.

        1) *See Rush v. Commercial Realty Co.*, where the A/R defense failed, since the plaintiff did not "voluntarily assume the risk" when going to a privy used as a restroom; he was forced to use the privy when "nature called."

  3. The effect of the A/R on the plaintiffs in states that have abolished contributory negligence varies.

    a. State statutes and judicial decisions that have adopted comparative negligence usually address how A/R will be dealt will in the state.

b.   Some states treat A/R as though it were contributory negligence, thus *barring the plaintiff from recovery.*

c.   Other states treat A/R in the same way as comparative negligence

    i.   *See Blackburn v. Dorta* (Fl. 1977), where the Fl. Supreme Court held that express and implied A/R was to henceforth have the same effect as comparative negligence: it would mitigate the defendant's recovery.

4.   The Different Kinds of Assumption of the Risk in Florida and in Other States

a.   Express Assumption of the Risk

    i.   The A/R is express in releases and other contractual provisions where the potential plaintiff expressly agrees to assume the risks.

b.   Implied Assumption of the Risk

    i.   Primary Assumption of the Risk

        1)   The primary assumption of the risk applies to when there is no duty.

        2)   Example: a party assumes the risk of being jostled about in an aircraft by winds. The A/R is no defense because the airline never had a duty of preventing the jostling about to begin with.

    ii.   Secondary Assumption of the Risk

        1)   Pure Assumption of the Risk

            a)   Pure A/R applies when the plaintiff goes into a situation knowing, appreciating, and voluntarily assuming a risk in a way that is *reasonable.*

            b)   Example: running into a burning building to save a child.

            c)   In these cases, the A/R is no defense.

        2)   Qualified Assumption of the Risk

            a)   Qualified A/R applies when the plaintiff goes into a situation knowing, appreciating, and voluntarily assuming a risk in a way that is *unreasonable.*

            b)   Ex.: running into a burning building to save a book or some other object.

            c)   In these cases, A/R *is* a defense.

X.   PARTIES THAT MAY BE HELD LIABLE

A.   JOINT TORTFEASORS: LIABILITY AND JOINDER OF DEFENDANTS

1.   When Joint and Several Liability Applies

a.   Introduction

        i.   We previously saw that joint and several liability (J/SL) applied when *res ipsa loquitur* was invoked, but the plaintiff could not prove which of multiple defendants caused the harm. *Ybarra v. Spangard.*

        ii.   In this section, we will explore four other situations under which J/SL may apply.

    b.   Determining Which Party Caused the Harm

        i.   When it is clear that one of a group of the defendants caused harm, but it is not clear which one, all may be ***jointly and severally liable*** (J/SL).

           1)   *See Summers v. Tice* (defendant) (Cal. 1948), where the defendants argued that, because the plaintiff could not prove which defendant's shot caused the plaintiff's eye injury, neither was liable because the plaintiff did not prove but-for cause. Held: since it is clear that one of the defendants was the cause of the injury, one or both are liable; the burden is on each the defendant to show that he was not the cause; otherwise, they are J/SL. The burden shifts to the defendants, who may untangle the facts.

        ii.   Carried to its logical conclusion, *Summers* allows an entire industry to be held liable to the plaintiff, when it is clear that some member of that industry caused the plaintiff's injury, but when it is not clear as to which one.

           1)   *See Sindell v. Abbott Laboratories* (Cal. 1980), where each company marketing the drug that caused the plaintiff's health problems was liable for its market share of the drug, even though only 90% of the companies that could have sold the drug to the plaintiff's mother were in the suit, and it was thus possible that none of them caused the plaintiff's injury.

    c.   Common Acts of Negligence

        i.   J/SL also applies when several actors are engaged in a *common act of negligence.*

        ii.   *See Bierczynski v. Rogers* (plaintiff), where the defendant argued that he should not be liable for the plaintiff's injuries, since it was Race, not the defendant, who had collided with and injured the plaintiff. Held: because both the defendant and Race were engaged in a common act of negligence (racing on a public way), both are jointly and severally liable to the plaintiff. But for the defendant's negligence, the plaintiff would not have been injured.

    d.   In addition, J/SL may be used in cases involving employer/employee and master/servant relationships.

  2.   Joint and Several Liability in Comparative Negligence States

a. Some states that have adopted comparative negligence still apply J/SL.

    i. *See Coney* (plaintiff) *v. J.L.G. Industries, Inc.*, where the defendant was held J/SL for injuries caused to the plaintiff when the plaintiff fell from the defendant's platform: comparative negligence is used to determine the plaintiff's comparative fault, not each the defendant's comparative fault.

    ii. *N.B.*: however, the first defendant may recover against the codefendant in a **contribution and indemnity suit** (*see infra.*), unless the codefendant is insolvent.

b. In other states, the adoption of comparative negligence eliminates J/SL.

    i. Rationale: since these states have already become accustomed to apportioning the plaintiff's fault, they apply the same calculus to each of the defendants.

    ii. *See Barlett* (plaintiff) *v. New Mexico Welding Supply, Inc.*, where the plaintiff was unable to collect the entire judgment against the defendant, who was only 30 % at fault, because NM abolished J/SL upon adopting comparative negligence. Since the codefendant, who was principally responsible for the accident, was "nowhere to be found," the plaintiff was able to recover only 30 %.

B. VICARIOUS LIABILITY

1. Introduction

a. Vicarious liability is the liability of a supervisory party for the acts of a subordinate. Employers, for example, are said to be vicariously liable for the acts of their employees.

b. The doctrine of *respondeat superior* (*Lat.*, "let the superior answer") points to vicarious liability, and holds that a master or principal is *vicariously liable* for the negligence of his employees or agents, even when he was not himself negligent.

c. *Respondeat superior* is thus in many ways like SL: an employer is held liable, *regardless of his faultlessness*.

d. There are two elements to *respondeat superior* vicarious liability:

    i. The damage was *actually and proximately caused* by an employee's negligence; and

    ii. The employee was working *within the scope of his employment or agency*, which includes both:

        1) *Work done for the employer* by the employee; and

        2) *Personal work* interconnected with the work done for the employer.

2. The Going and Coming Rule

a. The "going and coming rule" is an exception to the scope of employment rule.

b. When an employee is going and coming to work, he is not considered to be *within the scope of employment* (and the employer thus cannot be held liable for damages caused), *unless:*

   i. The negligence is triggered by a work incident and it is foreseeable that the employee will cause damage while coming or going to work.

      1) *See Bussard v. Minimed, Inc.* (defendant), where the defendant's employee, having left work while dizzy from insecticide sprayed at the work place, later collided with the plaintiff's car. Because the damage was foreseeable, the defendant employer was liable to the plaintiff for the injuries caused.

   ii. The employee is going or coming to work while on a company errand for the employer, even if the employee is on a *detour*.

      1) There is, however, a limit as to certain detours that take an employee *out of the scope of employment. O'Shea v. Welch.*

      2) Such detours are known as ***frolics***.

      3) The factors considered in determining whether a detour was a frolic include:

         a) How long the diversion took; and

         b) Whether it was related to work or to purely personal interests.

3. Independent Contractors

   a. Unlike employees, independent contractors are not given specific directions on how to do their work.

   b. Rather, they are asked to achieve a certain result, *regardless of how they go about doing it.*

   c. Employers of independent contractors are not liable for the negligence of those contractors.

      i. *See Murrell v. Goertz,* where the employer of a newspaper carrier was not liable for the negligence of the carrier towards a plaintiff that was struck by the carrier, because the carrier operated under broad guidelines outside of the control of the employer.

   d. The justification of this rule: to hold an employer liable for the acts or omissions of one over whom he had no control would be a *miscarriage of justice.*

   e. However, employers of independent contractors *can be held liable for their **direct negligence*** over acts and omissions that they control.

i.   Example: hiring a contractor that the employer should have reasonably known to be negligent.

f.   In addition, employers could be held vicariously liable for ***non-delegable duties***, such as assuring safety in one's car.

     i.   *See Maloney v. Rath*, where an employer is held vicariously liable for the negligence of her independent mechanic contractor. The general rule that employers are *not vicariously liable* for the negligence of their contractors does not apply when the question involves a non-delegable duty, such as the duty to maintain safe brakes.

C.   CONTRIBUTION AND INDEMNITY

1.   Contribution

a.   Under the old common law, a defendant was not entitled to contribution from a codefendant, even if the codefendant was simultaneously responsible for the plaintiff's injury.

b.   Under the intermediate common law, a defendant could recover 50 % of damages from his codefendant.

c.   Under the modern law, especially in states that have grown comfortable in allocating percentages of fault through comparative negligence, a defendant may recover whatever a codefendant's proportional share in damages was.

     i.   However, in states that have not adopted comparative negligence, the *per capita* ("by the head") system is used.

d.   Contribution is allowed in forty nine states, and is generally allowed only in negligence cases (intentional torts are barred).

e.   Elements of contribution:

     i.   Both the defendants are held liable through either:

          1)   The plaintiff's proving both parties' negligence in a single lawsuit;

          2)   A defendant's impleading of a codefendant; or

          3)   A defendant's suing a codefendant in a separate action.

     ii.   One defendant paid more than his proportionate share of the judgment.

f.   There are three approaches as to who pays the price of an insolvent defendant:

     i.   One defendant takes the full brunt of a codefendant's insolvency (J/SL approach);

     ii.   The plaintiff takes the full brunt of a codefendant's insolvency (the approach when J/SL is abolished);

        iii.   One defendant pays a codefendant's share in proportion to his percent of liability in comparison with that of the plaintiff.

            1)   Example: suppose the plaintiff was 20 % at fault, the defendant was 40 % at fault, and the codefendant was 40 % at fault.

            2)   The defendant, in addition to paying his own 40 % share of the plaintiff's damages, will pay two thirds of the codefendant's share of the damages; the plaintiff will pay the remaining one third.

2.   Indemnity

    a.   Indemnity is a contract **shifting liability from a defendant to another party** who is legally responsible to the defendant.

    b.   The common law recognized the right of indemnity in several relationships, such as that of an employer with his employees.

    c.   When the right of indemnity is recognized, then when one member of the relationship who did not act tortiously is held liable for the tortious conduct of the other member of the relationship, the former has the right to collect the entire judgment from the latter.

        i.   For example, if a non-negligent employer is held *vicariously liable* for a negligent employee's torts, the employer has a *right of indemnity* against the employee.

        ii.   Similarly, if a seller or a service agent, through no negligence of his own, sells or installs a *defective product* and is sued by an injured purchaser, he has a *right of indemnity* against the manufacturer.

            1)   Example: an electrician installs a light switch that later sparks and injures the plaintiff. If the electrician is held liable for negligence, he has a *right of indemnity* against the manufacturer.

APPENDICES

INTENTIONAL TORTS SUMMARY

Introduction and Background	ITs are unique in that they always require a volitional act as well as intent that a particular result come about.	
	Elements: volition, intent, a resulting tortious act.	
The Seven Intentional Torts: elements	*Assault*	Volition, intent to cause fear of harmful contact, resulting fear.
	Battery	Volition, intent to cause harmful contact, resulting contact.
	False imprisonment	Volition, intent to confine, resulting confinement
	IIED	Outrageous act, intent or recklessness, proximate cause, severe ED
	Trespass to land	Volition, intent to enter land, resulting trespass
	Trespass to chattels	Volition, intent to interfere with chattel, resulting interference
	Conversion	Volition, intent to exercise dominion, resulting serious interference
Privileges	*Consensual privilege*	Actual or implied consent (implied-in-law, implied-in-fact).
	Non-consensual privilege	Self-defense
		Defense of others
		Defense of property
		Recovery of property

CULPABILITY SUMMARY CHART

← Culpability / fault →

← *Strict liability*	← *Unforeseeable (no tort)*	→ *Foreseeable (negligence)*	→ *Recklessness*	→ *Intentional torts*
The defendant is liable, regardless of fault.	On this side of negligence, the behavior was reasonable or the event unforeseeable.	On this side of negligence, a reasonable person would have taken steps to avoid the danger.	IIED.	Assault, battery, FI, IIED, trespass to land, trespass to chattels, conversion.
The defendant is liable.	The defendant is not liable.	The defendant is liable.	The defendant is liable.	The defendant is liable.
Does not require fault.	There is no fault.	The defendant is at fault.	The defendant is at fault.	The defendant is at fault.
Blasting, fireworks displays, oil drilling, etc.	Leaving one's golf clubs in a backyard. *Lubitz v. Wells.*	Failing to have an attendee on board a barge, thus causing it to sink. *Carroll Towing Co.*	Threats of physical injury and the destruction of one's business. *Siliznoff.*	Intentional harm to a person or to his land or property.

SUMMARY CHART OF SPECIAL RELATIONSHIPS

Duty to Rescue	J/SL	Indemnity	Vicarious liability
Employer/employee	Employer/employee	Employer against an employee	*Respondeat superior* (employer for employee)
Invitor/invitee (common carriers, innkeepers, etc.)	When it is not clear which one in a group of the defendants caused an injury	Seller or service agent against a manufacturer	General contractors for non-delegable duties
Husband/wife, parent/child	Joint tortfeasors engaged in a common act of negligence	The insured against his insurer	A parent for his child's torts (if established by statute)

CHAPTER 4.
CIVIL PROCEDURE

I. INTRODUCTION

A. INTRODUCTION TO THE LAW OF CIVIL PROCEDURE

1. Defining Civil Procedure

   a. Civil procedure refers to the methods and practices within litigation between private parties.

   b. It can be contrasted to the domain governing the substance or content of the law. It can similarly be contrasted to criminal procedure, which governs cases prosecuted on behalf of the public against a criminal defendant.

2. Alternatives to Civil Litigation

   a. Alternative dispute resolution (ADR);

   b. Negotiation between parties coming to their own settlements;

   c. Mediation under the guidance of a third party; and

   d. Arbitration – dispute resolution "without the law" by a third party that usually has the power to make binding decisions.

3. Getting into Federal Court

   a. There are three "doors" to get into federal district courts:

      i. The United States as a party (plaintiff or defendant);

      ii. Diversity of citizenship; and

      iii. Federal question jurisdiction.

         1) This includes: (i) federal courts' exclusive jurisdiction (*e.g.*, on patent and copyright law, bankruptcy law, etc.), and (ii) federal courts' concurrent jurisdiction (*e.g.*, on the interpretation of the Constitution).

         2) The subject matter may involve, for example, questions of diversity, including cases involving admiralty and maritime jurisdiction, public ministers, ambassadors or aliens.

   b. In addition, a case involving a question over which the federal courts hold concurrent jurisdiction can be appealed to the U.S. Supreme Court if it has exhausted the state court appeals process.

B. THE HIERARCHY OF SOURCES OF CIVIL PROCEDURAL LAW

1. The U.S. Constitution

   a. Art. VI, cl. 2 (Supremacy Clause): "This Constitution, and the Laws of the United States . . . and all Treaties made . . . under the Authority of the United States . . . shall be the supreme Law of the Land."

b. By "Laws," the Constitution is referring to federal laws. Thus, the Constitution and federal laws trump state laws and municipal ordinances.

2. Federal Statutes

    a. These are passed by Congress and are contained in 28 USC, which deals with the Judiciary and Judicial Proceedings.

    b. In addition, they cover federal question jurisdiction (§ 1331); diversity jurisdiction (§ 1332); removal jurisdiction (§1441); supplemental jurisdiction (§ 1367); venue (§ 1391) and the FRCPs.

3. Federal Rules of Civil Procedure (FRCP)

    a. These rules govern civil actions in the United States district courts (in contrast, the Federal Rules of Appellate Procedure deal with the appeals courts).

    b. Over half of the states have adopted the FRCP, either in their entirety or with some changes.

    c. The courts are not given ***the discretion to disregard the federal rules***, even if doing so would be in the interests of justice.

        i. *See Carlisle v. United States* (U.S. 1872), where Carlisle was declared guilty and sentenced for possession with intention to distribute marijuana. The court granted a motion for judgment of acquittal, even though it was filed by Carlisle's attorney one day late, because disregarding the motion would have been a "miscarriage of justice." The Sixth Circuit declared that the District Court did not have the authority to disregard Federal Rule of Criminal Procedure 29, even though Carlisle may have been innocent, and even if the error was due to attorney negligence. On appeal, the Supreme Court affirmed the Circuit Court decision.

4. Local Rules

    a. FRCP 83(a) states that each district court, "acting by a *majority of its district judges*, may, after giving appropriate public notice and an opportunity for comment, *make and amend rules* governing its practice."

    b. When the FRCP are silent on a matter, the local rules fill in the gaps.

    c. The numbering scheme in the FRCP must be used in the local rules.

    d. Failing to observe a local rule, such as a deadline for submitting a legal brief, can cause a party to lose rights.

    e. However, the failure to comply with a requirement of form (*e.g.*, the spacing between paragraphs in a legal brief) will not be enforced in a way that causes a party to lose rights when the non-compliance is not willful (FRCP 83(b)).

5. Standing Orders (FRCP 83b)

a. A standing order looks forward to and applies to all of the cases pending before a court.

b. Some judges issue standing orders on a subject when there is no applicable local rule.

c. Standing orders are binding only on parties appearing before the judge who wrote them.

d. One often must contact the clerk of the court to obtain them.

e. The non-willful non-compliance of standing orders, unlike that of local rules, the FRCP, and statutes, cannot cause the breaching party to lose rights; ignorance is an excuse.

6. Orders

a. An order is a written direction or command that may be interlocutory or final that is delivered by a court or judge.

b. Parties apply to the court or judge for an order by making motions which, unless made during a hearing or trial, must be made in writing (FRCP 7(b)).

C. THE STRUCTURE OF THE FEDERAL COURT SYSTEM

1. The U.S. Judicial branch

a. U.S. district courts may decide the following cases:

    i. Cases where the U.S. is a party;

    ii. Cases involving the Constitution, federal laws and treaties ("federal question jurisdiction"). This includes cases involving admiralty and maritime jurisdiction, public ministers, ambassadors or aliens.

    iii. Questions of diversity.

b. The Supreme Court has jurisdiction over:

    i. Exclusive jurisdiction:

        1) Conflicts between two or more states

    ii. Original jurisdiction:

        1) The Supreme Court has original jurisdiction over:

            a) Conflicts between two or more states;

            b) Conflicts involving ambassadors, public ministers, or consults of foreign states;

            c) Conflicts between the U.S. and a state;

            d) Actions or proceedings by a state against citizens of another state or against aliens.

        2) These involve a very small number of cases, usually less than one dozen per year.

2. The Three Tiers of the Federal Courts

	Supreme Court	Circuit Courts	District Courts
Who created it?	Constitution	Congress	Congress
How many are there?	One	Thirteen	About one hundred
Jurisdiction discretionary or mandatory?	Discretionary	Mandatory	Mandatory
Oral argument allowed?	Always	Usually (ct. decides)	Maybe

3. *En Banc* Decisions

    a. Whereas one judge decides cases in the district courts, decisions are made *en banc* in the Supreme Court and in panels of three in the circuit courts.

    b. More judges participate in the decision-making in the higher courts because of the importance of higher court decisions, which apply over a greater geographic range.

4. Oral Argument

    a. Always allowed in the Supreme Court (one half of an hour is given to each side).

    b. Usually allowed in circuit courts (FRAP 34), depending on whether:

        i. The appeal is frivolous;

        ii. The law has been authoritatively decided; and

        iii. The facts and legal arguments are adequately presented in the briefs.

II. SUBJECT MATTER JURISDICTION

A. INTRODUCTION

1. There is a presumption against jurisdiction in the federal courts.

2. If the Constitution or USC does not specifically grant subject matter jurisdiction (SMJ) to the federal courts, the case must go to state court.

Federal Courts	State Courts
Federal Courts are courts of *limited* jurisdiction	The primary state courts are courts of *general* jurisdiction
They can *only* hear cases that the Constitution *or* Congress say they may hear. Their SMJ is defined entirely by these two entities.	They can hear any case unless Congress *or* the state legislature states otherwise.

3. The lack of SMJ in a court may be raised as a defense anytime, including on appeal.

B. THE FIRST "DOOR" TO THE FEDERAL COURTHOUSE: THE UNITED STATES AS A PARTY

1. The district courts have original, concurrent jurisdiction over any actions commenced by the U.S. (28 USC § 1345).

   a. These cases account for 4.3% of cases initiated in federal courts.

   b. Is knowing that U.S. is your client enough to establish that you may commence this case in federal court? Generally, yes, although Congress could create exceptions.

2. The district courts similarly have original jurisdiction over actions commenced against the U.S. (§ 1346).

   a. Cases with the U.S. as a defendant account for 15 % of cases initiated in federal courts.

   b. Is knowing that you are filing a case against the U.S. enough to establish that the federal courts have jurisdiction over your case?

      i.   There are times when the district courts have original, exclusive jurisdiction over claims against U.S. (such as for money damages accruing after 1945 for injury or loss of property).

      ii. However, § 1346 limits jurisdiction to a number of cases. For example, a claim arising under the Constitution or congressional acts must not exceed $10,000 in order to be heard in the federal district courts.

      iii. Such cases may, however, be heard in state courts, but only if a statute permits state courts to hear cases against the U.S.

C. THE BIGGEST DOOR: FEDERAL QUESTION JURISDICTION

1. Introduction

   a. Federal courts are given SMJ over federal question cases because federal judges have expertise over the Constitution, federal laws and treaties.

b.   USC § 1331 grants district courts original jurisdiction over cases arising under the Constitution, laws, or treaties of the United States. This jurisdiction is concurrent with the state courts.

2.   The Well-Pleaded Complaint

     a.   A well-pleaded complaint is one that sufficiently sets forth: (i) a claim for relief, including grounds for a court's jurisdiction; (ii) a basis for the relief claimed; and (iii) a demand for judgment in a way that allows the defendant to respond to each of the issues presented.

     b.   In federal court, when the plaintiff is seeking federal question jurisdiction, the well-pleaded complaint must raise the *controlling issue of federal law*.

     c.   The claim stated in the complaint must arise under federal law; the defenses raised are irrelevant to determining whether the district court has federal question jurisdiction.

         i.   *See Louisville and Nashville Railroad Co. v. Mottley* (U.S. 1908), where the plaintiff sued the defendant for breach of contract for having rescinded the plaintiff's railroad passes. In the complaint, the plaintiff anticipated the defendant's affirmative defense: a federal statute required the defendant to rescind the passes. Since the only questions to be litigated—whether rescinding the passes violated a federal statute and whether the statute was unconstitutional—were federal, the plaintiff filed the case in federal court. The Supreme Court held, however, that the relevant question was the claim made by the plaintiff in the complaint, which in this case was a breach of contract claim over which the state courts had exclusive jurisdiction.

3.   Centrality of the Federal Question

     a.   When an issue arises under federal law, but other issues arise under state law, the district courts have federal question jurisdiction *only if the federal issue is central to the claim*.

         i.   *See Merrell Dow Pharm., Inc. v. Thompson*, where the plaintiff filed in state court a complaint invoking a federal statute and five other counts involving state law against a company whose drug caused birth defects. When the defendant removed the case to federal court, the plaintiff filed a motion to remand the case back to state court, which was denied. The Supreme Court held that, although a federal question was involved, there was no basis for federal jurisdiction over the matter, since Congress, in passing the law that was invoked, never intended for private actions for violations of the statute.

     b.   If the plaintiff files a complaint in federal court in which two claims arise under state law and only one claim arises under federal law, the court could dismiss the state law claims and hear only the federal claim.

4.   Jurisdiction of the Supreme Court

a. The Supreme Court has original, *exclusive* jurisdiction over litigation between two or more states (28 USC § 1251(a)).

b. The Supreme Court has original, *non-exclusive* jurisdiction over:

    i. Actions in which ambassadors, other public ministers, or consuls are parties;

    ii. Controversies between the U.S. and a state;

    iii. Actions by a state against citizens of another state or against aliens (28 USC § 1251(b)).

5. Jurisdiction of the district courts

a. The district courts have both *original* and *exclusive* jurisdiction over:

    i. Admiralty, maritime and prize cases (28 USC § 1333);

    ii. Bankruptcy cases (28 USC §1334);

    iii. Patent, plant variety and copyright cases (28 USC § 1338);

    iv. Federal antitrust cases (15 USC §§ 15-26).

b. The district courts have *original, concurrent* jurisdiction over:

    i. Cases in which ambassadors, other public ministers and consuls are parties (over which the Supreme Court also has original, non-exclusive jurisdiction);

    ii. Cases between in which a state is a party (over which the Supreme Court has original, non-exclusive jurisdiction);

    iii. Interpleader cases ("suits to determine a right to property held by a stakeholder [usually a disinterested third party] who is in doubt about ownership and who therefore deposits the property with the court to permit interested parties to litigate ownership").

    iv. Commerce and antitrust cases;

    v. Unfair competition;

    vi. Postal matters;

    vii. Internal revenue;

    viii. Civil rights actions;

    ix. Election disputes;

    x. Actions to compel an officer of the U.S. to perform a duty owned to a plaintiff;

    xi. All civil actions brought by an Indian tribe arising under the Constitution, laws or treaties of U.S. (§ 1362)

c. It appears that some of these statutes, such as § 1362, are redundant with § 1331, which states generally that the district courts have original jurisdiction of civil actions arising under federal laws.

        i.   However, in § 1331's original form, the district courts had jurisdiction only over claims demanding more than $10,000 in remedies.

        ii.   Thus, these other statutes, which do not set a minimum amount in controversy, are not redundant with the original wording of § 1331.

D. FEDERAL DIVERSITY JURISDICTION

1. Diversity Jurisdiction in Lawsuits Between Individuals

    a. Diversity jurisdiction cases comprise 20 % of the federal docket.

    b. The district courts have *original* and *concurrent* jurisdiction when *more than $75,000* is sought in a controversy between citizens of different states (this is the majority of cases). 28 USC § 1332(a)(1).

    c. The courts also have jurisdiction when the conflict is between: (i) citizens of a state and citizens of a foreign state; (ii) citizens of different states and in which citizens of a foreign state are additional parties; or (iii) a foreign state, as plaintiff, and citizens of a state or of different states (28 USC § 1332(a)(1)-(4)).

    d. However, even if the case involves claims of more than $75,000 and diversity among the parties, the case cannot go to federal court if it involves domestic relations or probate claims.

    e. The Rules of Federal Diversity Jurisdiction

        i.   The parties must be from different states, without regard to the citizenship or location of the judge or his court.

        ii.   Specifically, they must be *citizens*, not *residents*, of different states;

            1)   The key is *citizenship*, or *domicile*, that is, the state in which the subject has or once had a physical presence and in which he intends to remain indefinitely.

            2)   Contrast this to *residency*, which refers to the state in which the subject has occasionally resided or is temporarily living without the intent to remain there indefinitely.

                a)   *See Mas v. Perry*, where the court accepted Mrs. Mas's contention that her domicile was not in Louisiana, since she did not intend to remain there indefinitely.

        iii.   There must be *complete diversity* between the parties.

            1)   Federal diversity jurisdiction requires *all of the plaintiffs* to be *completely diverse* from *all of the defendants*.

            2)   Thus, a citizen of a state will be unable to bring a case under diversity jurisdiction if any single one of the defendants named in the complaint is a citizen of that same state, unless the plaintiff drops that defendant from the complaint.

                a)   The source of this rule is *Strawbridge v. Curtis*, a case that was dismissed from federal court because all of the plaintiffs were not diverse from all of the defendants.

3) However, an exception is established with respect to class action lawsuits, where complete diversity is not required (28 USC § 1332(d)).

    a) Rather, minimal diversity suffices. However, if greater than one-third of the members of all plaintiff classes and the primary defendants are citizens of the state in which the action was originally filed, the district court may decline to exercise jurisdiction.

    b) Other differences include amount of money in controversy.

4) Realignment

    a) If a plaintiff puts other plaintiffs on the defendant side in order to establish federal diversity, the court may "realign" the parties and only afterwards decide if there is truly diversity.

    b) For example, if a New York plaintiff sues a New Jersey plaintiff and places a New Jersey co-plaintiff on the defendant side in order to keep complete diversity, the court may realign the parties.

iv. The court must determine citizenship and complete diversity *at the time the complaint was filed.*

1) For example, if a plaintiff from California sued a defendant in Texas and, after filing the complaint, moved to Texas, the requirements for diversity would be met.

2) However, if it can be shown that on the day that the plaintiff filed the complaint, he did not intend to remain in California, the court will conclude that he was not a California citizen at the time the complaint was filed and therefore, the requirements for diversity were not met.

v. The amount in controversy must exceed $75,000.

1) The amount in controversy is what the plaintiff states in the complaint, but it must be possible "to a legal certainty" that the plaintiff can get over $75,000.

2) The defendant may thus raise several defenses against federal diversity jurisdiction (e.g., a statute caps the amount recoverable to less than $75,000).

3) A judge may dismiss the complaint if it is virtually impossible that a jury would award more than $75,000 (e.g., in a case in which the plaintiff sues for a minor insult).

4) However, if there is even the slightest chance that the plaintiff would be awarded more than $75,000, judge must exercise jurisdiction.

5)   The Amount in Controversy for Preventing Frivolous Cases

     a)   The general rule in the United States is that each party pays its own attorneys' fees,[14] but the loser pays the winner's costs (docket fees, court reporters, court appointed experts, interpreters, etc.).

     b)   Furthermore, in order to dissuade plaintiffs from asserting federal diversity jurisdiction by exaggerating the amount in controversy, federal courts *may deny costs* to the winning plaintiff and *may impose the costs* of the losing defendant on the plaintiff (28 USC § 1332(b)).

Jury's Verdict	*What the Plaintiff Must Pay*
Awards nothing	His own attorneys' fees; all costs.
Awards $75,000 or less	His own attorneys' fees; possibly, his own costs and those of the defendant.
Awards over $75,000	His own attorneys' fees.

6)   Aggregate Claims

     a)   Plaintiffs will sometimes try to add up individual claims in order to reach the required $75,000 amount in controversy.

     b)   It is not clear as to when various claims may be added together, but it appears that the plaintiff can add up *all claims* (even transactionally unrelated claims) to reach the required amount if all of the claims are *against the same defendant*.

         i)   For example, if the plaintiff injured the defendant in a $30,000 negligence claim, he can add an unrelated $50,000 breach of contract claim in order to exceed the $75,000 amount in controversy requirement.

     c)   However, if there are multiple parties on either side, aggregation of different claims generally is not allowed, even if the claims are transactionally related.

         i)   For example, if co-plaintiffs hold claims of $50,000 each against a common defendant for

---

[14] The policy behind this rule is to allow more the plaintiffs access to the courts. If the losing side were always obliged to pay the winner's attorneys' fees, then due to the often exorbitant costs of such fees in the United States, far fewer potential the plaintiffs would exercise their legal rights. It is worth noting that in many European countries, where attorneys' fees are generally lower, the losing party pays both parties' attorneys fees.

The American rule has many exceptions. For example, some states, as a penalty for bringing frivolous cases to court, or as a punishment for egregious violations, impose attorneys' fees of both parties on the losing party.

two different injuries, the amount in controversy requirement is not met.

d) Nevertheless, if multiple parties share a common claim, aggregation is permitted.

i) For example, if the plaintiff is injured by two co-defendants who cause him damages that exceed $75,000, the amount in controversy requirement is satisfied, since there is only one claim.

e) It is always easier to bring in additional claims to reach the amount in controversy requirement, provided they do not bring in additional parties.

2. Diversity Jurisdiction in Lawsuits Involving Legal Entities

a. Corporations

i. A corporation is an entity that acts as a person distinct from the shareholders who own it. It may issue stock, pay taxes and is liable for its own torts.

ii. For the purposes of 28 USC §§ 1332 (diversity) and § 1441 (removal), a corporation has citizenship in both:

1) The state of its *principal place of business* (which may be the location of either: (i) the headquarters, or "brain" of the corporation; or (ii) the main manufacturing center); and

2) The state where it is *legally incorporated*. USC § 1332(c)(1).

a) *See Randozzo*, where the judge dismissed a case with prejudice after the plaintiff failed to mention *both* the state of incorporation *and* the state of the primary place of business when alleging diversity.

3) (For insurers, it is the state where any of their insured are citizens).

iii. The location of a corporation's principal place of business is not necessarily that of its corporate headquarters; it may be that of a major manufacturing plant.

1) *See J.A. Olson Co. v. City of Winona* (1987), where the plaintiff sued in Mississippi federal court based on diversity jurisdiction. The court dismissed the case, holding that the plaintiff was in fact a citizen of Mississippi, even though its corporate headquarters were in Chicago, since the plaintiff's only manufacturing plant was in Mississippi, many decisions were made in Mississippi, and most of its employees were Mississippians.

2) If a plaintiff sues a defendant whose *headquarters* or *main manufacturing center* are located in the same state as the plaintiff, it would be safest to file the case in state court, since the defendant's citizenship is not clear.

b. Non-Incorporated Businesses

    i. Limited liability partnerships (LLP)

        1) An LLP has citizenship in all of the states in which its members are citizens.

    ii. Limited liability companies (LLC)

        1) LLC's are hybrids between LLP's and corporations.

        2) They are statutorily authorized in many states.

        3) Under the majority rule, their citizenship is determined like that of LLPs; it is based on the citizenship of their members.

            a) *See Belleville Catering Co. v. Champaign Market Place LLC*, where the plaintiff, calculating the defendant LLC's citizenship based on what it would have been had the defendant been a corporation, concluding that there was complete diversity. The court, calculating the defendant's citizenship based on the citizenship of all of its partners, held that the complete diversity requirement was not met.

3. The Exception for Domestic Relations and Probate Cases

a. Perhaps rooted in the English tradition where ordinary courts of law or equity did not handle family matters (these were handled by the ecclesiastical courts), American federal courts may refuse to hear family matters. Federal courts will also not take cases that seem to interfere with state probate claims.

b. This may be appropriate, since state courts tend to be in better touch with the local agencies that deal with probate and family issues (divorce, alimony and child custody).

c. The origins of this rule are not found in 28 USC § 1332, which governs diversity, but rather, in *Barber* (1859), which held that Congress did not intend for the federal courts to handle these cases.

    i. Later, *Ankerbrandt*, acknowledging that *Barber* may have been wrong, stated that since Congress did not annul *Barber* over for the last one hundred years, Congress has tacitly endorsed the decision.

d. Note that there is nothing in the domestic relations and probate exceptions that would prevent a plaintiff from bringing tort suit in federal court against, for example, a father who abuses a child he has custody over. Although family issues are related, the central tort claim can be brought into federal court.

E. **SUPPLEMENTAL JURISDICTION IN FEDERAL QUESTION CASES**

1. Introduction

a. Supplemental Jurisdiction

i.   Also known as ancillary or pendent jurisdiction, supplemental jurisdiction is codified under 28 USC § 1367.

ii.   Whenever a district court has original jurisdiction over a claim (federal question or diversity jurisdiction), all other claims arising under the same § 1367(a) "case or controversy" as the original claim can be heard in the district court, even if they do not have an independent basis for subject matter jurisdiction.

1)   *See United Mine Workers v. Gibbs (plaintiff)*, where the plaintiff accused the defendant of intentional interference with the plaintiff's contracts and of a concerted union plan against him. The plaintiff sued the defendant for violation of Labor Management Relations Act and included a state law claim for the defendant's malicious harm to the plaintiff's contracts. Because the state contract claim arose from the same core facts, or "case or controversy," as the federal claim, the Court allowed both to be tried in the federal courts.

b.   Pendent Parties Jurisdiction

i.   Pendent parties jurisdiction is jurisdiction to adjudicate a claim against a party who is otherwise not within court's jurisdiction, because the claim by or against that party arises from the same core facts of another claim that is properly before the court.

ii.   Pendent parties jurisdiction was limited in *Finley v. United States*, where Finley was barred from bringing a state torts action against new defendants (from which there was no diversity), even though this new claim arose under the same common core of facts of the original claim, which arose under a federal claim (the Federal Torts Claim Act) over which the District Courts had original, exclusive jurisdiction. The Court held that the District Courts did not have jurisdiction over the state claims, since there was no independent basis for jurisdiction (there was neither diversity nor a federal question). Pendant party jurisdiction was not allowed when only the federal question, not the additional claim, arose under federal law.

iii.   Congress overruled *Finley* with USC § 1367, which allows pendent parties jurisdiction *unless otherwise banned by statute*. "Such supplemental jurisdiction shall include claims that involve the joinder or intervention of additional parties."

iv.   However, with respect to federal diversity, § 1367(b) places several limits on pendent parties jurisdiction. Neither supplemental jurisdiction nor pendent parties jurisdiction may be used to circumvent the complete diversity requirement in cases founded on diversity jurisdiction.

When Supplemental Jurisdiction is Permitted

	In a Federal Question Case	*In a Diversity Case*
To Join a	Permitted. This is the most	There is no need, since in a

New Claim	compelling reason to join claims. Ex: codifying *Gibbs*.	diversity case, another claim against the same defendant will also be diverse and thus can be aggregated.
To Join a New Party	Permitted. Ex: *Finley* overruled by Congress.	Maybe; see § 1367 Example: the court may have PJ over the defendant, but not over the codefendant.

2. Courts have the discretion to decline jurisdiction over the state claim when:

    a. It raises a novel or complex issue of State law;

    b. It substantially predominates over the federal claim;

    c. The district court has dismissed all claims over which it has original jurisdiction; or

    d. For other compelling reasons. USC § 1367(c).

3. USC § 1367(d) deals with gifts to plaintiffs. If a plaintiff mistakenly believes that a case falls under supplemental jurisdiction, the statute of limitations is tolled.

    a. Rationale: unlike cases dismissed from federal court under federal question jurisdiction or federal diversity jurisdiction, here, the courts have a degree of discretion that plaintiffs cannot predict. Thus, it would not be their own fault if the case was dismissed.

4. Original Jurisdiction Distinguished

    a. Supplemental jurisdiction is different from original jurisdiction in that it provides a way for a federal court to hear a *claim* (a cause of action), not a *case* (a civil action). The case must still enter the federal court through one of the "front doors" (federal question, diversity, or United States as a party).

    b. While the federal courts generally do not have discretion in hearing cases under their original jurisdiction,[15] they may exercise some discretion in exercising supplemental jurisdiction.

F. SUPPLEMENTAL JURISDICTION IN DIVERSITY CASES

1. USC § 1367(b) limits when the district courts may exercise supplemental jurisdiction when they have original jurisdiction founded solely on 28 USC § 1332.

2. This sub-rule is for benefit of defendants, since it makes bringing them into federal court much more difficult.

---

[15] Exceptions: 28 USC § 1332(d) allows for the exercise of discretion in diversity jurisdiction in class action lawsuits.

3. Claims (causes of action) within a case with § 1332 diversity jurisdiction may not enter federal court if they are made by plaintiffs against defendants who were made parties under:

    a. Rule 14 (when the defendant or the plaintiff may bring in a third party);

    b. Rule 19 (joinder of persons needed for just adjudication);

    c. Rule 20 (permissive joinder of parties);

    d. Rule 24 (intervention);

    e. Or under anyone claiming to be joined to the action through Rule 19 or seeking to intervene as the plaintiff through Rule 24, when exercising such supplemental jurisdiction conflicts with § 1332 diversity requirements by destroying complete diversity.

4. Example: Alice, Betty, and Carol have a three-way collision. A's damages are $90,000 and B's are $25,000. A and B join as co-plaintiffs against Carol and their citizenship presents no problem for diversity jurisdiction. A's claim meets § 1332's amount in controversy requirement, but B's does not. Under the rules of aggregation, they cannot be added up. Can they be added together through §1367?

    a. Under § 1367(a), this is possible, but under § 1367(b), there is no supplemental jurisdiction over diversity cases when parties are joined through Rule 20, but 20 is about prohibiting federal jurisdiction when defendants, not plaintiffs, are added to the claim.

        i. Courts have disagreed, and the Supreme Court is looking at this issue. But if it allows it the claims to be aggregated, isn't it overruling the complete diversity rule?

        ii. Example: suppose B and C are from the same state. There would not be complete diversity, even though § 1367 would allow it.

        iii. In such a situation, wouldn't a judge be required not to hear the case since *Strawbridge v. Curtis* requires complete diversity?

    b. The Supreme Court has held that a federal court in a diversity case may exercise supplemental jurisdiction over additional plaintiffs whose claims *do not satisfy the amount-in-controversy requirement*, provided the claims are part of the same case as the claims of plaintiffs who do satisfy the requirement.

        i. *See Exxon Mobil Corp. v. Allapattah Services, Inc.* (2005), where the Court ruled that if the other elements of jurisdiction are present, and at least one plaintiff satisfies the amount in controversy requirement, 28 USC § 1367 permits supplemental jurisdiction over *all of the other plaintiffs' claims*, even if they are for less than the required amt in controversy.

    c. However, in order to join a co-plaintiff with a claim that does not exceed $75,000 under supplemental jurisdiction where jurisdiction of the original claim is based on diversity, the original claim must *exceed $75,000* and ***complete diversity must not be destroyed***. *Ortega v. Star-Kist Foods*.

    d.   Thus, a non-diverse party may *not* be joined. The *Exxon Mobil Corp. v. Allapattah Services, Inc.* Court went to great lengths to explain that it was not overruling *Strawbridge*.

G. REMOVAL JURISDICTION

1. Removal jurisdiction allows defendants to remove from state to federal court.

    a.   It must be a case that could have been brought to federal court in the first place.

    b.   Under the majority rule, a case may be removed no later than thirty days after receipt of the initial pleading by the first defendant.

        i.   It can be thirty days from the original pleading, or from an amended pleading that now has jurisdiction in federal cts when original pleading did not (for example, non-diverse defendants are dropped out)

        ii.   Exception: after one year has passed, a diversity action cannot be removed, even if the defendant receives a pleading that allows for diversity jurisdiction .

    c.   In some minority jurisdictions, later defendants may remove if they can get former defendants to agree, even if former defendants did not originally file for removal.

2. Generally, those cases over which the district courts have original jurisdiction may be removed.

3. Removal Procedures

    a.   Removal must take place within thirty days of when the defendant receives the complaint, or when the defendant receives the pleading that allows for removal (through creating federal SMJ).

    b.   The defendant may remove by filing a ***notice to remove*** and delivering all of the pleadings to the district court.

    c.   If the property procedures are followed and the district court has SMJ, then the remand is automatically granted. There are no pleadings or hearings.

    d.   However, if the courts lacks SMJ, any party or the court may then seek to have the case remanded to state court.

    e.   If the plaintiff seeks a remand for any other reason (*e.g.*, for a defect in the removal procedure, because it is a case that may not be removed, etc.), he has thirty days to file a ***motion for remand***.

    f.   Remanding, unlike removing, involves the judge, pleadings, and a court decision to determine a disputed issue of law.

4. There are some cases over which the federal courts do *not* have original jurisdiction, but which may nonetheless be removed to federal court:

    a. 28 USC § 1442 cases against federal officers or agencies; and

    b. 28 USC § 1443 civil rights cases (where the defendant feels that because of his race, he will not receive a fair trial in state court).

5. There are other cases over which district courts *do have jurisdiction*, but which nonetheless may not be removed to federal court:

    a. 28 USC § 1445 provides a list of these cases, which include cases brought under the Violence Against Women Act, workmen's compensation actions, etc.

    b. In these cases, the plaintiff has the advantage of not only being able to choose the court, but also being able to keep the case there.

    c. Furthermore, when the defendant in a diversity case is a citizen of the forum state, he may not remove to federal court, since the rationale of avoiding the jury prejudice against out-of-state parties would not apply to a defendant who is a citizen of the forum state.

III. PERSONAL JURISDICTION AND VENUE

A. INTRODUCTION

1. The Limits on Personal Jurisdiction

    a. Constitutional Limitations

        i. In order for a court to hear cases before it, the Constitution requires both ***adequate notice*** and ***nexus*** between the defendant and the forum state (see *infra.*, "Constitutional Limitations on *In Personam* Jurisdiction").

    b. Statutory Limitations

        i. If no statute grants the court the power to hear cases involving the parties in the case, there is no personal jurisdiction (PJ).

        ii. However, a statute does not create valid PJ unless it is within the limitations of the Constitution.

    c. Personal Jurisdiction in the Federal Courts

        i. Under FRCP 4(k), a federal court must analyze personal jurisdiction with all of the same rules that the courts of the state in which the federal court is located must follow.

2. Three Kinds of Personal Jurisdiction

    a. *In Personam* Jurisdiction

        i. Also termed "personal jurisdiction," *in personam* jurisdiction refers to a court's power to bring a person (as opposed to property) into its adjudicative process.

ii. Judgments are entitled to full faith and credit in all fifty states (art. IV, Constitution).

iii. Thus, if the forum state abided by the statutory and constitutional limitations on PJ and the plaintiff is awarded a judgment, the plaintiff can enforce the judgment against the defendant's property in all fifty states.

b. *In Rem* Jurisdiction

i. This refers to a court's ability to adjudicate the rights of *all the world* with respect to property located within the borders of the state in which the court is located.

ii. The state can bind *all persons* regarding the property's ownership in, for example, a forfeiture proceeding.

c. *Quasi in Rem* Jurisdiction

i. *Quasi in rem* jurisdiction is jurisdiction over the person that is based on the presence of the person's *property* within the forum state, as opposed to the *presence or contacts* of that person with the forum state.

B. CONSTITUTIONAL LIMITATIONS ON PERSONAL JURISDICTION

1. Constitutional Limitations on In Personam Jurisdiction

a. Introduction

i. The Due Process Clause of the Fourteenth Amendment limits states' jurisdiction over nonresident defendants.

ii. If a state has a statute giving its courts personal jurisdiction over the defendant, the statute must recognize two constitutional conditions: *notice* and *nexus* (sufficient contacts).

b. Sufficient Notice under the Constitution

i. Constitutional due process requires that the parties before the court receive *adequate notice* of the action.

ii. Some ways of satisfying the due process notice requirements include:

1) Personal service;

2) Leaving service with a responsible person at the defendant's home; and

3) Delivering service to the defendant's agent.

iii. When an agent is appointed to the defendant by law (*e.g.*, state motor vehicle agencies under state long-arm motor vehicle statutes that bring nonresidents into state court PJ), the agent must notify the defendant of the charge.

iv. When the defendant's address is unknown, making mailing of the notice impossible, publication is a viable alternative.

c. The Constitutional Requirement of Nexus

i. Nexus requires both *reasonableness* and *minimum contacts* between the defendant and the forum state.

ii. This is the limit to which state long arm statutes may reach.

iii. Traditionally, the state where the defendant is a resident or where he was served with process has sufficient nexus.

 1) *See Pennoyer v. Neff*, where Neff (plaintiff) brought an action against Pennoyer for taking his land which was sold to Pennoyer in a default judgment. Court held that a state holds exclusive jurisdiction over persons and property within its borders. Therefore the plaintiff, who was not a resident of Oregon, could not have had a judgment against him by an Oregon court, *unless* it was with his consent. He also was not properly notified. Service within the state is not only sufficient, but also necessary to establish PJ. Therefore, the only ways to have personal jurisdiction over a defendant is to sue him in his resident state, to serve him with process in the state in which he is not a resident, or to sue him in a state of non-residence with his consent.

iv. *Pennoyer v. Neff* has created the following rules:

 1) A state has PJ over the defendant *only* if he is served within its borders.

  a) This rule has been greatly expanded in the modern era.

 2) Serving the defendant within a state's borders is *sufficient* grounds for establishing PJ.

  a) This rule continues today (see below, "Transient Jurisdiction").

 3) *PJ is statewide*; if any judge in a state has PJ over a defendant, then any judge in that state also has PJ.

  a) This rule continues today.

v. In the Modern Era, the due process standard is fairness. The requirement of consent or being served in-state under *Pennoyer v. Neff* was largely expanded to the requirements of only *minimum contacts* and *reasonableness*.

 1) *See International Shoe v. Washington* (plaintiff), which held that defendants can be brought into a state even when they were neither present nor served in-state, as long as certain "*minimum contacts*" were met and jurisdiction was "*reasonable*." In *Shoe* the State of Washington sued to require the defendant to conform with a statute requiring the defendant to pay unemployment benefits to its employees in Washington. The defendant argued that Washington did not have jurisdiction over it, since it was a Delaware corporation with its principal place of business in Missouri, with no offices in Washington. The court held that the company's employees, being located in Washington,

established systematic and continuous contacts that are sufficient to establish PJ.

vi.   Reasonableness

     1)   A court can use its discretion in deciding whether it is reasonable for a state to hold jurisdiction over a defendant.

     2)   Many factors may be considered, including the burden over the defendant in defending himself in the forum state and the interest of the state in holding defendants within their jurisdiction for certain claims.

     3)   In some cases, the court might decide that although the forum state has minimum contacts with the defendant, it would be unreasonable to exercise PJ over him and that the case should be heard in another state.

         a)   *See Asahi Metal Industry Co. v. Superior Ct.*, where Asahi, a Taiwanese Co., had minimum contacts with California, since it knew that its tires would wind up there, but PJ in California was unreasonable, given the interest of Asahi and California in litigating in California and the burden of having the defendant litigate in a foreign legal system. The defendant's knowledge that some of its products might end up in California was not enough to give California PJ.

         b)   *Compare Worldwide Volkswagon*, where although it was reasonable to adjudicate a claim in Oklahoma (the claim arose there, all of the witnesses were there, and it was more convenient for the parties to litigate there), the Court held that Oklahoma did not have PJ because the defendant did not have the requisite minimum contacts with the state.

vii.   Three Kinds of Minimum Contacts

     1)   General Jurisdiction

         a)   If the defendant engages in **systematic and continuous activity**, the court will have "general jurisdiction" over him in any cause of action arising against him, even those that occur outside of the state.

         b)   Examples of systematic and continuous activity include presence, domicile, or having a business or employees in the state.

         c)   Regular visits to a state or substantial purchases made from the state do *not* constitute systematic and continuous activity.

             i)   *See Helicopteros Nacionales de Colombia, S.A. v. Hall*, where the defendant had trained, negotiated a contract, accepted checks from, and purchased helicopters in Texas, yet the court held that such contacts were insufficient in order to establish the "systematic and continuous contacts" required to establish general jurisdiction, since the claim did not arise in Texas.

    ii)   *Compare International Shoe v. Washington*, where having employee in Washington *did* constitute systematic and continuous contacts.

2)   Specific Jurisdiction

    a)   The state may exercise "specific jurisdiction" over the defendant if the claim arose from activities within the state.

    b)   Example: if a California citizen, which he was visiting New York for the first time, hit the plaintiff's car while driving, New York will be able to exercise specific jurisdiction over him.

        i)   *See McGee v. Int'l Life Insurance*, where the California courts had PJ over a Texas Co. whose only contact with California was limited to its one customer in California.

        ii)   *See Burger King Corp. v. Rudzewicz*, where the defendant enters into a franchise agreement with Burger King, which is incorporated in Fla. The agreement required the defendant, a Mich. resident, to send fees to franchisor's home office in Fla. Court held that Fla. courts had PJ over the defendant because he purposefully directed his activities toward Fla.

3)   Purposeful Availment

    a)   A state may exercise PJ over a defendant when he *purposefully avails* himself of the court's legal system.

    b)   The defendant's contacts with the forum state may not be casual, isolated, or accidental.

    c)   It is possible for a court to have PJ over the defendant even if the defendant has never entered the state, as long as the defendant knows that his activities would have a consequence in the state.

        i)   *See Keeton v. Hustler Magazine*, where a magazine should have known that it would have damaged the plaintiff's reputation through libel in the forum where the plaintiff brought suit, since the magazine was distributed there.

    d)   However, the plaintiff's unilateral activity cannot satisfy the defendant's requirement with forum state; the defendant must ***purposefully avail*** himself of the privilege of conducting activities in the forum State.

        i)   *See Hanson v. Denkla*, where the question arose as to whether a Florida court could have jurisdiction over a Delaware bank over a trust. The trust holder was a Pennsylvania resident who established the trust in Delaware, and then later moved to Florida. Since the bank had no connection with Florida when the trust was created, the Supreme Court held that Florida did not have PJ).

     e)   Where the defendant is not purposefully availing himself of the laws of a state, simply knowing of the possibility of a claim arising in the state does not establish sufficient nexus.

        i)   *See World-Wide Volkswagen Corp. v. Woodson*, where the corporation's awareness that its sales in New York could have resulted in injuries in Oklahoma was not enough to establish "purposeful availment," since one's products could end up *anywhere* in the world without creating sufficiently minimal contacts.

     f)   Even where there are minimum contacts, a court may dismiss a claim for lack of PJ when there is a large burden on the defendant or the state has no interest in the case.

     g)   For example, in *Kulko v. Superior Ct.*, a father's compliance with the request of his children to live with his ex-wife in California and his purchase of a one-way ticket for one child to go there (while the mother sent the other ticket) is not sufficient grounds to bring him within California's PJ. The father did not act to benefit himself of the laws of California, but rather, he acted in the interests of his family. He did not thus avail himself of the laws of California.

2.   Constitutional Limitations on *In Rem* Jurisdiction

    a.   Defined

        i.   *In rem* jurisdiction refers to a court's power to adjudicate the rights of *all parties* to property within the state.

    b.   Nexus

        i.   The property's presence within a state is sufficient grounds for granting a court *in rem* jurisdiction, since states have a strong interest in adjudicating the rights of *all the world* regarding property within their borders.

    c.   Notice

        i.   Notice requires that the defendant be notified of an action through the best methods available.

   ii. Publication is insufficient process when the addresses of defendants are known. However, when personal notification of each defendant is cost-prohibitive, the plaintiff has a duty only to use the best methods available. *Mullane v. Central Hanover Bank and Trust Co.*

 3. Constitutional Limitations on *Quasi in Rem* Jurisdiction

  a. Defined

   i. *Quasi in rem* jurisdiction is *in personam* jurisdiction based on a defendant's property in a state.

  b. Nexus

   i. Traditionally, under *quasi in rem* jurisdiction, any plaintiff could sue any defendant in any state as long as the defendant owned property within that state.

   ii. A court could grant judgment up to the value of the property.

   iii. Today, all actions, including *quasi in rem* actions, are subject to the same minimum standards test to which *in personam* jurisdiction is subject.

    1) *See Shaffer v. Heitner* (1977), where the plaintiff, a stock holder, brought suit in Delaware against the officer defendants of Greyhound through *quasi in rem* jurisdiction by sequestering defendants' stock, which was located in Delaware, since the stock was deemed to be in the state of incorporation of the organization (Greyhound was a Delaware corporation). Although traditionally, the defendant's ownership of property in the forum state was a sufficient nexus for personal jurisdiction in the forum state, after *Shaffer*, the ownership of such property was only *evidence* of jurisdiction. If the claim is related to the defendant's property, the state would have jurisdiction; if the claim is unrelated, then minimum contacts would not be met by showing mere ownership of property.

  c. Notice

   i. The best available method is required for notice.

C. STATUTORY LIMITATIONS ON PERSONAL JURISDICTION

 1. Statutory Limitations on *In Personam* Jurisdiction

  a. Federal Courts

   i. In the federal court, the FRCP govern the requirements for notice.

   ii. Rule 4 leaves several possibilities for service of process, including:

    1) Those methods allowed under state law;

    2) Personal service;

    3) Leaving process with an agent; or

4) Leaving service at one's home with a person of suitable age and discretion.

a) In an age where many people own multiple abodes, service of process can be met at any one of the defendant's homes.

b) *See National Dev. Co. v. Triad Holding Corp.*, where the court held that the defendant's Manhattan apartment was his "house" for the purposes of FRCP 4(e)(2), even though the defendant had multiple homes throughout the world and his permanent residence was in Saudi Arabia.

iii. Rule 4(d) Requests to waive service

1) From the defendant's perspective, the only time to allow it is when a) you are immobile and can't just take off or b) there is a long time before the 120 day service period ends.

2) But if there is very little time before the time window runs out, and you are not immobile (like a corporation that can't go off and hide), then do not allow waiver of service and take off!

iv. Rule 4(k) defines the territorial limits of effective service. It explains that a court has jurisdiction over *any* defendant who receives a summons and meets general jurisdiction or other conditions.

v. Rule 12(b) defines two errors that can be made with respect to notice:

1) Insufficiency of process (Rule 12(b)(4)), which is hardly ever is an error; and

2) Insufficiency of service of process (Rule 12(b)(4)) which often is an error.

a) The issue with service of process is deciding how to serve a summons on a defendant in a way that will bring him within the court's jurisdiction.

b) "Actual notice" is not enough for proper service. For example, one may receive a summons that was left on his porch, but this will not constitute proper service.

3) It may seem that if a defendant makes a motion to dismiss for improper service of process, the plaintiff can personally serve the defendant when the plaintiff arrives to court to argue.

a) However, the defendant does not always show up in court, and even if he did, he would have immunity.

b) Furthermore, the defendant's lawyer may not be an agent appointed to receive service of process on behalf of the defendant.

b. State Long-Arm Statutes

  i. States do not have the power to hear all cases; they only have jurisdiction over cases when their legislatures have granted them powers to hear them.

  ii. All states have long-arm statutes that specify the scope of cases that can be brought within their courts.

  iii. All state long-arm statutes granted state courts PJ over:

    1) The state's domiciliaries; and

    2) Those served with process within the state (see "Transient Jurisdiction," *infra.*)

  iv. States generally also grant their courts *in personam* jurisdiction over defendants when the defendant commits a certain act within the state, whether or not the defendant is served within the state.

  v. All states also appear to have nonresident motor vehicle statutes, which have been held to be constitutional.

    1) *See Hess v. Pawloski* (plaintiff), where the defendant, a resident of Pennsylvania that was allegedly driving recklessly in Massachusetts injured the plaintiff. Under a Massachusetts statute, drivers in Massachusetts give implied consent to Massachusetts Motor Vehicles to be their agent. The Court held that this statute did not violate the Fourteenth Amendment, which does not preclude states from enforcing statutes to bring safety to their roads, even if such statutes are enforced against nonresident drivers.

  vi. Beyond these elements, which all states have in common, the states vary in their long-arm statutes.

    1) Some states, such as California, have "unlimited long arm statutes," which grant their courts PJ to the extent allowed under the Constitution's nexus and notice requirements.

    2) Other courts have limited long arm statutes, permitting only certain defined actions to be within the state's jurisdiction.

2. Statutory Limitations on *In Rem* Jurisdiction

 a. Many states have statutes granting *in rem* jurisdiction allowing the state to adjudicate the rights of all parties regarding property, as long as the property is in-state.

 b. *In rem* jurisdiction relates to condemnation proceedings, forfeiture proceedings of property to the state, settlement of decedents' estates, etc.

3. Statutory Limitations on *Quasi in Rem* Jurisdiction

 a. Most states have statutes that allow two kinds of *quasi in rem* jurisdiction:

  i. Claims arising out of the property within the state.

1)   The minimum contacts requirement is fulfilled when the claim relates specifically to the property.

ii.   Claims unrelated to property within the state.

1)   Since the constitutional requirements for *quasi in rem* jurisdiction have been so significantly limited by *Shaffer v. Heitner*, and since plaintiffs still have the burden of proving the defendant's minimum contacts with the state (even though he owns property in the state), plaintiffs will usually opt for *in personam* jurisdiction in order not to be limited by the value of the in-state property.

D.   TRANSIENT JURISDICTION AND THE INTERNET

1.   Transient Presence

     a.   If the defendant does not have minimum contacts in the forum state, does not fall within the state's long arm statutes, and does not consent, a state will nevertheless have jurisdiction over him if he is **served** *while in the forum state*.

     b.   Where the claim arose is irrelevant for the purpose of transient jurisdiction; all that is necessary is that the defendant *purposefully avail himself of the laws* of the state by voluntarily going there (vacationing there, driving his car through the state, etc.).

     c.   Minimum contacts between the defendant and the forum state are considered satisfied when the defendant avails himself of the laws of the state.

         i.   *See Burnham v. Superior Ct. Cal.*, where the defendant, passing through California to do some business and to visit his children who were with his ex-wife, was served by her in California for divorce. The court held that the California courts had PJ over the defendant because his presence in the state was voluntary.

     d.   Exceptions

         i.   There is no PJ when the defendant is served while in the foreign state because he was subpoenaed there as a witness to another case.

         ii.   Similarly, there is no jurisdiction over the defendant who is served while forced into the forum state (*e.g.*, beat up and dragged over state lines) or deceived into the forum state (*e.g.*, defendant's ex-wife tells the defendant he must come see their sick son, who really is not sick).

2.   The Internet

     a.   Just as increased mobility has lead to an expansion of *Pennoyer*, some commentators have stated that PJ will be changed with respect to the Internet, which poses many challenges to PJ.

     b.   However, this is not yet clear.

i. *See Revell v. Lidov*, where the plaintiff sued the defendant and Columbia University in Texas for defamation for an article written by him and posted on Columbia University's website. The defendant had no systematic and continuous contacts with Texas and he did not know that the plaintiff even lived there. The court held that there was no PJ because the web site and Columbia University did not have sufficient contact with Texas to lead to them anticipate the possibility of being haled into court there.

E. Venue and Transfer of Actions

1. Introduction

   a. Venue and transfer are additional limits on the plaintiff's selection of a forum.

   b. If a plaintiff brings a case in an improper venue, the remedy is either dismissal or transfer.

   c. If the judge choose to transfer a case in a state court, it will be transferred to a proper venue within the same state; if the case is in a federal court, it will be transferred to a proper venue *anywhere in the country*.

   d. The law of venue has both similarities and differences with PJ.

Differences Between Personal Jurisdiction and Venue

Fora that have PJ over the defendant	Districts that Have PJ	Districts that Have Proper Venue
Virginia (his domicile)	Eastern District Western District	*Eastern District* Western District
Indiana (where the cause of action arose)	Northern District Soutern District	Northern District *Soutern District*
Alabama (where he is on vacation now)	Northern District Middle District Southern District	Northern District *Middle District* Southern District

2. Determining Where Venue Is Proper

   a. In local actions, venue is where the property is located. However, these are a small minority of cases.

   b. The vast majority of cases are transitory cases, and state and federal statutes prescribe where they can be brought.

   c. Proper Venue in State Court

      i. When the defendant is a natural persona, states generally have statutes that allow venue in a *county*, *parish* or other *subdivision where the defendants reside* or have *systematic and continuous contact* or where the *claim arose.*

    ii.   When the defendant is a corporation, it can generally be sued in the county of its principle place of business.

    iii.   In certain actions, such as divorce, states allow venue in the county where the plaintiff resides.

  d.   Proper Venue in Federal Court

    i.   If a case is being removed from state court, then in the judicial district corresponding to the forum where the case was originally brought in state court will have proper venue.

    ii.   If the case is originally brought in federal court, then the following federal districts will have venue:

      1)   If all the defendants reside in the same state, then a district where *any* of the defendant resides;

      2)   Otherwise, in a district in which a substantial part of the events occurred;

      3)   If there is no district in which the action may otherwise be brought:

        a)   When it is founded on diversity only, it should be brought in a district where any defendant is subject to PJ;

        b)   When it is not founded only on diversity, it should be brought in any district where any defendant may be found.

    iii.   Corporations are considered to reside in any district that has PJ over it (apply *International Shoe v. Washington's* minimum contacts test as if it were a natural person).

      1)   When a state has more than one district, each district can be examined and analyzed as though it were a state in order to determine whether that district would have had PJ over the corporation.

  3.   Venue Mistakes

  a.   If the plaintiff files a case to an improper venue, the defendant may move to dismiss.

    i.   The motion must be made within twenty days.

    ii.   The court in its discretion may dismiss the case or transfer the case to a proper venue.

  b.   If the plaintiff files a case in a permissible but inconvenient forum, the defendant may move to transfer.

    i.   No time limit is imposed on the defendant for the purpose of filing this motion.

   ii.   The court will transfer the case to another venue if that venue is also proper and if it is more convenient for the parties, witnesses, or is in the interest of justice.

4.   Transfer and Forum *Non Conveniens*

   a.   Transfer and forum *non conveniens* are similar in that both can get a case moved to a better place for trial.

   b.   However, forum *non conveniens* is used when the case belongs somewhere where the judge's transfer powers do not reach.

      i.   Thus, in state courts, it is invoked when the proper forum is outside the state.

      ii.   In federal court, it is only invoked when the proper forum is outside the United States.

   c.   Forum *non conveniens* is a dismissal, but unlike other dismissals, the judge makes dismissal contingent on the defendant's waiving any defenses that would make it harder for the plaintiff to start over (statute of limitations; lack of PJ; venue, etc.).

Summary of the Mistakes a Plaintiff May Make

Plaintiff's mistake	*Can the mistake be fixed by transfer?*
Subject Matter Jurisdiction	No, never (except, for example, if it was filed in one federal court, such as a bankruptcy court, when it needed to be filed in a federal district court).
Personal Jurisdiction	In state court, it can never be fixed by transfer, since a state court can only transfer a case to other courts within that state, but if the original court did not have PJ, then none of the other state courts would. In federal court, one court may transfer the case to another court in the country that has PJ.
Venue	Always, if PJ is correct. However, a court may choose instead to dismiss the case.

IV.   STATE LAW IN FEDERAL COURT

A.   THE EVOLUTION OF THE DOCTRINE FOR DETERMINING WHAT LAW APPLIES

1.   Historical Approach

   a.   Historically, the federal courts, assuming that there was no federal law on point, were to apply state local laws (statutes and laws inherently local in character, such as state real property principles), but not general laws (state case law).

   b.   *See Swift v. Tyson*, which held that under the Federal Rules of Decisions Act, the federal courts were to apply state law only when there was applicable statue ("local law") on point; otherwise, the federal courts could create the law (a federal common law).

2. *Erie* Approach

   a. The *Erie* doctrine, applying to both state local laws and general law, overruled *Swift v. Tyson*, and held the **federal common law to be unconstitutional**.

   b. In *Erie Railroad Co. v. Tompkins,* the plaintiff sued to recover injuries sustained while on a footpath on railroad's right of way. The plaintiff argued to apply the federal common law, which recognized him as a licensee, but the defendant argued to apply the Pennsylvania state law, which would have held the plaintiff to be a trespasser. Held: the state common law should be applied.

      i. *N.B.*: despite *Erie*, which essentially held that there is to be no federal common law, many urge the federal courts to create a new federal common law based on international law and on the law of nations.

3. Substantive v. Procedural Approach

   a. In his concurrence in *Erie Railroad Co. v. Tompkins*, Justice Reed articulated for the first time the *substantive v. procedural approach* to determining what law applies in federal court.

   b. Under this approach, the federal courts should apply state substantive law and federal procedural law ("no one doubts federal power over procedure").

4. The *Guaranty Trust Co. v. York* Outcome Determinative Approach

   a. Under *Guaranty Trust Co. v. York* (1945), the test is not whether the law in question is substantive or procedural, but rather, whether applying a federal law over a state law would lead to a different outcome.

   b. If it would, then the state law should be applied.

5. *Byrd* Countervailing Federal Interest Approach

   a. Finally, under *Byrd v. Blue Ridge Rural Electrical Cooperative, Inc.*, the Court held that the *York* outcome determinative test should be applied, unless there is a **countervailing federal interest**, in which case the Federal Rule or practice should be applied.

   b. *See Byrd v. Blue Ridge Rural Electrical Cooperative, Inc.* (1958), where the federal practice of allowing trials by jury conflicted with a South Carolina practice that would have required a bench trial. The federal practice was applied because of the countervailing federal interest in allowing trials by jury.

B. ***HANNA'S* MODERN APPROACH**

1. The Rules Enabling Act Prong (*Hanna II*)

    a. When there is a Federal Rule on point, the Rules Enabling Act prong of *Hanna v. Plumer* (see *infra.*) applies and the following must be determined:

        i. Whether the Federal Rule is valid.

            1) The validity turns on whether it is constitutional. A Federal Rule is constitutional if it was within Congress's power to legislate over federal procedure.

            2) The test looks to whether the Rule is arguably procedural; if it is, then it is valid and constitutional.

        ii. Whether the Federal Rule abridges, enlarges, or modifies any state substantive rights (the 28 USC § 2072(b) inquiry).

            1) The purpose of a substantive law is to abridge, enlarge, or modify any legal right.

            2) There are two ways that a law may be substantive:

                a) It may primarily deal with areas of human conduct (*e.g.*, a tort law); or

                b) It may appear to be procedural, but when applied, is outcome determinative in a way that undermines the twin aims of *Erie* (discouraging forum shopping and avoiding the inequitable distribution of justice).

    b. If the Federal Rule is valid and does not abridge, enlarge, or modify any state substantive rights (this is almost always the case), then the Federal Rule trumps the state law and should be applied.

    c. If the Federal Rule is invalid, or if it is valid but it abridges, enlarges, or modifies state substantive rights, then the state procedural rule should be applied.

2. The Rules of Decision Act Prong (*Hanna I*)

    a. When no Federal Rule is on point, the Rule of Decision Act prong of *Hanna v. Plumer* applies and a modified outcome determinative test should be applied by first determining:

        i. Whether applying the federal practice will lead to forum shopping; and

        ii. Whether the federal practice will lead to an inequitable distribution of justice.

    b. If following the federal practice undermines the twin aims of *Erie*, then the state rule should be applied, *unless* there is a *Byrd* countervailing federal interest, in which case the federal practice should be followed.

c. *N.B.*: this analysis only applies to procedural questions. When there is a substantive question, the federal courts are required to apply *state law* when no Federal Rule is on point.

   i. *See Gasperini* (plaintiff) *v. Center for Humanities, Inc.*, where the court followed the New York "materially deviates" standard for reviewing jury verdicts over the federal double jeopardy provision of the Seventh Amendment. Since the question was substantive, the federal court was obligated to apply the state law under *Erie*. The Seventh Amendment "shocking to the conscience" requirement does not apply to state courts, so no federal law on point applies. Between a state substantive law and an inapplicable federal practice, the state law must be followed.

3. Summary

   a. Thus, there are two situations in which a federal procedural practice or law would be applied over a state law or practice:

      i. There is no *valid* Federal Rule on point, but there is a countervailing federal interest; or

      ii. There is a valid Federal Rule on point;

         1) *S Hanna v. Plumer* (1965), where the defendant argued for application of a Massachusetts state law, since under *York*, there was an outcome determinative difference between Rule 4 service of process requirements and the Massachusetts rule requiring process to be personally served. Held: where there is a Federal Rule on point, it is to be applied when it is (i) valid (arguably procedural) and (ii) does not abridge, enlarge, or modify any state substantive rights (§ 2072(b)). Rule 4, passing these tests, is a valid federal law and therefore trumps the state rule.

   b. This is true even when there is an outcome determinative difference that compromises the twin aims of *Erie*.

C. DETERMINING THE STATE LAW TO APPLY

1. Once a federal court decides that it should apply state law, it has the obligation of deciding *which* state's laws to apply.

   a. As a general rule, the federal courts are required to apply the laws of the state in which the action was brought (the forum state), which states which laws to apply. When there are no laws on point, the court is to do what it believed the state supreme court would have done.

      i. Example: if a complaint was filed in a Massachusetts federal court, then that court would apply the Massachusetts rules as to the applicable laws. Thus, if in a diversity suit, the Massachusetts state courts would apply New York state laws in a given case, then a Massachusetts federal court must also apply the New York state laws.

   b. This is true even if a case is transferred.

        i.   If the case in the above hypothetical were then transferred to Ohio, the Massachusetts choice of law rules would still govern and the New York state laws would apply.

        ii.   Rationale: the plaintiff should have the benefit of the laws of the venue where he originally **properly** sued.

        iii.   However, when the plaintiff originally sues in a wrong venue, and it is transferred under 28 USC § 1406, this rule does not apply, since the plaintiff should not benefit of the choice of law rules of a venue where he improperly originally sued.

    c.   This can lead to gamesmanship among the plaintiffs

        i.   *See Ferrins v. John Deere*, where the Court allowed the plaintiff to adjudicate a claim in Pennsylvania even though he originally properly brought the claim in Mississippi merely to later transfer it without being subject to the Pennsylvania SL.

        ii.   *N.B.*: a defense that the defendant could have raised was that this transfer was against the interests of justice, which are recognized by 28 USC §1404(a).

D.   FEDERAL LAW IN STATE COURT

1.   When adjudicating **non-exclusive federal question claims**, state courts must apply only those federal procedural laws "essential to effectuate" the purposes behind the federal law.

V.   PLEADINGS AND MOTIONS

A.   AN OVERVIEW OF PLEADINGS

1.   Introduction

    a.   Pleadings are documents filed by a litigant that set forth the material facts and legal arguments of his claims or defenses.

    b.   The purposes of pleadings are to: (i) give notice of the suit; (ii) give factual and legal information about the nature of the claim; (iii) establish jurisdiction; and (iv) narrow the issues.

    c.   The plaintiff initiates suit by filing what most jurisdictions call a "complaint."

    d.   The defendant may respond to the complaint by:

        i.   Filing her own pleading, called the "answer," and raising any affirmative defenses;

        ii.   The plaintiff may then respond to any affirmative defenses in his "reply."

2.   Pleadings Allowed; Form of Motions

    a.   Under Rule 7, the following pleadings are required in an action:

        i.   A **complaint** and **answer**;

        ii.   A *reply*, if there is a *counterclaim* (an independent cause of action made by the defendant against the plaintiff in order to defeat the plaintiff's claim) denominated as such;

        iii.   An answer if there is a *cross-claim* (a claim under FRCP 13(g) by one party against a co-party);

        iv.   A *third party complaint*;

        v.   A *third party answer*.

    b.   No other pleadings are permitted, except that the court may order a reply to an answer or a third-party answer. Rule 7(a).

    c.   The deadline for service of all of these pleadings is twenty days from the date of receipt.

    d.   When counting days, the following rules must be followed:

        i.   If the amount of time is less than eleven days, weekends and holidays are not counted;

        ii.   If the amount of time is eleven days or more, weekends and holidays are counted.

    e.   Receipt is effectuated by the mailbox rule: the day the pleading is dropped in the mailbox is the day that it is served.

3.   General Rules of Pleading

    a.   Under Rule 8(a), all pleadings setting forth a claim for relief against another party (original claim, counterclaim, cross-claim, third-party claim) must contain:

        i.   A short, plain statement of the court's jurisdiction;

        ii.   A short, plain statement of the claim showing that the pleader is entitled to relief; and

        iii.   A demand for judgment.

4.   Pleading Inconsistent Facts and Alternative Theories

    a.   Under Rule 8(e)(2), the plaintiff may plead inconsistent facts or theories in a complaint when the plaintiff has insufficient knowledge.

        i.   *See McCormick* (plaintiff) *v. Kopmann*, where the plaintiff was permitted to claim that the defendant negligently drove his truck and the plaintiff's husband was not contributorily negligent or, in the alternative, a co-defendant's serving him liquor caused his death.

    b.   There are two limitations on pleading inconsistent facts:

        i.   Ethical considerations: one may not plead what he knows to be untrue. Rule 11.

        ii.   Tactical considerations: pleading inconsistent facts may negatively affect the jury's perception of the case.

5.   Form of Pleadings.

a. All pleadings require a ***caption*** containing: the name of the court, the file number, the title of the action (*e.g.*, "Smith v. Jones"), and the name of the pleading. Rule 10(a).

b. Each set of circumstances must be set forth in separate, enumerated paragraphs. Rule 10(b).

c. Statements in a pleading may be adopted by reference to exhibits, which become part of the pleading. Rule 10(c).

B. REQUIREMENTS OF THE COMPLAINT

1. General Requirements

a. The complaint, like claims made in other pleadings, must contain a short and plain statement of the court's *jurisdiction*, a claim entitling the plaintiff to *relief*, and a statement of the *relief sought*.

b. The complaint requires legal sufficiency in that the case must state a valid claim.

2. Factual (or "Formal") Sufficiency

a. Rule 8(f) reflects a policy that places substantive justice over rigid, technical procedural rules.

b. Within this context, the Court has taken a relaxed view as to factual, or formal sufficiency, by interpreting the Federal Rules as moving away from the rigid requirements of code pleading.

c. The plaintiff need only plead with specificity sufficient to put the defendant on notice of any claims against him.

   i. *See Dioguardi* (plaintiff) *v. Durning*, where the plaintiff sued the defendant for conversion. The defendant moved to dismiss for failure to state facts sufficient to constitute a claim. Held: stating facts is not necessary; rather, stating a claim upon which relief may be granted is required and sufficient. Judgment for the plaintiff.

3. Heightened Specificity Requirements in Certain Cases. Rule 9.

a. There are two exceptions to the liberal pleading requirements in federal courts:

   i. When the Federal Rules require heightened specificity (Rule 9(b) fraud or mistake; Rule 9(g) special damages); and

   ii. When Congress requires it.

b. In all other cases outside of these exceptions, the federal courts do not have authority to impose heightened standards. *See Leatherman v. Tarrant County* (lower courts were not permitted to require heightened specificity for actions alleging municipal liability).

c. When heightened specificity is required, six questions must be pleaded in the complaint: who, where, what, when, why and how.

4. Rule 41(a) Voluntary Dismissals

    a. By the Plaintiff

        i. The plaintiff may file a *notice* to dismiss his own action at any time between his filing of an action and the defendant's filing of an answer or motion for summary judgment (SJ), whichever comes first.

        ii. The dismissal is without prejudice, unless the plaintiff formerly brought and dismissed the same action in any other federal or state court in the United States.

    b. By Stipulation of the Parties

        i. The plaintiff may stipulate dismissal with the signatures of all other parties to the action.

        ii. The dismissal is without prejudice, unless the parties stipulate otherwise.

    c. By Court Order

        i. If the plaintiff wishes to dismiss his action *after* the defendant files an answer or a motion for SJ, the court may order such a dismissal without prejudice, unless prejudice is specified in the order.

5. Rule 41(b) Involuntary Dismissal

    a. The defendant may have an action dismissed if the plaintiff violates *any court order* or for his *failure to prosecute*.

        i. *N.B.:* these are different from Rule 12(b) motions, which are raised by the defendant before he serves his answer, and thus, before the defendant has the opportunity to move to dismiss against the plaintiff for failure to prosecute, for violating court orders, etc.

    b. Such a dismissal is considered to be with prejudice, unless otherwise specified by the court.

    c. An action may also be involuntarily dismissed by the initiative of the court.

        i. *See Link v. Wabash*, which established that a court may make an involuntary dismissal *sua sponte* (by order of the court "of its own will" (Lat.), without motions by either party).

    d. Courts will consider several factors in granting involuntary dismissals, such as whether a lawyer intentionally violated a judge's order.

C. VERACITY IN PLEADING

1. Introduction

    a. Attorneys and unrepresented parties must sign their pleadings, written motions, and other papers. Rule 11 (a).

b. By presenting a document to the court, they are representing that to the best of their knowledge (a subjective element), formed after reasonable inquiry (an objective element):

    i. It is not being presented for any improper purpose;

    ii. The claims and defenses are warranted by existing law or there are non-frivolous arguments for the extension, modification, or reversal of existing law;

    iii. The allegations have evidentiary support, or if so indicated, the party believes they will likely have evidentiary support; and

    iv. The denials have evidentiary support, or if so indicated, the party does not have enough knowledge. Rule 11(b).

c. The violation of Rule 11(b) can be through *signing, filing, submitting, or later advocating* such positions. Thus, more than one lawyer could be sanctioned under Rule 11(b) (*e.g.*, the one who signed and the one who filed).

d. Rule 11(b) may be violated by attorneys, unrepresented parties, represented parties, and law firms who violate Rule 11(b). Rule 11(c).

    i. Thus, if a party makes false representations to his lawyers, *the party himself*, and not his lawyers, may have sanctions ordered against him.

    ii. Furthermore, if an attorney violates Rule 11(b), then the whole firm may be sanctioned.

2. The Twenty One Day "Safe Window"

a. When a party moves for sanctions, he is obligated to abide by the twenty one day "safe window."

b. This gives the party receiving the motion twenty one days from the day that he is served with the motion to correct his conduct. If he fails to do so, the motion may be filed with the court.

c. This safe window is mandatory, but not jurisdictional. The party raising Rule 11 must provide the other party with notice, but this requirement may be waived.

    i. *See Rector* (plaintiff) *v. Approved Federal Savings Bank*, where the court held that the safe window rule was like a statute of limitations; it was mandatory but could be waived if not raised as an affirmative defense in the trial court.

    ii. *N.B.*: not all courts would accept this court's reasoning; some would see the safe window as jurisdictional (*e.g.*, like SMJ).

d. The safe window provision provides protection for lawyers who do not disclose contrary authority.

    i.   Thus, if a lawyer fails to cite a case that is against his position, he may withdraw the paper within the safe window period and not be required to pay monetary sanctions.

    ii.   However, failing to disclose such authority may not be ethical.

  3. The Nature of Sanctions

    a. Monetary sanctions include attorney fees and costs to court.

    b. Non-monetary sanctions include admonition, the suspension of practice before a court, and the publication of an opinion criticizing an attorney by name.

    c. Attorneys' fees and other expenses may only be rewarded by motion, not by the court's initiative (even if the court issues an order to show cause).

     i.   Thus, while both fines and attorneys' fees may be requested by motion, only fines may be ordered by court's initiative.

     ii.   As a limitation, monetary sanctions may not be imposed on a represented party for violations of Rule 11(b)(2), which requires that the representations made to a court are warranted by existing law or by a nonfrivolous argument for the modification of existing law or the establishment of new law. Rule 11(c)(2)(A).

      1) Example 1: Party pressures Lawyer into filing a frivolous claim. Lawyer tells Party that he has no case, but Party insists that he file the case anyway. May Party be monetarily sanctioned?

       a) No, since this would be a violation of Rule 11(b)(2).

      2) Example 2: same as above, only Party knows that the claim is frivolous, but wants to harass the other Party. Can Party be sanctioned?

       a) Yes, for the violation of Rule 11(b)(1), which deals with bringing a pleading for an improper purpose.

      3) Example 3: Party pressures Lawyer into filing a frivolous claim. Lawyer says Party has no case, but Party convinces him to file it anyway. May Party be non-monetarily sanctioned?

       a) Yes; Rule 11(c)(2)(A) does *not* state that a party may not receive a *non-monetary* sanction; it applis only to monetary sanctions.

    d. For monetary sanctions to be imposed, one of the following must occur:

     i.   A party must make a motion for attorneys fees or other costs; or

     ii.   A court must enter an order describing the problematic conduct, give the party a chance to show cause, and then impose a penalty while describing the conduct determined to constitute a violation of Rule 11.

D.   DEFENDANT'S OPTIONS IN RESPONSE TO THE COMPLAINT

1.   In response to the plaintiff's complete, the defendant may raise any of the following ***motions***:

    a.   Rule 12(b) Motions

        i.   The defendant may make motions to dismiss under Rule 12(b) based on the following causes: (i) lack of SMJ, (ii) lack of PJ, (iii) improper venue, (iv) failure to state a claim, (v) insufficiency of process, (vi) insufficiency of service of process, or (vii) failure to join a party under Rule 19.

        ii.   The defendant has only one chance to make such a motion, and that is before serving his answer or motion for SJ.

        iii.   Alternatively, the defendant may raise these defenses in his answer, but if he does, he may lose the defenses that require express invocation (PJ, venue, process, service of process), unless he amends his responsive pleading under Rule 15(a).

        iv.   Once a Rule 12(b) motion is raised, it cannot be amended or raised another time.

    b.   Other Motions

        i.   The defendant may also make any of the following motions:

            1)   A Rule 12(e) motion for a more definite statement (this may also be made by the plaintiff if the defendant serves a pleading requiring a reply).

            2)   A Rule 12(f) motion to strike (this may also be made by the plaintiff).

            3)   A Rule 56 motion for SJ, if the defendant introduces evidence outside of the complaint (this may also be raised by the plaintiff after receiving the defendant's answer);

            4)   Rule 12(c) motions for judgment on the pleadings are *not* permitted by the defendant, because these can only be made after all the pleadings are made and the pleadings are closed. Thus, the defendant must first file his answer.

2.   In the alternative, the defendant may answer the plaintiff's complaint.

    a.   Introduction

        i.   The defendant must file his answer within twenty days of being served or, if the defendant waives service of process, within sixty days.

        ii.   In his answer, the defendant may raise Rule 12(b) defenses and also respond to the plaintiff's allegations, raise affirmative defenses, and make counterclaims.

b.   Responses to the Plaintiff's Allegations

    i.   The defendant has three options as to what he may do in response to each of the plaintiff's allegations:

        1)   Admissions

            a)   The defendant may admit some or all of the plaintiff's allegations.

            b)   If the defendant knows that some or all of the plaintiff's allegations are true, the defendant is ethically required to admit this in the answer.[16]

            c)   If an averment is not explicitly denied, it will be treated as admitted.[17]

        2)   Denials

            a)   In a *general denial*, the defendant denies *everything* in the complaint.

                i)   This is generally what one should do when ethically possible.

                ii)   If the defendant denies all of a claim, but fails to admit one part that is true, that can have serious consequences later on.

                iii)   If it prejudices the plaintiff, it is possible for a court to require the defendant to proceed as though the entire claim were true.

            b)   *Specific denials* deal with each averment separately, admitting some and denying others.

        3)   Denials for Lack of Knowledge or Information

            a)   When the defendant lacks knowledge or sufficient information, he may deny make a denial based on the same.

c.   Rule 8(c) Affirmative Defenses

    i.   In his answer, the defendant may raise an affirmative defense, which is based on the notion that, even if everything that the plaintiff claims is true, the defendant is still entitled to a judgment in his favor.

    ii.   These defenses vary by state. For example, some states require the plaintiff to plead lack of contributory negligence as part of his *prima facie* case; other states require it as an affirmative defense.

    iii.   In federal court, regardless of what states require, affirmative defenses including the nineteen mentioned in Rule 8(c) must be included in the defendant's answer.

---

[16] This does not apply to criminal defendants.

[17] However, the amount in damages is not considered waived if not denied by the defendant.

iv. If they are not included, the defendant may not raise them. However, courts give liberally leave to amend.

v. Nevertheless, the defendants should err on the side of caution and raise anything that may seem to be an affirmative defense in the answer.

vi. How does one know if something is an affirmative defense?

1) If it is included in the Rule 8(c) list of defenses (accord and satisfaction, arbitration and award, assumption of risk, contributory negligence, discharge in bankruptcy, duress, estoppel, failure of consideration, fraud, illegality, injury by fellow servant, laches, license, payment, release, *res judicata*, statute of frauds, statute of limitations, waiver), it is automatically an affirmative defense.

2) If it is not, one of the following three tests should be used:

a) If the defendant's defense is based on some fact that the plaintiff did not have to prove to win the case, then it is an affirmative defense;

b) If the defendant's defense substantially resembles one of the other defenses listed in Rule 8(c), then it is an affirmative defense;

c) If the defendant's defense would catch the plaintiff off-guard if raised for the first time in trial, then it is an affirmative defense under the "Surprise Test."

d. Counterclaims or Cross-Claims

i. The defendant may raise counterclaims against the plaintiff.

1) A counterclaim is an independent cause of action made by the defendant in order to defeat the plaintiff's claim.

2) It does not need to be transactionally related and requires the plaintiff's reply.

ii. The defendant may also raise a cross-claim against a co-party.

1) Cross-claims must be transactionally related.

3. Failure to Respond: Default and Default Judgment

a. Rule 55(a) Entry of Default

i. Either party may file an affidavit for and obtain an entry of default when the other party fails to respond to its claims (*e.g.*, a defendant's failure to answer a complaint; the plaintiff's failure to reply to counterclaims in an answer, etc.).

ii. It is even possible for a party to get an entry of default when the other party defends a case on the merits.

1) Example: the plaintiff files complaint against the defendant; the defendant files motion for SJ arguing on the merits; the court rejects the defendant's motion; the defendant never

serves answer; the plaintiff files affidavit with the court for entry of default, which the court grants.

  iii. The court has no discretion on this matter.

 b. Rule 55(b) Judgment of Default

  i. There are two possibilities regarding what the plaintiff may do in order to obtain a default judgment.

   1) When the defendant *has neither appeared nor responded* and the plaintiff's claim is for a *sum certain* (or for a sum that can be calculated into a sum certain), the plaintiff files an affidavit with the clerk and the clerk is obligated to grant the plaintiff the exact amount requested.

   2) When the defendant has *appeared but has not responded*, or has neither responded nor appeared, but the plaintiff's damages are *not for a sum certain*, the plaintiff must make an application to the court explaining why the plaintiff is entitled to a default judgment, and there must be a hearing on the matter.

    a) This hearing may be as simple as the plaintiff's stating the damages and the court's granting it or it may as complicated as a full evidentiary hearing on the matter.

    b) If the defendant **has appeared** (through a letter to the court from a lawyer saying he will represent the defendant, through the defendant's making any motion, etc.), he must be served with written notice of the application for a default judgment at least three days prior to the hearing on the application.

    c) If the defendant **has not appeared**, the plaintiff is not required to serve the defendant with written notice of the hearing on the application for default judgment.

  ii. Both plaintiffs and defendants may ask the court for an entry of default and may make application to the court for a default judgment.

  iii. However, only plaintiffs may obtain a default judgment by the clerk. Rule 55(b)(1).

E. DEFENDING FOR LACK OF PERSONAL AND SUBJECT MATTER JURISDICTION

 1. Two Ways of Defending for Lack of Personal Jurisdiction

  a. Collateral Attacks

   i. A collateral attack on personal jurisdiction takes place outside of the original proceeding (after a default judgment has been handed down).

   ii. The advantage to a collateral attack is that the hearing for PJ takes place in the defendant's home state (unless the plaintiff goes to collect judgment in a foreign state where the defendant holds property). Thus, the defendant does not have to show up in a distant court.

    iii.   The disadvantage, however, is that the defendant loses his right to defend the case on the merits and waives all other defenses.

    iv.   Once a case is adjudicated, a collateral attack cannot be made.

    b.   Direct Attack

        i.   A direct attack is made *before* a case becomes final in all courts.

        ii.   The advantage to a direct attack is that the defendant does not waive his right to defend the case on the merits.

        iii.   The disadvantage is that the defendant may be forced to undergo the inconvenience of traveling to a distant forum and finding local counsel.

            1)   In some PJ motions, this may include the added expense of discovery and moving evidence to the forum state, as well as the defendant's psychological discomfort of being in foreign territory.

            2)   If the defendant loses, he is often required to litigate in the distant forum before having the chance to appeal for lack of jurisdiction.

            3)   This is even true when he is right and the distant forum has no PJ over him.

2.   Defending for Lack of Subject Matter Jurisdiction

    a.   Under Rule 12h(3), lack of SMJ can be raised as a defense at any time, even after the case is decided, so long as it is through a direct attack in the trial court, on appeal, or in the Supreme Court.

    b.   Although the defendant can raise lack of SMJ on appeal, it appears that the defendant may *not* raise lack of SMJ in a collateral suit. *See Chicot County Drainage Distr. v. Baxter State Bank.* SMJ challenges must be made in the suit in which they are being asserted, since courts have jurisdiction to decide their own jurisdiction.

    c.   Regarding default judgments, the Restatement (Second) on Judgments allows collateral attacks for lack of SMJ on default judgments. Very few courts, however, have actually allowed for collateral attacks on SMJ on their own.

F.   IMPLEADER (THIRD-PARTY PRACTICE) (RULE 14)

1.   Procedural Aspects

    a.   Impleader allows a defendant to join a person not a party to the action in limited circumstances.

    b.   To invoke impleader, the defendant becomes a third-party plaintiff claiming that a third party would be liable to him for part or all of his liability to the plaintiff.

c.   Generally, impleader is allowed against one who owed the third party plaintiff contribution and indemnity.

     i.   Example: the plaintiff sues the defendant for crashing into her with the defendant's car. The defendant claims mistaken identity as his defense, and claims that a thief who stole his car is liable. May the defendant implead the thief?

     ii.   Here, the defendant's theory is based on his *not being liable*, not on indemnity or contribution. Therefore, impleader is not available.

d.   Impleader allows a court to determine all liabilities, including the liability of third-party defendants to third party plaintiffs, in one action.

     i.   *See Markvicka* (plaintiff) *v. Brodhead-Garrett Co.* (third party plaintiff), where Brodhead-Garrett Co. (third party plaintiff) successfully brought a school district third party defendant into an action to determine whether it (the school district) was liable to the plaintiff, who was injured while using a jointer machine manufactured by Brodhead. Brodhead proceeded on the theory that if it was liable to the plaintiff, then the school district was liable to Brodhead for failure to properly maintain the machine and supervise children.

e.   To bring in a third party, the defendant (third party plaintiff) must serve a summons and complaint. He may do so within ten days of filing the original answer. Otherwise, he must seek leave of court.

f.   The third party defendant may make defenses against the third party plaintiff's direct claims against him as well as defenses against the plaintiff's claims against the third party plaintiff.

g.   The plaintiff and the third party defendant may make additional claims against one another when such claims arise out of same "transaction or occurrence." Rule 14(a).

2. Jurisdictional Aspects

a.   To determine whether there is jurisdiction, first look for an independent basis for SMJ.

     i.   Example: the plaintiff, a New York citizen, sues the defendant, a California citizen, in a claim that exceeds $75,000. The defendant impleads a Florida third party defendant for indemnity claims of over $75,000, and the third party defendant brings a claim against the plaintiff of under $75,000. Which of these claims has no independent basis for SMJ?

     ii.   The third party defendant's claim against the plaintiff.

b.   If there is no independent basis for SMJ, there will always be supplemental jurisdiction in the third party plaintiff's case against the third party defendant for indemnity or contribution.

        i.   Since it operates under the third party defendant's liability to the third party plaintiff for the plaintiff's claim against the third party plaintiff, it always involves a common case or controversy for the purpose of article III of the Constitution.

      c.   Similarly, the third party defendant's case against the plaintiff and the plaintiff's case against the third party defendant always involves a common "case or controversy," under § 1367(a), since it must arise from same "transaction or occurrence" as the underlying dispute.[18]

      d.   However, if the original claim is based *only* on diversity, this claim may not destroy that diversity. *Owen Equipment and Erection Co. v. Kroger*.

G. AMENDED PLEADINGS (RULE 15)

1.   Rule 15(a) Guidelines for Determining When Pleadings May be Amended

    a.   Amending pleadings is permitted once as a matter of course without the consent of the parties or of the court under the following guidelines:

      i.   When the original pleading is one that **requires a responsive pleading**, an amended pleading may be filed anytime *before the other party serves its responsive pleading*;

      ii.   When the original pleading is one that **does not require a responsive pleading**, an amended pleading may be filed within either of the following periods, whichever is shorter:

        1)   Within twenty days of serving the original pleading; or

        2)   Before the action is placed on the trial calendar.

    b.   Otherwise, party must amend the pleading by either:

      i.   The **written consent** of the other party; or

      ii.   **Leave of court**, which is freely given when in the interests of justice.

        1)   When deciding whether to grant leave to amend, courts consider the following factors: whether such leave would engender undue delay or undue prejudice, the repeated failure of the party to cure deficiency, bad faith, and futility.

        2)   Furthermore, amendments on the eve of trial are discouraged.

2.   The Problem of Variance under Rule 15(b)

---

[18] Most courts consider the § 1367(a) "same case or controversy" standard to be equivalent to the Federal Rules' common "transaction or occurrence" standard. Some Circuits, however, such as the Second Circuit, consider the former to be broader than the latter. Even in the Second Circuit, then, all impleaded cases fall under federal supplemental jurisdiction, since they will necessarily involve the "same case or controversy" as the original claim.

a. There has been a debate over specificity and the need for correlation between what is pleaded in a complaint and what the judge or jury may decide.

b. *Variance* refers to the plaintiff's introducing evidence in trial proving a legal theory different from that which he pleaded in his complaint (*e.g.*, the plaintiff claims fraud in the complaint, but proves negligence).

c. Under the common law, this was fatal; but under the Federal Rules, which elevate substance over form, this is permitted.

d. Under Rule 15(b), the plaintiff is not required to amend the complaint when the issue of variance arises, as long as the defendant expressly or impliedly consents (by not objecting).

e. However, a party may object to evidence not within issues raised in pleadings. A court will then freely allow pleadings to be amended, unless the objecting party can show prejudice.

    i. *N.B.*: prejudice means more mere general detriment; it must be detriment in a way that is *inherently unfair* to a party, such as when evidence is suddenly sprung on the defendant in such a way that he has not opportunity to respond.

    ii. Often, in such cases, the judge may cure such prejudice by granting the disadvantaged party a continuance in order to conduct the requisite discovery to respond to the additional claims and evidence.

    iii. However, judges have the discretion to deny such continuances, and may do so if such a continuance will affect other cases on the trial calendar.

f. The final determination of the issues to be tried is definitively decided at the final pretrial conference. Rule 16(d).

g. After this conference, a ***pretrial order*** stating the issues to be tried is made. It may only be modified if it is shown to lead to manifest injustice.

h. Thus, if, after a pretrial order, a party brings in evidence relating to separate legal claims, the opposing party may object on two bases:

    i. The new claim was not in the original pleadings (in which case the court will freely grant leave to the first party to amend, unless the opposing party shows that such an amendment would prejudice him); or

    ii. Such a legal claim introduces new issues that are not within the scope of the pretrial order (in which case the judge will not allow the amendment, unless refusing the same would lead to manifest injustice).

3. Amendment and the Statute of Limitations under Rule 15(c)

a. ***Amendments to claims or defenses*** are treated the same as though they had been in the original pleadings and thus relate back to the time of the complaint when one of the following elements are met:

   i. The state law allows them to relate back. Rule 15(c)(1).

   ii. The new claim arises out of the same transaction or occurrence as the claims set forth in the original pleading. Rule 15(c)(2).

      1) Policy rationale: the purpose behind SL's is to put parties on notice. In a case in which a transaction is tried before a court under one legal theory, it is reasonable to expect parties to be on notice for liability under other potential legal theories linked to the same transaction.

      2) The question of whether a new legal claim is based on the same transaction or occurrence is a subjective question over which courts will differ.

         a) *See Marsh* (plaintiff) *v. Coleman Company*, where the plaintiff sued the defendant for wrongful discharge when the defendant allegedly fired the plaintiff in 1988 in violation of federal statute for the plaintiff's age. Later, the plaintiff brought another, related action, for fraud that occurred in 1985. The defendant raised the SL and the plaintiff argued that it was the same transaction and that the new claim would relate back. Held: because the two events are not based on the same events in time or space, the fraud claim does not relate back.

         b) *N.B.:* some courts would have read the Rule more openly than this court did and would have allowed the fraud claims to relate back, since they were intimately connected with the plaintiff's termination case.

   iii. The amendment changes a party or the naming of a party against whom a claim is asserted. Rule 15(c)(3). Such amendments relate back only when the following elements are met:

      1) The new claim arises out of the same transaction or occurrence as the claims set forth in the original pleading; *and*

      2) Within Rule 4(m) for service of summons and complaint, the party to be brought in by amendment has:

         a) Received notice of the lawsuit under Rule 15(c)(3)(A); and

         b) Knows that but for the other party's mistake with respect to the identity of the proper party, the action would have been brought against him. Rule 15(c)(3)(B).

4. Rule 15(d) Supplemental Pleadings

a. A supplemental pleading is a pleading that sets forth *all events* that occurred ***after the pleading was filed*** that a ***party could not have included*** in the original pleading.

b. It is therefore different from an amended pleading, which includes facts or legal theories that ***a party could have included*** in the original pleading, but did not.

c. Permission for a supplemental pleading may be granted even though the original pleading is defective in its statement of a claim for relief or defense. If the court deems it advisable that the adverse party plead to the supplemental pleading, it will order such pleading. Rule 15(d).

VI. PARTIES, JOINDER, AND SUPPLEMENTAL JURISDICTION

A. INTRODUCTION

1. Background

   a. *Joinder* is the uniting of distinct claims or parties in an action. SMJ, venue and PJ all may affect the possibility of joinder.

   b. Joinder is possible when: (i) the FRCP's permit it; and (ii) the court has power (SMJ) to hear the case.

2. Rule 17 Real Party in Interest and Capacity

   a. Real Party in Interest

      i. A suit may generally only be brought if a party has suffered injury.

      ii. However, the person suing is not always the person who will receive the benefit of a favorable judgment. Examples when the two do not align include:

         1) When a trustee sues on behalf of a real party in interest;

         2) When a claim is assigned by *subrogation*, by operation of law, as often occurs in insurance cases.

   b. Capacity to Sue or Be Sued

      i. The capacity to sue or be sued is determined by the state law of the individual's domicile.

      ii. In all other cases, it is to be determined by the law of the state in which the district court held, except that: (i) partnerships may be sued in their common name to enforce rights they have under the Constitution; and (ii) Title 28 governs receivers appointed by U.S. courts.

      iii. *N.B.*: generally, all states include infants and incompetent persons among those who lack capacity to sue or be sued.

B. CLAIM JOINDER BY PLAINTIFFS AND DEFENDANTS (RULE 18)

1. Procedural Aspects

a.   Under Rule 18(a), a party may join "as many claims ... as the party has against an opposing party." They do not need to be transactionally related.

b.   Since claims may be joined to "an original claim, counterclaim, cross-claim, or third-party claim," any party, including the defendant, may use joinder.

c.   The standard is permissive in that parties are not *required* to join claims.

d.   When a claim is cognizable only after another has been prosecuted to a conclusion, the two claims may be joined. Rule 18(b).

e.   This applies not only to the original plaintiff, but also to any party seeking relief against another party, whether it is through a counterclaim, a cross-claim, or a third-party claim.

f.   However, an unrelated cross-claim may not be asserted under Rule 18(a) unless it is being added to a valid, related cross-claim under Rule 13(g).

2.   Jurisdictional Aspects

a.   A claim must first have SMJ before being joined.

b.   When there is no independent basis for an additional claim, there may be a basis for SMJ through supplemental jurisdiction.

i.   In any civil action over which the district courts have original jurisdiction, they will also have supplemental jurisdiction over all other claims that arise from the same case or controversy under article III of Constitution

1)   Such supplemental jurisdiction will include claims that involve joinder or intervention of additional parties.

2)   However, even when an additional claim or party arises from the same claim, 28 USC § 1367(b)-(c) limit supplemental jurisdiction.

ii.   Yet when jurisdiction is based only on diversity, there is no supplemental jurisdiction when diversity is destroyed by additional claims by the plaintiffs (but not third party plaintiffs, etc.) against persons made parties under Rules 14, 19, 20, 24.

1)   But when a claim is brought by the defendant as a cross-claim against a second the defendant, there is supplemental jurisdiction even if it destroys diversity in an action based solely on 28 USC § 1332, as long as the additional claim arises from the same transaction or occurrence as the original claim.

2)   *N.B.*: 28 USC § 1367(b) makes efforts to protect diversity only when:

a)   The original claim is brought *only* under § 1332 diversity; *and*

b)   The joined claim is one brought by a plaintiff. Thus, claims brought by the defendants may destroy diversity, yet still be joined.

iii.   The district courts may decline supplemental jurisdiction over claims under § 1367(a) in certain circumstances, such as when the additional claim is one that involves a novel state law question.

C.   COMPULSORY JOINDER (NECESSARY AND INDISPENSABLE PARTIES) (RULE 19)

1.   Procedural Aspects

   a.   Rule 19 applies when a party *must* be joined.

   b.   A party is considered *necessary* in an action when:

   i.   Complete relief cannot be accorded absent the party; or

   ii.   It is a person with an interest in the subject matter of the action such that his absence may (i) impede his ability to protect that interest; or (ii) leave those parties that are already named subject to substantial risks.

   1)   A joint tortfeasor is not considered to be a "necessary" party under Rule 19(a).

   2)   *See Temple v. Synthes Corp.*, where the plaintiff's claim was dismissed for failure to join a joint tortfeasor. On appeal, the court held that jointly and severally liable defendants are not indispensable under Rule 19; the plaintiff *may* join any or all of them, but is not required to do so. Reversed and remanded.

   c.   A *necessary* party *must* be joined when it is *feasible* to join him: he can be found and served with process, is subject to PJ, and does not affect diversity jurisdiction.

   d.   If it is *not* feasible to join him, the court must determine whether it should proceed in equity and good conscience without him or whether there is a way to get around the problem (*e.g.*, by transferring the case to a court in another state).

2.   Jurisdictional Aspects

   a.   Under Rule 19, there is always a common case or controversy; 28 USC § 1367(a) is met as a matter of course.

   b.   Jurisdiction may, however, be limited by § 1367(b), which requires that parties joined under Rule 19 by plaintiffs *not destroy diversity*.

   c.   In such an event, the plaintiffs may sometimes align the parties to preserve diversity. Courts may react to this by "realigning" parties to where they should have been.

D. PERMISSIVE PARTY JOINDER BY PLAINTIFFS (RULE 20)

1. Procedural Aspects

   a. Rule 20 allows additional parties to be joined.

      i. Permissive joinder

         1) All persons may join in one action as plaintiffs if:

            a) As plaintiffs, they assert any right to *relief jointly, severally, or in the alternative*, or, as defendants, there is asserted against them any right to relief jointly, severally, or in the alternative;

            b) Arising out of the same *transaction or occurrence*; and

            c) A *common question of law or fact* to all these persons will arise in the action. Rule 20(a).[19]

         2) The plaintiff or the defendant need not be interested in obtaining or defending against all the relief demanded.

         3) Judgment may be given for one or more plaintiffs or defendants, according to their respective rights and liabilities.

      ii. Under Rule 20(b), the court may order *separate trials* and make other orders to:

         1) Prevent a party from being embarrassed, delayed, or put to expense by the inclusion of a party against whom the party asserts no claim and who asserts no claim against the party; or

         2) Prevent delays or prejudice.

      iii. Usually, it is not difficult to determine whether a right to relief arises out of the same transaction or occurrence.

         1) However, some ambiguous situations may arise.

         2) *See Schwartz* (plaintiff) *v. Swan*, where Swan and Brey injured the plaintiff in an auto accident, and on a separate occasion, Polivick exacerbated the plaintiff's injuries in a second accident. The plaintiff sued Swan and Brey, and joined Polivick under Rule 20. The trial court severed the joinder, holding that the two incidents were not the same transaction or occurrence. On appeal, the court held that the claims could be joined because the accident with Polivick had an effect on the injuries caused by the accident with Swan and Brey. It would be impossible for Schwartz to prove who caused which injuries, since the two were so closely intertwined.

---

[19] This element will generally be met if the right asserted arises out of the same occurrence or transaction.

        iv.   Rule 42 (Consolidation; Separate Trials) parallels Rule 20 in that it allows for actions involving a common question of law or fact to be joined for hearing or trial.

            1)   The standard for Rule 42 is more lax than that of Rule 20; Rule 42 merely requires a ***common question of law or fact***; it does not require a common transaction or occurrence.

            2)   The difference between Rule 20(a) and Rule 42(a) is that the former is invoked by the parties; the latter is used by the court.

            3)   Both Rules 20(b) and 42(b) allow a court to *order separate trials* within the same action.

    b.   Rule 21 Misjoinder and Non-Joinder of Parties

        i.   Courts are not to dismiss a case because of a misjoinder.

        ii.   Rather, they may "sever" parties, dropping or adding them by court order on motion of any party or *sua sponte* at any stage of the action and on such terms as are just.

        iii.   Any claim against a party may be severed and proceeded with separately.[20]

2.   Jurisdictional Aspects

    a.   Although Rule 20 allows additional parties to be joined whenever they assert any right to relief arising out of the same occurrence or transaction, the joinder of new parties is still subject to SMJ in federal courts.

    b.   Additional parties may be joined even if they do not have their own, independent basis for SMJ, since under 28 USC § 1367(a), supplemental jurisdiction includes "claims that involve the joinder or intervention of additional parties."

    c.   Thus, there will be supplemental jurisdiction as a matter of course for parties joined under Rule 20, since those parties are joined in when there is a common transaction or occurrence, which necessarily means that the case passes the § 1367(a) common case or controversy.

    d.   However, in a case of which the district courts have jurisdiction founded soley on diversity, the complete diversity and jurisdictional amount in controversy requirements apply over claims made by plaintiffs against persons made parties under Rule 14, 19, 20, or 24. 28 USC § 1367(b).

    e.   The jurisdiction of the federal courts over additional parties is also limited when the claims raises a novel issue of state law or falls into the other enumerated exceptions of 28 USC § 1367(c).

---

[20] Severance is not the same as a Rule 20(b) order of separate trial.

E.   CLAIM JOINDER BY DEFENDANTS

1.   Counterclaims

    a.   Introduction

        i.   Counterclaims may exceed the plaintiff's claims and may even be added with leave of court if the defendant leaves them out negligently.

        ii.   Counterclaims may be *compulsory* or *permissive*.

    b.   Compulsory Counterclaims (Rule 13(a))

        i.   Procedural Aspects

            1)   Compulsory counterclaims arise out of the same occurrence or transaction as the original claim.

            2)   When a counterclaim is compulsory, the defendant *must raise it in his answer*.

            3)   Rationale: plaintiffs have an interest in having any claims that will ever be brought regarding a specific transaction or occurrence tried all at one time.

            4)   Generally, compulsory counterclaims not raised in a case are considered waived, *even when the case is settled*.

                a)   *See Dindo v. Whitney* (defendant) (1971), where the defendant originally sued the plaintiff for injuries sustained while the plaintiff driving. Through later consulting independent counsel, the plaintiff learned that he could have asserted a counterclaim for the defendant's putting hands on the wheel. Rather, however, the case was settled. Held: the plaintiff's failure to raise a compulsory counterclaim and the settling of the case constitute a waiver of the right to later raise the counterclaims, *if the plaintiff was aware of the his right to raise the claim* at the time that he waived them. Remanded to a jury to determine if the plaintiff knew.

            5)   Many courts consider compulsory counterclaims waived, *even when not raised due to a default*.

                a)   *See Carteret Savings and Loan Assn. v. Jackson* (defendant), where the defendant was barred from bringing counterclaims in an action because he failed to raise them in a separate action where they would have been compulsory. He failed to raise them in the first action because he defaulted.

        ii.   Jurisdiction Aspects

            1)   Compulsory counterclaims must be supported by SMJ.

            2)   There will often be an independent basis for SMJ, such as federal question or diversity.

3) However, if there is not, there is generally SMJ over the counterclaim through supplemental jurisdiction.

4) If, however, the counterclaim has an independent basis for SMJ, but the original claim does not, then under the ***well-pleaded complaint rule***, supplemental jurisdiction does not bring the original claim under the jurisdiction of the court, since the claims of the *complaint*, not of any other pleading, must fall within federal SMJ in order to be heard in federal court.

c. Permissive Counterclaims (Rule 13(b))

   i. Procedural Aspects

      1) Permissive counterclaims do *not* arise from the same transaction or occurrence as those of the original claim.

      2) At his option, the defendant *may* make permissive counterclaims in the same case in which the plaintiff sues the defendant. Alternatively, he may do so in a different proceeding.

   ii. Jurisdictional Aspects

      1) Each claim must be assessed separately to determine whether it has SMJ.

      2) First, one should inquire whether there is an ***independent basis*** for SMJ.

      3) If there is not, one should inquire whether the case would fall within ***supplemental jurisdiction***.

         a) To have supplemental jurisdiction, a case must arise from the same case or controversy.

         b) Thus, for the majority of courts, supplemental jurisdiction does not apply, since permissive counterclaims do not arise from a common transaction or occurrence (if they did, they would be compulsory).

         c) Since most courts consider a common "transaction or occurrence" to be the same as a § 1367(a) common "case or controversy," a permissive counterclaim automatically does not qualify.

         d) However, for those few circuits (such as the Second Circuit) that consider the § 1367 "common case or controversy" standard to be broader than the Federal Rules' common "transaction or occurrence" standard, there are some cases that may arise from a common case or controversy, but not from a common occurrence or transaction. Such permissive counterclaims may fall within supplemental jurisdiction.

2. Cross-Claims (Rule 13(g))

a.   Procedural aspects

    i.   Cross-claims are not compulsory; the defendant *may* make them against a co-party in the action.

    ii.   Rule 13(g), which implicitly permits the defendants to seek contribution and indemnity, requires cross-claims to arise under *same transaction or occurrence* as:

        1)   The original action;

        2)   A counterclaim; or

        3)   Property that is the subject matter of the original action.

b.   Jurisdictional aspects

    i.   For there to be a cross-claim, the cross-claim must arise under the same transaction or occurrence. Therefore, it will automatically be of the same case or controversy.

    ii.   There will always therefore be at least supplemental jurisdiction as long as the original claim had supplemental jurisdiction.

3.   Intervention (Rule 24)

a.   Introduction

    i.   Intervention implies that a third party initiates a joinder in an action already in progress.

b.   Procedural Aspects

    i.   ***Intervention by right*** allows an applicant who is not a party to an action to become a party upon *timely application* when:

        1)   A US *statute* confers an unconditional right to intervene. Rule 24(a)(1); or

        2)   The applicant claims an *interest* in an action that risks being *impaired* and the applicant is not adequately *represented* by existing parties. Rule 24(a)(2).

    ii.   ***Permissive intervention*** allows an applicant who is not a party to an action to become a party upon *timely application* when:

        1)   A US *statute* confers an unconditional right to intervene. Rule 24(b)(2); or

        2)   The claim or defense shares a *common question of law or fact* with the main action. Rule 24(b)(2).

    iii.   No duty to intervene

        1)   If a party having an interest in the subject matter of a case fails to intervene, and a judgment negatively impacts his interest, the failure to intervene does *not* waive his defense to that judgment, which he may later challenge in a separate suit.

2)   One is never legally bound by a judgment in a case in which he was not a formal party.

c.   Jurisdictional Aspects

    i.   To assure that the claim of an applicant falls within the SMJ of the court, one should first check for an independent basis for SMJ (federal question or diversity between the plaintiff-intervener and all of the defendants or the defendant-intervener and all of the plaintiffs).

    ii.   Otherwise, there may be a basis for SMJ under supplemental jurisdiction.

        1)   Traditionally, 28 USC § 1367(a) supplemental jurisdiction is met with respect to *interventions by right*, since the joined claim is so closely related to the controversy that the third party's interest may be impaired absent the intervention.

        2)   There is, however, a tendency to exclude *permissive interventions* from § 1367(a) supplemental jurisdiction, since a "common question of law or fact" is broader than the same "case or controversy." When, however, the "common question of law or fact" is substantially related to the original claim, supplemental jurisdiction will apply.

VII.   DEPOSITIONS AND DISCOVERY

A.   INTRODUCTION

1.   Detailed factual allegations come not in the pleadings, but in *discovery*, which serves the following purposes:

a.   To allow parties to narrow their issues;

b.   To facilitate settlements by allowing each side to know how much its case is worth; and

c.   To give each party more comprehensive information on the claims that will be raised at trial.

2.   Other methods for obtaining information include the following:

a.   Interviews with voluntary witnesses;

b.   Visiting the scene of a crime; and

c.   Hiring private investigators.

B.   OVERVIEW OF DISCOVERY DEVICES

1.   Required Disclosures

a.   Parties are required to turn over any information that is useful to that party's claims or defenses.

b.   This does not, however, include information that is harmful to those claims or defenses that aid the other side.

        i.   *N.B.*: contrast this to criminal cases, where prosecution must turn over exculpatory information to the defense.

  c.   There are three kinds of required disclosures:

        i.   *Initial disclosures*, which are disclosed at a very early stage in the case. Rule 26(a)(1);

        ii.   Disclosures of *expert testimony* of those expected to testify at trial. Rule 26(a)(2); and

        iii.   *Pretrial disclosures*, which refer to what will be done at the trial. Rule26(a)(3).

2.   Depositions

  a.   Oral Depositions (Rule 30)

        i.   Oral depositions are conducted as though the witness were testifying at trial, but no judge is present.

        ii.   They may be done without leave of court.

        iii.   They can be quite expensive, with $1,000 expended for a court reporter to transcribe a day-long deposition.

        iv.   There is a presumptive limit of ten depositions per side.

        v.   One may depose:

            1)   *Parties*, with a Rule 30(b)(1) notice of deposition; or

            2)   *Non-parties* (some of whom are not under the court's jurisdiction), with a court order.

  b.   Written Depositions (Rule 31)

        i.   Written depositions, or depositions "upon written questions," allow parties to serve a set of questions to be asked to a witness.

        ii.   A court officer asks the questions and the lawyer need not be present.

        iii.   Disadvantages to written depositions include the inability to:

            1)   Ask follow up questions; and

            2)   Watch how the witness reacts to certain questions.

3.   Interrogatories to Parties

  a.   Rule 33 interrogatories to parties are like depositions, except that in interrogatories, it is the parties that are required to give answers reflecting what they actually know and information available to them.

  b.   There is a presumptive limit of twenty five interrogatories to each party. This limit may be modified by stipulation or court order.

  c.   Usually, a party will begin with interrogatories to develop the follow up questions needing to be later asked in depositions.

d.   Upon receiving an interrogatory, a party may answer or object (privilege, irrelevance, undue burden, etc.). If a party does not object, the objection is waived.

4.   Productions and Entry Upon Land for Inspection and Other Purposes

    a.   Rule 34 requires a party to produce documents and other data compilations to the other side for inspection; or

    b.   To permit entry upon land or property for inspection, surveying, photographing, testing, etc.

5.   Physical and Mental Examinations of Persons

    a.   Rule 35 requires a party that causes a physical or mental examination to be made to deliver a copy of a detailed written report of the examination, if requested.

    b.   The examined party waives the privilege that he may have in requesting and obtaining a report of examination.

    c.   This applies to examinations made by agreement of the parties, unless otherwise provided.

6.   Requests for Admission

    a.   Parties may use Rule 36 requests for admission to determine the undisputed facts.

    b.   Admissions save resources by requiring each side to make direct admissions.

    c.   Admissions are considered *conclusive*, unless the court permits their withdrawal or amendment. Rule 36(b).

C.   SCOPE OF DISCOVERY (RULE 26(B))

1.   General Scope

    a.   Parties may obtain discovery regarding any non-privileged matter that (i) is **relevant** to claim of any party; (ii) may **lead to discovery** of admissible evidence; (iii) is requested in **good faith**; and (iv) is **not prejudicial** to other party.

    b.   *See Anderson* (plaintiff) *v. Hale* (N.D. Ill. 2001), where an African American sued the defendant, a member of a racist church, while the defendant was on a shooting spree. The plaintiff demanded a document production from the state bar in the hope to getting insight into the defendant's character and fitness. The defendant objected on basis that information was irrelevant and that its purpose was to harass him. Held: if information seems reasonably calculated to lead to other evidence that will be used to prove a case, such information is discoverable. The defendant's motion is denied.

2.   Relation to the Rules of Evidence

a. Rule 26(b)(1) does not require that information be admissible to trial in order to be discoverable; it requires only that information reasonably lead to evidence that *would be admissible in trial*.

b. ***Hearsay*** may be considered sufficiently relevant for discovery, but not sufficiently relevant for admission to trial.

  i. Thus, although hearsay may not be admissible in trial, it is discoverable if ***reasonably calculated to lead to discovery*** of admissible evidence.

  ii. Example: Mrs. Smith heard brakes making a screeching sound. Is her testimony admissible in trial? Yes.

   1) What if it was her husband who told her that he heard brakes screech?

   2) This would not be admissible in trial, since it was hearsay, but it would be within the scope of a deposition, since it appears *reasonably aimed at leading to discovery of other evidence*.

c. Additionally, evidence of other similar incidents that would be prejudicial to a party would not admissible in trial but would be discoverable if it would reasonably lead to relevant information.

3. Privileged Material (Rule 26(b)(5))

  a. Overview

   i. The scope of privileged communications is generally determined by state law.

   ii. Among the categories of communications classified by state laws as privileged are those between an attorney and his client, a physician and his patient, a priest and his parishioner, and a husband and his wife.

   iii. Rule 26(b)(1) limits discovery to ***non-privileged materials***. A communication is *not* privileged merely because its disclosure would be embarrassing or detrimental.

    1) *See Coca-Cola Bottling Co. v. Coca-Cola Co.* (defendant), where the plaintiff sought discovery of the defendant's secret formula in order to prove that Diet Coke and Coke were indeed the same product. When the defendant refused to disclose the formula due to potential detriment, the court held that the plaintiff was entitled to non-rebuttable factual finding in favor of the plaintiff.

  b. Waivers of Privilege

   i. Failure to claim a privilege may be viewed as a waiver.

    1) Example: The client, while being deposed, admits privileged information without his attorney's objecting. The privilege will be considered waived.

        ii.   Revelation of the privileged information to another non-privileged party (someone other than a priest, spouse, etc.) destroys the confidentiality of the communication and also constitutes a waiver.

4.   Work Product (Rule 26(b)(3))

    a.   Work product is different from privileged material in that it is not *absolutely protected.*

    b.   However, work product has some protections. It is not discoverable on mere demand; rather, the other party must show that (i) it has substantial need of the materials in the preparation of the party's case; and (ii) that the party is unable without undue hardship to obtain the equivalent of the materials by other means. Rule 26(b)(3).

        i.   *See Hickman* (plaintiff) *v. Taylor*, where the plaintiff, a representative of a crew member who drowned when a boat sank, sent interrogatories asking the defendant to produce all records of memoranda, statements, records, and reports from the crew members. The defendant refused. Held: in order for a party to obtain another party's work product, it must show why that work product is substantially significant to its arguments and why it cannot otherwise acquire the required information without undue hardship. Here, the plaintiff failed to make such showings, and the information and witnesses are easily available to the plaintiff. Judgment for the defendant affirmed.

            1)   *N.B.*: the work product doctrine was first recognized in this case.

        ii.   *See also Holmgren v. State Farm Mutual Insurance Co.* (defendant), where handwritten notes written by the defendant's adjuster estimating the value of the plaintiff's claims was held to be discoverable, due to substantial need.

    c.   Material that will gain the most protection as work product is that which reveals an attorney's thoughts, legal strategies, and mental impressions.

5.   Experts

    a.   Introduction

        i.   An expert is someone with special knowledge or skill that will assist the trier of fact in a case to determine evidence pertaining to an issue.

        ii.   Experts may *testify in court* ("testifying experts") or they may *consult and educate* the lawyers on the issues ("non-testifying experts").

    b.   Testifying Experts

        i.   The parties generally pick the testifying experts that bolster their arguments for trial.

ii. The parties must disclose their testifying witnesses' identities. Rule 26(a)(2)(A).

iii. Additionally, they must disclose a written report containing all testifying experts' opinions, reasons therefore, list of publications, other cases where testified, and other matters. Rule 26(a)(2)(B).

c. Non-Testifying Experts

i. The work and opinions of non-testifying experts are generally treated and protected to the extent of work product.

ii. A party may depose or serve non-testifying experts with interrogatories only with a showing of *exceptional circumstances* under which it is impracticable for the party seeking discovery to obtain facts or opinions on the same subject by other means. Rule 26(b)(4)(B).

iii. Some courts consider *only* the experts' work products to be protected, but not their names and identities. Other courts consider experts' work products as well as their names and identities to be protected.

1) *See Ager v. Jane C. Stormont Hospital and Training School for Nurses* (defendant) (1992), where the plaintiff's lawyer refused to reveal information regarding his non-testifying witnesses, in contempt of court. On appeal, the Court held that since information by one party regarding experts who will not testify is work-product, it is not to be disclosed absent *extraordinary* circumstances. Order vacated and remanded.

D. TIMING AND PRETRIAL DISCLOSURES, CONFERENCES, AND ORDERS

1. Timing

   a. Rule 26(f) deals with the time limits for discovery.

   b. It requires the parties to confer to make arrangements for discovery and to make proposals regarding the subjects for which discovery will be needed and the limitations that should be made by the court as to what is discoverable.

2. Pretrial Disclosures

   a. Rule 26(a)(3) requires that a party disclose, in addition to those disclosures required by subsections (1)-(2), the documents, exhibits, and names of witnesses to be called on or used in trial.

   b. These disclosures generally must be made thirty days before trial.

3. Pretrial Conferences and Orders

   a. Rule 16 sets out the rules for pretrial conferences to expedite the case.

   b. Rule 16(b) allows the courts to hold a scheduling conference in order to create a scheduling order and as many pretrial conferences as necessary.

      c.   Rule 16(d) deals with the final pretrial conference.

          i.   The judge enters the "final pretrial conference order" reciting what happened in the conference.

          ii.   The statement of issues to be tried, etc., trumps over the parties' pleadings.

          iii.   The final order is only modified to prevent "manifest injustice."

E.   SANCTIONS (RULE 37)

1.   Introduction

      a.   Rule 37 allows parties to make motions to *compel discovery* (Rule 37(a)) and *provides sanctions* for failure to comply with court orders (Rule 37(b)) and for failure to disclose information required by Rule 26 (Rule 37(c)).

2.   Mechanics of the Rule

      a.   If a party fails to produce materials requested by the other side, the other side may move the court for a Rule 37(a) Order Compelling Discovery.

      b.   If the party disobeys the court order as well, the court may *find him **in contempt***; *presume that the **evidence stands against him***; ***dismiss** the case*, or ***grant judgment by default*** against him under to 37(b).

      c.   Factors to be considered are whether the party's actions were done intentionally or negligently and in good faith or in bad faith.

      d.   Under Rule 26(g), all discovery requests, responses, and objections must be signed by an attorney of a represented party or by an unrepresented party certifying that, to the best of the signor's knowledge formed after reasonable inquiry, the paper is (i) consistent with the federal rules; and (ii) not interposed for any improper purpose.

      e.   Otherwise, sanctions may be imposed.

          i.   *See Washington State Physicians Ins. Exchange and Association v. Fisons Corp.* (defendant), where during discovery, the defendant failed to turn over self-incriminating documents that pointed to the defendant's recklessness in continuing to market harmful drugs. Held: sanctions are warranted because in the defendant's stating that all relevant documents were disclosed, the defendant was being dishonest in artificially narrowing the scope of the requests being made.

      f.   A party failing to abide by Rule 36(a) requests for admission by refusing to admit certain facts may be punished under Rule 37(c)(2), for failure to admit. *See Holmgren v. State Farm Mutual Automobile Ins. Co.*

VIII. TRIALS AND ADJUDICATION

A. THE RIGHT TO A JURY (RULE 38)

1. Scope of the Constitutional Right

    a. Assuming that a case passes the initial hurdles of PJ, SMJ, and venue, two questions must be asked: (i) will the case proceed to trial? and if so, will it be a trial by a judge or a jury?

    b. The Seventh Amendment "preserves" the right to trial by jury in cases at common law.[21] Rule 38(a) employs this same language.

    c. Thus, courts must look to the state of the law at the time that the Seventh Amendment was passed to determine the nature of the right that is to be preserved.

    d. At that time, the right to a trial by jury applied only to cases at law, not to cases at equity.

    e. Today, however, the question is complicated by the fact that: (i) the federal courts have **merged law and equity**; and (ii) **new causes of action** that did not exist at the time of the drafting of the Bill of Rights cannot be neatly classified as either law or equity.

2. The Complications of Merger and the Federal Rules

    a. Ever since the federal courts merged actions at law and actions in equity, the rules governing when trials by jury are available have become more complicated.

    b. Generally, actions involving an equitable issue and an issue at-law may have a jury decide the issue at-law.

    c. Usually, the issue at-law will be decided first, since trials by juries are constitutional and since, through preclusion, whatever facts are found in the first issue tried will be binding facts on the second issue to be tried.

    d. When, however, the court tries an equity issue before an issue at-law, the court's factual findings in the equity issue will not be binding on the jury for the issue at-law because of claim preclusion (since doing so would abridge parties' right to trial by jury).

3. New Causes of Action

    a. As a result of the merger of law and equity, a two-prong historical test has been adopted that allows a court to examine (i) the closest historical claim at the time that the Seventh Amendment was passed and (ii) the remedy sought, in order to establish whether the current case more closely resembles law or equity.

---

[21] The Sixth Amendment, in contrast, grants the right to a speedy and public trial by jury in *criminal* proceedings.

b. When the closest historical claim and remedy sought differ as to whether they resemble a remedy at law or at equity, the remedy sought has more sway.

    i. *See Chauffers Local v. Terry* (plaintiff), where the plaintiffs sued the defendant for not fairly representing them in a back pay action. The plaintiff requested a trial by jury and the defendant claimed that the plaintiff had no such right, since the cause of action more closely resembled what would have been an equity action at the time of the ratification of the Seventh Amendment. However, since the remedy sought (damages) more closely resembled a remedy at-law, and since this factor held more weight than the closest historical claim, the claim was recognized as a legal claim entitled to a trial by jury.

4. Juries in State Courts

a. Although the Seventh Amendment does not require trials by jury in actions at-law in state courts, most states provide for the right of trials by jury in at least *some* causes of action.

B. SUMMARY JUDGMENT (RULE 56)

1. Requirements for Summary Judgment

a. Summary judgment (SJ) is granted when there is "***no genuine issue of material fact.***" Under such circumstances, "the moving party is entitled to a ***judgment as a matter of law***." Rule 56(c).

b. There is a ***genuine issue*** of material fact when a record contains evidence from which a reasonable jury could find either way on an issue. A genuine issue would exist even if there was only one witness against twenty, even if that one witness was the plaintiff.

c. A ***material fact*** is one whose outcome affects the outcome of the case.

d. SJ may be invoked in the following cases:

    i. There is no factual dispute (*e.g.*, the parties stipulate the facts and disagree only on the law); or

    ii. There is a factual dispute, but it is not genuine (*e.g.*, one side has so little evidence that the other side wins as a matter of law).

e. The court interprets the evidence in a light most favorable to the non-moving party.

2. Summary Judgment Contrasted with Rule 12(b)(6) and 12(c) Motions.

a. There are three kinds of motions that provided for decisions without adjudication:

    i. Rule 12(b)(6) (and 12(b) generally) motions for dismissal for failure to state a claim;

    ii. Rule 12(c) motions for judgment on the pleadings; and

    iii. Rule 56 motions for summary judgment.

b.   In the Rule 12 motions, the court *only* considers the pleadings.

c.   In contrast, in SJ, the court may consider outside evidence. SJ is thus essentially a Rule 12(c) motion with additional evidence.

d.   SJ is similar to directed verdicts, which have the same standard. However, while in SJ, the court makes a ruling based on affidavits, a Rule 50 directed verdict is granted on basis of evidence presented at trial.

3.   Questions Requiring a Heightened Summary Judgment Standard

a.   Some issues require a party to plead a case under heightened standards of evidence.

b.   In these cases, the same heightened standard used in trial applies to the standard required for SJ.

   i.   *See Anderson v. Liberty Lobby, Inc.* (plaintiff), applying a heightened standard for malice in a libel case in the SJ proceeding, just as it would have done had the case gone to trial. SJ cannot be determined without considering the standard that the fact finder will ultimately use to determine if there was liability.

4.   Procedural Considerations

a.   There are two ways that a defendant can obtain SJ against a plaintiff:

   i.   Present affirmative evidence showing that there is no way that the plaintiff can prove an element; or

   ii.   Point out that the plaintiff has not and cannot produce evidence proving an element.

      1)   *See Celotex Corp. v. Catrett* (plaintiff), where the plaintiff sued a asbestos product manufacturers on the theory that her husband's exposure to their products caused his death. The defendant moved for SJ, arguing that the plaintiff *did not and could not prove that her husband had the requisite exposure* to the defendant's products. The defendant pointed to the plaintiff's not having responded to the defendant's interrogatory asking the plaintiff to identify witnesses who could testify that her husband was exposed to the defendant's products. This created the presumption that the plaintiff had not in fact had such witnesses or other proof. SJ for the defendant.

      2)   *N.B.*: had the plaintiff responded to the defendant's motion by submitting an affidavit or other evidence proving the plaintiff's husband's exposure to the asbestos, the defendant would not have been granted SJ.

b.   If the defendant successfully meets his burden, the burden shifts on the plaintiff to produce evidence to the contrary.

   i.   The plaintiff may meet the burden of proof through affidavits or further testimony. Rule 56(e).

      ii.   If the plaintiff is unable to do so, he must move the court to grant more time. Rule 56(f).

      iii.   The court will only grant more time if it believes that there is a reasonable chance that the plaintiff will be able to do so.

      iv.   Factors a court will look at include:

           1)   How long it has been since the start of the case; and

           2)   How much time the plaintiff has already had to produce the requisite evidence.

C. SECOND-GUESSING JURIES (RULES 50, 59)

1.   Judgments as a Matter of Law

    a.   A court may enter a judgment without a trial by jury when it concludes that no reasonable jury could find for one side.

    b.   In the alternative, a court may submit a case to a jury and if a jury returns a verdict that is not reasonably supported by evidence, the court may enter a judgment *non obstante veredicto* (JNOV).

    c.   The standard for granting SJ, a directed verdict, or a JNOV considers whether a reasonable jury could return a verdict in favor of one of the parties on the presented evidence.

    d.   Rule 50 controls directed verdicts and refers to them as, "judgments as a matter of law" (JMOL). JNOV's are now known as "renewed motions for judgment as a matter of law" under Rule 50(c).

    e.   If a party's motion for a JMOL is denied and an issue is submitted to a jury and the moving party loses, that party may move for a renewed JMOL.

    f.   A JMOL is similar to SJ, except that SJ motions are made outside of the context of trial.

    g.   As with SJ, a court may grant JMOL on some but not all issues.

    h.   The timing for JMOL motions in trial is as follows:

      i.   Opening statements;

      ii.   The plaintiff introduces evidence and closes his case in chief;

      iii.   The defendant may move for JMOL, or alternatively, may introduce evidence and close his case in chief;

      iv.   The plaintiff or the defendant may move for JMOL;

      v.   Closing arguments;

      vi.   The judge instructs the jury, the jury deliberates, and gives its verdict; the judge enters a judgment on the verdict;

      vii.   Within ten days, either party may renew its JMOL motion, but only if it had formerly moved for a JMOL during the trial, or may move for a new trial.

viii. Whether a party makes a Rule 50(b) renewed motion for a JMOL or a Rule 59 motion for a new trial affects the amount of time that that party has to appeal.

    1) The thirty day limit time to appeal is no longer based on when the entry of judgment on the verdict was made.

    2) Rather, it is based on the time of the entry of judgment for the renewed motion (provided that the motion is made in a timely manner).

i. The standard for granting a renewed JMOL (JNOV) requires that the jury's findings be clearly erroneous. A verdict is not considered to be clearly erroneous merely because it involved some degree of speculation.

    i. *See Lavender v. Kurn*, where the court denied a renewed JMOL because, although there was some speculation on the part of the jury, the verdict was *not* clearly erroneous. When a case goes to a jury, it usually means that there is some uncertainty. In such cases, it is best to allow the jury decide the facts, even if it involves some level of speculation.

2. New Trials

    a. Sometimes, there is sufficient evidence such that a JMOL would not be permitted or warranted.

    b. Nevertheless, under Rule 59, a court may be able to exercise influence over the verdict when the court finds that the verdict is not supported by the *preponderance* of the evidence. In such cases, new trials are allowed, in both actions at law and actions in equity.

    c. Thus, it may be possible for a party's case to survive the adverse party's motion for a JMOL, but *not* its motion for a new trial.

        i. *See Dadurian* (plaintiff) *v. Underwriters at Lloyd's of London*, where the jury found for the plaintiff, a jewelry buyer, even though there was substantial evidence that the plaintiff had been misleading on several of the facts, including how he purchased the jewelry. Held: since the preponderance of the evidence is against the plaintiff, a new trial is ordered.

    d. New trials may be granted for both trial error (*e.g.*, in the jury instructions given or in the evidence admitted) as well as error in the verdict, which finds contrary to the overwhelming weight of the evidence.

    e. As with renewed JMOL's, parties have ten days to make motions for a new trial.

3. Bench Trials

a. When the judge is the trier of fact (through parties' waiver of trial or when the action is in equity), the judge must record his fact findings and legal conclusions in a written opinion.

b. This opinion is not a Rule 58 separate document.

c. According to Rule 52(b), the parties may move for the court to amend its findings.

4. Motions to Set Aside the Judgment (MSAJ)

a. Rule 60(b) allows parties to move to set aside the judgment.

b. A motion to set aside is not an appeal. Rather, it is made directly to the trial court.

c. A judge's granting of a MSAJ is very rare. There are two kinds:

i. Rule 60(a) MSAJ's for clerical error; and

ii. Rule 60(b) MSAJ's for jury error (extremely rare).

IX. PRECLUSION DOCTRINES

A. COLLATERAL ESTOPPEL (ISSUE PRECLUSION)

1. Introduction

a. Collateral estoppel, which is sometimes referred to as "issue preclusion" or "estoppel by judgment," is the doctrine that prohibits a factual issue from being litigated in any lawsuit if it was litigated and decided in a previous proceeding.

2. For collateral estoppel to apply, the following elements must be met:

a. The same issue must have been *previously litigated*;

b. The issue must have been *actually litigated* in the previous suit;

c. The issue must have been *decided* in the first suit;

d. The decision must have been *necessary to the court's judgment* in the first suit.

3. Mutual Collateral Estoppel

a. Mutual collateral estoppel is the use of collateral estoppel by someone who was not a party in the first action to prevent a person who was a party in the first action from bringing a suit against him.

i. Example: A sues B for a transaction. B successfully raises contributory negligence. Later, A sues C under the same transaction. C is not required to re-litigate contributory negligence; it automatically applies as a defense.

b. In the above example, if in litigating the issue of A's contributory negligence, A was *not* contributorily negligent, C would not be estopped from a contributory negligence defense

c.   This is because one is not bound by a judgment from a lawsuit to which he was not a party.

B.   *RES JUDICATA* (CLAIM PRECLUSION)

1.   Under the doctrine of "*res judicata*" (Lat., the "the thing already adjudicated"), or "claim preclusion," a party *may not litigate **claims*** that he raised or could have raised in a previous suit that reached a final judgment.

2.   Claim preclusion applies when the following elements are met:

a.   Two lawsuits must involve the same claims.

   i.   Under the federal standard of *res judicata*, for federal courts, a "same claim" means any claim that arises out of the ***same transaction or occurrence***.

   ii.   However, defining the scope of a claim is often difficult, since a "cause of action" has never been precisely defined.

   iii.   Under the majority view, any claim that ***could have been brought*** but were not brought in a former suit is precluded from being re-litigated.

   iv.   Under the minority approach, the plaintiff is precluded only from bringing claims that were actually brought in a previous suit. Claims that could have been brought but were not are not precluded.

      1)   *See Carter v. Hinkle* (plaintiff), where the plaintiff was permitted to bring a personal injury claim arising out of the same occurrence from which a property damage claim that he had formerly adjudicated, even though he brought it in a separate, second action.

b.   The parties to the two suits must be the same or in privity.

c.   The first lawsuit must have ended in a final valid judgment.

   i.   Majority view: whether a party can appeal is irrelevant for this calculus;

   ii.   Minority view: the case must have been appealed or the time frame for appeals must have run and expired.

d.   The final judgment must have been on the merits.

   i.   Examples of judgments on the merits: a case that went to trial and was decided; SJ; and Rule 12(b)(6) dismissals for failure to state a claim when they are amended and again dismissed.

   ii.   Examples of judgments *not* on the merits: dismissal for lack of SMJ, PJ, or venue; and Rule 12(b)(6) dismissals for failure to state a claim.

APPENDICES

TABLE OF CASES

THEMATIC INDEX

GLOSSARY

***Ad coelum* doctrine** Under this doctrine, for the purpose of immovable minerals, "to whomever the soil belongs, he also owns to the sky and to the depths." It refers to the right of the owner of property to the space that extends vertically upward and downward from his property.

Arson The malicious, willful, and unlawful burning of a structure which, at common law, had to be the dwelling place of another.

Assignment A transfer of property that grants the possession of land for the *entire period of a lease*. By default, an assignment grants *all of the property* for the lease period. A *partial assignment* may however, be granted for only *part of the property* during the lease period. Compare SUBLEASE.

Bailment A legally recognized property relationship between a bailor, who gives personalty to another to be held for a particular purpose, and a bailee, party that receives the property.

Bill of attainder An uconstitutional legislative action that singles out an individual or group for punishment without the benefit of a trial.

Burglary At common law, the specific intent crime that consisted of the breaking and entering of the dwelling of another at night with the intent to commit a felony therein.

Causation in fact Actual causation that links an act with a result through implementing the "but-for" test (*i.e.*, "but for A, B would not have occurred"). Compare PROXIMATE CAUSE.

Circumstantial evidence Secondary facts and other evidence that lead to primary fact inferences.

Chattel An item of personal, as opposed to real property; any moveable object.

Claim preclusion *See* RES JUDICATA.

Closing (real property) The final meeting between the seller and the purchaser in a land sale contract, whereby the executory period is concluded and the payment and property are exchanged.

Closing of escrow *See* CLOSING.

Collateral estoppel Under the doctrine of collateral estoppel, a factual issue *may not be litigated* in any lawsuit if it was litigated and decided in a previous proceeding. Also referred to as ISSUE PRECLUSION.

Constructive notice Legal notice derived from the circumstances.

Construction The act of interpreting the sense or intention of a constitution, statute, contract, or some other text; the process of construing the meaning of a writing.

Constructive possession doctrine Doctrine by which control or dominion of property is granted to the owner of the *locus in quo*, in situations in which it would otherwise go to the finder (*e.g.*, in cases of treasure trove and findings generally). The doctrine is applied, for example, when an object is found in a private place of a store. The owner of the *locus in quo*, rather than the finder, obtains possession.

Conversion A tortious act of willful interference with the property of another without lawful justification, in a way that *deprives the owner of the use of his property*. Examples of conversion include illegal takings, the assumption of ownership, and the destruction of the property of another.

Counterclaim An independent cause of action made by the defendant against the plaintiff in order to defeat the plaintiff's claim.

Criminal negligence Extremely negligent conduct that creates a risk of death or serious bodily injury beyond that of mere civil negligence.

Cross-claim A claim under FRCP 13(g) by one party against a co-party arising out of the transaction or occurrence that is the subject matter either of the original action or of a counterclaim therein or relating to any property that is the subject matter of the original action.

Dead Man's Act A statute that disqualifies a party from testifying *against the estate* of the deceased because of the party's incentive to lie based on: (i) his interest in the case; and (ii) the unavailability of the deceased to contradict him.

Detinue An action at common law to recover PERSONALTY or its value when it is unlawfully held by another.

Devise To make a gift of real property by will. Property that can be given in such a gift is referred to as "devisable."

Duress A defense that applies when the defendant acts illegally and against his own will as a result of another's *unlawful threat* of bodily harm. Duress excuses an actor from the legal effects of his actions (*e.g.*, a defendant is not guilty for a theft committed under duress).

Easement The right to use part of land owned by another for a special purpose. *See* EASEMENT APPURTENANT and EASEMENT IN GROSS.

Easement appurtenant An easement that benefits the grantee's (dominant tenant) land. When there is an easement appurtenant, there are *both dominant* and *servient tenements*. Compare EASEMENT IN GROSS.

Easement in gross An easement that does not benefit the grantee's land. Although there is a servient estate, but there is no *dominant estate*. Compare EASEMENT APPURTENANT.

Equitable servitude Covenants restricting the use of land that run with the land at equity and thus offer remedies at equity (*e.g.*, injunctions). Compare REAL COVENANTS.

Executory period In a land sale contract, the period between the formation of the sale contract and the closing.

Ex post facto **law** (Lat., a law "after the fact"). A law that does any of the following retroactively: (i) makes conduct criminal; (ii) establishes a stricter punishment for a crime; or (iii) alters the procedural or evidentiary rules in favor of the prosecution.

False pretenses A specific intent crime consisting of the acquiring of title to the property of another through making false statements or misrepresentations with the intent of defrauding the owner.

First degree murder Under the modern statutory approach to murder, first degree murder is generally defined as all forms of murder having malic aforethought *and* premediation and deliberation. Compare SECOND DEGREE MURDER.

Freehold estate An estate where the possessor is the owner of the property (at least for a temporary period of time).

Grand theft The commission of LARCENY when the value of the property unlawfully taken exceeds some predetermined amount.

Habeas corpus Legal proceeding where a writ is brought to determine whether a person is being lawfully detained.

Holdover tenant A tenant who keeps possession of the property beyond the expiration of the lease.

Implied easement by prior use An easement that comes into being when an owner of two parcels of land uses one of them, the servient estate, to benefit the other in such a way that when he sells one of them, the purchaser can *reasonably expect* that the servient estate will continue to be used in a way that is consistent with its prior use.

In-court identification Modality of identification where an attorney asks a witness if she recognizes the perpetrator of a crime in court.

Indictment Since a defendant may not cross-examine witnesses presented against him in a grand jury indictment, the Confrontation Clause does no apply. Compare PRELIMINARY HEARING.

Infant A person who has not yet reached the legal age of majority (generally, eighteen years of age); a minor.

Intent (torts) The *mens rea* element for intentional torts, which is formed when the defendant possesses either: (i) purpose (a wanting or desiring) that a certain result come about; or (ii) knowledge to a substantial certainty that a result is substantially certain to come about as a result of his act (based on belief or knowledge).

Intervening cause An act that intervenes in the series of events after an act, such that it alters the resulting consequence. When intervening causes are strong enough to relieve wrongdoer of liability, they become SUPERSEDING CAUSES.

Involuntary manslaughter An *unintentional* killing lacking malice aforethought committed either with criminal negligence or during the commission of an unlawful act.

Issue preclusion *See* COLLATERAL ESTOPPEL.

Joinder The uniting of distinct claims or parties in an action.

Knowledge to a substantial certainty (torts) Knowledge of an extremely high risk that a particular consequence will materialize as a result of one's act. It may be based on knowledge or belief and, like purpose, satisfies the *mens rea* required in intentional torts.

Larceny A specific intent crime consisting of the unlawful taking and carrying away of the property of another with the intent to permanently deprive him thereof.

Leasehold estate An estate where the possessor is not the owner of the property (*e.g.*, in the case of a rental property). Possession will spring back to the owner after the current possessor's lease or rental comes to a close.

License (property law) A right to use another's property that is terminable at the will of the possessor of the land.

Malum in se (Lat., "a wrong in itself"). An inherently evil or immoral act, regardless of whether it is prohibited.

Malum prohibitum (Lat., "a prohibited wrong"). An act or offense which is prohibited but is not inherently wrong (*e.g.*, failing to stop at a stop sign).

Merchantable title Title not subject to such reasonable doubt that it would create a just apprehension of its validity in the mind of a reasonable prudent person. Merchantable title is not necessarily good title; it may have *slight defects*.

Mortgage Security for a debt given by a mortgagor (a debtor) to a mortgagee (a creditor) to secure a loan given to the mortgagor, usually for the purpose of purchasing land or some other real estate.

Mortgagee In a mortgage, the creditor, loan company, or bank that lends to the debtor, or mortgagor.

Mortgagor In a mortgage, the party that borrows from a creditor, loan company, or bank; a debtor.

Negligence *per se* Negligence established as a matter of law such that the plaintiff need not establish duty and breach. The violation of civil and criminal statutes gives rise to negligence *per se* in most states, such that the jury is instructed that the violation of a statute constitutes the breach of duty for the purposes of negligence.

Nonjusticiable political question A question that involves the exercise of *discretionary power* by either the Legislative or the Executive Branch; it does not involve a *judicial* question to be decided by the judiciary.

APPENDICES

Nuisance A condition or activity on another's land that unreasonably affects the other's right to enjoy and use his land. The standard is one of a person of *ordinary sensibility*.

Parol evidence Oral or written evidence of a bargain that occurred before the final terms of the contract were laid down and that was not made part of the final contract.

Parol evidence rule Rule of substantive law that states that supplementary oral or written evidence of any agreement prior to or contemporaneous with the laying down of the final terms of the contract cannot be used to contradict or vary the final agreement.

Pendent parties jurisdiction The jurisdiction to adjudicate a claim against a party who is not otherwise within court's jurisdiction, because the claim by or against that party arises from the same core facts of another claim that is properly before the court.

Personalty Personal property, which is moveable, as contrasted with REALTY (real property).

Photographic lineup Modality of identification where a witness identifies one suspect among others in a spread of photographs.

Pleading Documents filed by a litigant that set forth the material facts and legal arguments of his claims or defenses.

Police lineup Modality of identification in which suspects are lined up at a police station and a witness is asked if he recognizes the perpetrator among them.

Preliminary hearing Permits a defendant to cross-examine witnesses presented against him. Compare INDICTMENT.

Prima facie case A case in which the plaintiff presents sufficient evidence "on its first appearance" (Lat.) supporting the cause of action. If no contrary or rebutting evidence is presented, the plaintiff is entitled to a decision in his favor.

Profit à prendre An easement that grants the right to enter and remove timber, minerals, oil, gas, game, and other substances from another's land.

Proximate cause is legal causation that serves as a limitation on actual cause. The law limits those acts that are said to be "causes" of some consequence, requiring the acts to be related to the consequence through some foreseeable sequence of events. If an act is foreseeably related, it is said to be the proximate. Compare CAUSATION IN FACT.

Quantum meruit A Latin expression meaning "as much as he deserves." This is a doctrine at equity that allows a party to recover for the value of the labor or materials delivered to another, even if there was no actual contract or if there was a contract and the party breached it, in order to prevent the other party will not be unjustly enriched.

Rape Under the common law, rape was defined as "the carnal knowledge of a woman forcibly and against her will." The modern law has departed from this view by defining rape in gender-neutral terms.

Ratione soli **doctrine** Under this doctrine, also known as the "*ad coelum* minor doctrine," the owner of the soil *is the first occupant* and owner of whatever is found on the soil, including minerals and *ferae naturae*, regardless of who the finder is.

Real covenant A promise relating to land use that runs with the land at law and is enforceable at law (offering monetary damages as remedies) between the original covenanting parties as a contract. Compare EQUITABLE SERVITUDE.

Realty Real property, which is immovable and fixed to the ground (*e.g.*, buildings, land), as contrasted with PERSONALTY.

Recklessness (torts) The purposeful disregard of a high probability of a resulting consequence (*e.g.*, of resulting emotional distress, in the case of the intentional infliction of emotional distress).

Replevin An action at common law to recover *the possession* of personalty wrongfully taken from the plaintiff. Compare TROVER.

Replevy To exercise the common law action of REPLEVIN.

Res ipsa loquitur A negligence circumstantial evidence doctrine that is invoked when the facts create such a strong presumption of negligence that "the thing speaks for itself" (*Lat.*). The plaintiff is not required to introduce direct evidence.

Res judicata Under the doctrine of *res judicata* (Lat., the "the thing already adjudicated"), a party *may not litigate claims* that he raised or could have raised in a previous suit that reached a final judgment. Also referred to as CLAIM PRECLUSION.

Respondeat superior (*Lat.*, "let the superior answer") The doctrine that a master or principal is *vicariously liable* for the negligence of his servants or agents, even when he was not himself negligent. This doctrine usually refers to the liability of employers for their employees.

Robbery The specific intent crime that consists of the unlawful taking of property from another person or in the person's presence by the use of force or by threatening the imminent use of force.

Second degree murder Under the modern statutory approach to murder, second degree murder is generally defined as all forms of murder having malice aforethought, but, unlike FIRST DEGREE MURDER, lacks premeditation and deliberation (*e.g.*, depraved heart murder, felony murder committed in tandem with a non-inherently dangerous felony, etc.).

Shelter principle Under this principle, if a possessor of some chattel or other property became the legitimate owner of the property under some theory of ownership (*e.g.*, adverse possession, accession, etc.), then all subsequent possessors may claim that good title was also passed to them if they legitimately acquired the good.

Showup Modality of identification in which police seize a suspect, bring him to the victim of a crime, and ask the witness if the suspect is the perpetrator. A showup usually occurs before an indictment, when time is of the essence.

Solicitation The act of entreating, imploring, inducing, or encouraging another person to engage in some unlawful behavior.

Sua sponte By order of the court, "of its own will" (Lat.), without motions by either party.

Sublease A transfer of property that grants possession of the land to a new tenant for *part of the duration of a lease period*, even if it is as little as one minute. Compare ASSIGNMENT.

Suicide pact An agreement whereby two or more people agree to kill one another.

Superseding cause An INTERVENING CAUSE that is strong enough to relieve a wrongdoer of liability.

Supplemental jurisdiction The jurisdiction that a court has over a claim that is *part of the same case or controversy* as another claim over which the court has *original jurisdiction*.

Tort A civil wrong, other than a breach of contract, for which the law provides a remedy.

Tortfeasor A person who has committed a tort.

Trover A remedy that allows the rightful owner of property to recover possession or to recover damages for the wrongful taking of his property. Compare REPLEVIN.

Voidable title Title that is fraudulently transferred or transferred through the owner's negligence. Although it is imperfect, it has the potential of becoming full title (if transferred to a *bona fide* purchasaer, for example). Compare VOID TITLE.

Void Title Fatally flawed title that no action can cure or transform into full title. Compare VOIDABLE TITLE.

Voir Dire Judicial procedure in which attorneys examine prospective jurors to determine competency and potential bias. The process leads to the selection or rejection of those who will ultimately serve on the jury in a particular case.

Voluntary manslaughter An intentional killing mitigated by provocation in the heat of passion or other circumstances that negate malice aforethought.